FINDING
YOUR WAY
IN A
WILD NEW
WORLD

FINDING YOUR WAY
IN A
WILD NEW
WORLD

Reclaim Your True Nature
to Create the Life You Want

MARTHA BECK

ATRIA PAPERBACK

NEW YORK   LONDON   TORONTO   SYDNEY   NEW DELHI

ATRIA PAPERBACK
A Division of Simon & Schuster, Inc.
1230 Avenue of the Americas
New York, NY 10020

First Atria Paperback edition January 2013

ATRIA PAPERBACK and colophon are trademarks of Simon & Schuster, Inc.

For information about special discounts for bulk purchases,
please contact Simon & Schuster Special Sales at 1-866-506-1949
or business@simonandschuster.com.

The Simon & Schuster Speakers Bureau can bring authors to your live event.
For more information or to book an event, contact the Simon & Schuster Speakers
Bureau at 1-866-248-3049 or visit our website at www.simonspeakers.com.

Designed by Mspace/Maura Fadden Rosenthal

Manufactured in the United States of America

10   9   8   7

The Library of Congress has cataloged the Free Press edition as follows:
Beck, Martha Nibley, 1962–
Finding your way in a wild new world : reclaiming your true nature / Martha Beck.
p. cm.
Summary: "A transformative guide readers can use to become miracle workers, harnessing healing
power for themselves and for the world"—Provided by publisher.
1. Self-actualization (Psychology) 2. Success. I. Title.
BF637.S4B3958 2011
158.1—dc23
2011029265

ISBN 978-1-4516-2448-9
ISBN 978-1-4516-2460-1 (pbk)
ISBN 978-1-4516-2461-8 (ebook)

Note to Readers
Names and identifying details of the clients and some others described herein
have been changed. Quotes are intended to be illustrative or to reflect the essence
of a conversation, and are not necessarily verbatim.

CONTENTS

INTRODUCTION: MEET YOUR RHINOCEROS, HEAL YOUR LIFE

The imminent possibility of being killed by a rhinoceros isn't bothering me nearly as much as I would have expected. True, my heart fluttered when I first saw her, but from awe, not fear.

Well, maybe a little from fear.

Until this exact second, my friend Koelle Simpson (her first name sounds like "Noelle," but with a K) has been so focused on the rhino's footprints that she forgot to look up—a common mistake for people who, like both of us, are just learning to track. By the time Koelle raises her eyes and leaps backward six inches, nearly bumping into me, we're within about twenty feet of the rhinoceros.

Trust me on this: observing an animal in a zoo, particularly an animal the size of a Subaru Forester, is very different from encountering it on foot in its own neck of the woods. I can be startled into a cardiac emergency by a reasonably robust spider, so realizing that I'm close enough to spit on a mountainous animal who has two enormous pointy horns is . . . disconcerting. I open my mouth to yip like a wounded poodle. But then the awe kicks in, and I simply stare.

The rhino, half hidden behind a thorn bush, cocks her primordial-looking head—which is roughly the size of a grocery cart—and swivels her satellite-dish ears toward us. She seems edgy. I soon realize why. A rustle in the brush reveals the presence of a second animal, her calf. He's tiny in rhinoceros terms, no bigger than, say, Shaquille O'Neal. He appears to be circling around behind me, putting all four of us humans between himself and his loving mother. I'm no woodsman, but I suspect this means Mamacita will soon have not only the means and the opportunity, but also the motive, to commence goring and stomping.

And I feel just *great* about that.

It's like waking up in Ionesco's absurdist play *Rhinoceros*; instead of panicking, I find the possibility of death by skewering in the African wilderness weirdly pleasing. I mean, how many middle-aged moms from Phoenix get to go out that way?

The mother rhino paws nervously, and I feel the impact tremor in the ground beneath my own feet. She is huge. She is nervous. She could kill me as easily as I clip my fingernails. But my mind is filled only with wonder, distilled into two basic questions.

Question 1: How the hell did I get here?

Question 2: What the hell should I do now?

Both issues seem equally mysterious. Oh sure, I could follow the breadcrumb trail of choices that brought me on this jaunt into the African wilderness. But how did I even stumble into the opportunities to make such choices? I defer answering this first question in favor of the second, which seems more pressing: How, exactly, does one extricate oneself from the close proximity of an alarmed rhinoceros? I hope my African friends have at least a two-pronged plan for such emergencies, seeing as how the rhino is tossing her own two prongs repeatedly in our direction, like a placekicker warming up for a field goal.

As if reading my mind, my friend Boyd Varty, who grew up here in the African bush, outlines Escape Plan Prong One. "Breathe," he whispers.

Oh. Right. After an initial gasp, I've been holding my breath, a typical fight-or-flight reaction that's spiking my adrenaline and heart rate. Technically I know better than that, but I forgot. Most of my knowledge, after all, is secondhand. I've spent the past few years interviewing all sorts of experts on human consciousness, from neurologists to psychologists to monks to medicine women, and prosaic as it sounds, they all agree that deep breathing is a profoundly powerful act, the cornerstone of everything from longevity to enlightenment. This is especially true when dealing, up close and personal, with a wild animal that outweighs your entire family.

Breathe. Just one long exhale will transform my whole body: change my brain, my hormone balance, my intuitive abilities, and my effect on other creatures. I know this intellectually. My friends know it viscerally. Koelle might look like a fitness model, but thousands of hours as a real-life "horse whisperer" have made her super-cool when dealing with large, nervous animals. Boyd is so tuned in to the wilderness he's practically a wild African animal himself. The fourth and final member of our party, Solly Mhlongo, is a Shangaan tracker of legendary skill and courage. He once sprinted across a river to drag Boyd from the jaws of a crocodile who was gnawing his leg like a drumstick until Boyd, thinking fast, shoved his foot *down* its throat, opening the membrane that keeps water out of its lungs (the so-called gular flap or pouch), setting Boyd free and inspiring the song "Kick Him in the Gular Pouch," which is sung by Boyd's entire family on festive occasions involving alcohol, and would make an excellent hip-hop number.

But that is not my point.

My point is that, of the four people in our little expedition, I am definitely the weakest link. Nevertheless I'm feeling as bubbly and joyous as a four-dollar box of sparkling wine. I give Boyd a clumsy thumb's up, and he flashes me his movie-star smile. (It seems unfair enough that these people are brave and smart—do they also have to be good-looking?) As the rhino mother squares up with us, snorting, and her baby continues to mosey toward our rear flanks, Boyd silently launches Prong Two of our escape plan, which is to edge sideways into a thorn bush. We place our feet carefully to avoid rocks, animal burrows, and snakes. The thorns rip at my clothes and hair and skin. I'm well aware that any misstep could result in exceptionally stimulating consequences. I can't stop smiling.

How the hell did I get here? What the hell should I do now?

It occurs to me, as I tiptoe, that I've been asking these questions all my life, certainly by school age, when I began to suspect I'd disembarked from the universe's light-rail system onto the wrong planet. Slowly evading the rhinoceros, I flash back several decades, to other moments when my hair was full of sticks, my arms covered with scratches, and my attention fully invested in some animal—a bird, a squirrel, a feral kitten—for whose friendship I would gladly have risked death.

HOW I GOT HERE

At age four, when most of my memory begins, I still half-believed my favorite books: fairy tales with talking mice and deer; Arthur, the Once and Future King, whom Merlin could change into any beast; Tarzan and Mowgli, who were raised by animals. When people asked me, "What do you want to be when you grow up?," I said, "An archer," not because I wanted to shoot things with arrows, but because I thought that that job title would qualify me to live like Robin Hood, hanging out in a forest with a bunch of idealistic friends.

This felt not only like a normal life ambition, but like the one, inevitable occupation of my core being, my "true nature." I thought it up myself. No one ever told me to think that way, to learn the names of several hundred mammalian species or to spend hours outside watching birds and munching random plants to see what happened. No one even urged me to read—but I did, obsessively, because how else could I travel to distant wildernesses, have great adventures, learn about animals I could never hope to see in real life? The great gift I got from my family, as the seventh of eight children, was the absolute freedom to read what I wanted, dive into any patch of wilderness I could find, and assume that I'd keep doing it my whole life. Unlike thousands of clients I've counseled in adult life, no one ever tried to stop me from following my true nature. Until I was five, anyway.

Perplexingly, once I started school I found that my first teachers were not convinced I'd grow up to learn animal languages and live in the woods. After a few quizzical, critical responses from adults, I realized that none of my literary heroes or their sylvan lifestyles was real. Chasing stray cats around empty lots wasn't going to get me anywhere in polite society; to succeed I had to focus completely on my education. Which I did. In fact, I focused long and intensely enough to grind my way through three Harvard degrees. By my late twenties I was well on my way to being a professor of sociology or social psychology or organizational behavior or sociobehavioral organopsychology or whatthehellever.

There was one tiny fly in my career ointment: the thought of spending my life writing for academic journals and attending faculty meetings made me want to beat myself to death with my own shoes. So in my early thirties I went back to that five-year-old self, the one with dirty fingernails and a passion for field biology, and asked her what she'd like to do. Within reason, of course. She said that she wanted to write hopeful thoughts for other people who felt imprisoned by offices, bureaucracies, or family pressures. She wanted to write books that made people feel free, the way *Tarzan* and *The Jungle Book* made her feel free. She wanted to tell readers they could create their own rules.

This sounded marginally acceptable to my schooled self. I pictured myself living The Writing Life in the country, wearing a billowy blouse, churning out prose, and collecting checks from a quaint, rustic-looking mailbox down by the front gate. By the time I realized I'd joined the entertainment industry, it was sort of too late. But as writers go, I was lucky. I ended up on a kind of endless book tour, traveling constantly to give luncheon speeches, conference addresses, and TV appearances. Then the Internet arrived. Information was being spread in fabulous new ways. Now, in addition to writing, speaking, and doing media interviews, people told me I had to blog, tweet, and post on Facebook. I did my best, but whenever I tried to join the Internet revolution, I felt like the creepy middle-aged high school teacher showing up at a student kegger. I was running as fast as I could while again becoming miserable and overworked, defined by rules about How to Succeed in Business by Really, Really Trying.

In the midst of this I'd received an unusual request. A man named Alex van den Heever, who was a game ranger (whatever that was), invited me to come see what was happening at a game preserve in South Africa called Londolozi. I'd been to Londolozi once, during a book tour, and fallen utterly in love with the place. Because of this, Alex's email had forcefully grabbed my attention—or rather, the attention of my thorn-scratched, twig-haired, four-year-old self. The very word "Londolozi" had sounded a clear tone somewhere inside me, a note that resonated purely and perfectly with my true nature. I'd begun to cry as I read Alex's email, not quite knowing why.

But at this moment, having responded to Alex's email, become a frequent visitor to Londolozi, and arrived face-to-face with Mama Rhino and her calf, the reason for those tears dawns on me. As I carefully pull a thorn from my cheek, hoping the rhino won't charge but not really minding if she does, things start clicking together in my mind, like the pieces of a jigsaw puzzle settling into their proper positions.

Londolozi is a Zulu word meaning "protector of all living things." The people who gave that name to this wilderness have spent their lives doing something they call "restoring Eden." The land under my feet was once a bankrupt cattle farm, almost devoid of life. This ecosystem was restored to its original state by just a few people, including Alex, my friend Boyd Varty and his family, and Shangaan trackers like Solly. These folks have already helped restore an area of the Earth larger than Switzerland, and they have no intention of stopping.

So—it all seems to me clear now—it was my uncivilized four-year-old self, with her passion for animals and love of running around in places with few humans, who dragged me ten thousand miles to this wild, magical place with these wild, magical people. Right now, I'm creeping into a bush with an African tracker, a conservationist, and a woman who really can talk to animals. The reality hits me as hard as any rhinoceros: the world I believed in, back in my most innocent, uninformed, childish mind— the world I long ago stopped hoping to find, the one I'd buried under decades of thankless work toward "civilized" goals—is *real*. That's why, right now, I could die happy—happier than I've been in forty years. My life will have been worth living for this one moment, with these friends, this place, those primordial animals, this joyful pounding heart. I'm finding out what it feels like to reclaim my true nature. It's one of the most wonderful things I've ever experienced. And because ecstasy loves company, I want you to experience it too.

The wild new world of the twenty-first century is the perfect setting for reclaiming your true nature. And your life will work much, much better if you let that nature direct your choices. It will bring you freedom, peace, and delight; give you the optimal chance of making a good living; and help you create the best possible effect on everything around you. I'm not certain exactly how it will play out in your case, but here's what I do know: it's time you met your rhinoceros.

HOW DID *YOU* GET HERE?
WHAT SHOULD *YOU* DO NOW?

Your "rhinoceros" is anything that so fulfills your life's real purpose that if someone told you, "It's right outside—but watch out, it could kill you!," you'd run straight out through the screen door without even opening it. Barefoot. Right now, you know what your rhinoceros is, but you may not yet *know* that you know, because the part of you that clearly sees your right life is your true nature, and it doesn't talk much (as we'll see later). Your rhinoceros may not be quite as attention-getting as mine. But it will awaken in you such happiness you'll want it to return again and again.

Maybe you'll have a rhinoceros moment while playing a cool new video game, or decorating a room with your soul mate, or helping a toddler grow a flower, or nourishing a circle of friends who rarely stop laughing and never stop helping one another. Maybe your rhinoceros hasn't been invented yet. When the younger of my two daughters asked me what to choose for her college major, I told her, "Design your own major.

Then take all the classes that make you want to jump out of bed in the morning—or afternoon, or whatever—because your real career probably won't exist for a few more years."

As we begin the second decade of the twenty-first century, the pace of technological and social change has reached what statisticians call "the knee of the curve" in an exponential growth pattern. That means that, after many centuries of slow progress from basic fire-making to the Industrial Revolution, we are now inventing more powerful technologies at such a pace that soon the human brain won't be able to keep up with the machines it has built. Even professional futurists have no idea what the world will look like in the coming decades, though they do highlight a few key trends that will almost certainly continue. For example:

- Individuals like you and me now have the power to do things, such as getting information to billions of people, that only large organizations, like governments and corporations, could do at any earlier point in human history.

- The means for achieving objectives like this are becoming cheaper, more accessible, and more ubiquitous by the day.

- Knowledge is no longer power, because knowledge is no longer scarce. What is scarce is human attention. Directing human attention is the way people trade goods and services—thus how they survive financially—in the wild new world.

- The qualities that capture positive attention these days aren't slickness, blandness, and mass consensus (boring), but authenticity, inventiveness, humor, beauty, uniqueness, playfulness, empathy, and meaning (interesting).

- The scarcest, most coveted resources aren't high-tech machines or highly developed cities, but "unspoiled" places, people, animals, objects, and experiences.

Once we figure out what constitutes your rhinoceros, your best bet for living happily and prosperously is to go interact with it. Maximum positive attention (the most valuable resource in this wild new world) comes from *being absolutely yourself,* operating from your true nature, to connect with the true nature of people, animals, plants, events, and situations.

THE FUNCTION OF YOUR TRUE NATURE

Having received some social science training in my day, I knew all this before I finally met my own actual, flesh-and-blood rhinoceros. I also knew that the true nature of all humans—indeed true nature broadly defined—has always been limited by survival pressures, including those the sociologist Max Weber called the "iron cage" of rationalization. As long as people keep making money by rational means, Weber wrote, society's iron cages will keep imprisoning them, obliterating their desires and differences, turning human workers into mere components of the great financial machine of society.

As a graduate student reading Weber's work, it did not surprise me to learn that the great theorist tended to get a little blue; in fact he sometimes lay in his room for years on end, and described humanity's future as a "polar night of icy darkness." Nor was I surprised that Weber (like me) had chronic physical pain that crippled him for decades. Whenever I took breaks from my graduate studies to lie down and watch wildlife documentaries (the better to tolerate my own chronic pain), I'd invariably hear predictions that a literal "polar night of icy darkness" was on its way, whether it was nuclear winter or some other form of global disaster. How the hell did we get here? What the hell should we do now?

I was super fun at parties.

Yet even though I had long ago accepted that true nature—yours, mine, Earth's—was damaged beyond repair, when I went to Londolozi I heard my true nature whispering a new message. I'd thought I was just stealing a few moments from the iron cage of my work to glimpse one last piece of the vanishing natural world, but the instant I accepted death-by-rhino, a different thought entered my awareness. For that wordless instant I let go of the false self I carry around in my mind. In the single beat of inner silence that followed, I heard the message from my sunburned, grubby-fingered four-year-old self, the message that the very existence of Londolozi, the people who had restored it, the anxious mother and her healthy, strapping calf all represented: *Nature can heal.*

HEALING YOUR TRUE NATURE

That one short sentence became a watershed in my life. It told me that, if we give ecosystems a chance (as humans have at Londolozi), whole landscapes can begin to repair themselves. It said that, despite the years I'd spent in various iron cages, my own true nature could repair itself too. So can yours. Even if you're a devout city-dweller, even if you see nature solely as that deplorably mall-deprived space you must drive through to get to the airport, even if you believe, with W. C. Fields, that "anyone who hates children and animals can't be all bad," *that very expression of your unique preferences is part of your true nature.* Your job, now and for the rest of your life, is to heal that true nature and let it thrive.

These days the iron cages of many industries are collapsing, taking with them the jobs of many people who traded their happiness for supposed economic security. Change is reaching a scope and pace that has left few social or economic institutions unchanged (and is quickly getting around to changing the rest). The wild, fluid world of the twenty-first century means that you not only *can* free yourself from your iron cage, but you *must.* Freedom and health for your deepest, truest self is essential for thriving in this strange, unprecedented time, when (as we'll see later) authenticity often equals attention, which equals value, which equals prosperity.

How the hell did you get where you are? By making your way, as best you could, through a maze of social pressures that were often destructive to your true nature. What the hell should you do now? Find a new way. A better way. *Your* way. The unknown, uncharted path through this wild new world that allows you—yourself, in your uniqueness—to reclaim the full measure of your true nature.

Can you accept this challenge? If you can't, I hope that you're comfortable living in your cage—and seeing it smashed by a tidal wave of escalating change. If you can, congratulations. Your future will be filled with adventures and excitement. It will also find you charting your course in a new peer group. The decision to heal your own true nature, by definition, makes you one of nature's healers. And as it happens, healers play a unique, powerful, perhaps unprecedented role in the wild new world.

To get something done, as any murder mystery will tell you, we need motive, means, and opportunity. Your true nature provides the motive for creating the life you really want. The fluidity of our civilization is creating the opportunity. The means you'll use to realize your "right life" may not be as obvious. I believe they must come from ancient traditions created and used by wise healers in many different cultures and places. These ways of mending were developed to fix any precious, complex, broken thing. Our culture, while zooming far past previous societies in its ability to manipulate the physical world, has lost or deliberately discarded these ways of repairing what is broken in people and in the world. Teaching you to use them is the central purpose of this book.

THE HEALING TEAM

Way back when I was teaching in college and business school, something incongruous started happening to me: for some reason, people kept showing up at my office and asking me questions, not about school but about their lives. "How the hell did I get here?" they would ask me. "What the hell should I do now?"

I had no idea. Fortunately, I realized that if I just sat there, people always figured it out for themselves. That's the reason I ultimately became a life coach, part of a profession so cheesy it fairly screams to be covered in nuts (and some would argue that it is). I didn't choose life coaching as a career; I wanted to be something more prestigious, like a professor, or a convenience-store clerk, or a crack addict. But as a coach, I gradually noticed that many of the people who hired me were oddly similar. Though they looked very different superficially—all flavors of gender, age, race, nationality, and occupation—they *sounded* weirdly alike. Here are some examples to show you what I mean.

- Kendra was a nineteen-year-old college student, sent to me by her parents after an academically disastrous first semester at Columbia. "I can't focus," said Kendra, who was once an excellent student. "I walk around New York feeling trapped by concrete. I don't belong. I want—I *need* to be somewhere else, doing something else. Something that, I don't know, somehow *helps*." Her voice trembled as she said this; it made no sense to her, but the emotions behind it were clearly overwhelming.

- Born to a wealthy New York City family, Jack once aspired to be either a mounted policeman or a dog walker in Central Park.

"Those were the only professions I knew about that involved being outside, with animals," he laughed. When he was fifteen, Jack met a boy who had autism, and a lightbulb went on in his mind. "I saw how Denny relaxed around animals, and I became obsessed with facilitating that." Jack studied special education in college and graduate school and eventually began doing occupational therapy with children with special needs, using interaction with animals as part of their therapy. "This is simply not what we do in my family," Jack said. "But it's the only thing I've ever wanted to do."

• "I'm ridiculously busy, but almost every day I find myself putting everything aside and just listening to people," Lorrie, a middle-aged mom, told me. "Sometimes people I hardly even know. I'm not sure why they want to confide in me, but they do. And then I hear myself giving them advice that never, until that very moment, entered my head. I feel like I'm taking time away from everything I'm supposed to do, but when I'm in the moment, none of that seems to matter. What's wrong with me?"

• Pete was my driver from a conference in the Catskill mountains to the Albany airport. He grew up hunting for fun, but began soul-searching about the morality of taking a life, any life, when he joined protests against the war in Vietnam. Frustrated with the government, Pete went to live on an Apache reservation, where he became best friends with the local medicine man. Many years later Pete still lives to connect with the wilderness and thinks constantly about healing it. "During hunting season," he told me, "I put on my camouflage, go out into the woods, and scare animals away from hunters." When I pointed out that this sounded just a tiny bit dangerous, he laughed. "It's not the way I was supposed to risk my life serving my country, but it's the best way I know."

• All April ever wanted was a good, steady job with a decent salary, benefits, and room for advancement. But her job with a prominent bank "wasn't completely fulfilling," she said. "Actually, if I'd stayed I would have randomly stabbed someone in another cubicle." April found fulfillment elsewhere: "I love talking with my friends about how we're going to change the world. We're just goofing off, but I'm half serious. I do feel as if something is happening, and I'm not supposed to watch it from a corporate job."

See what I mean? Though very different in terms of demographics, all these people shared a querying, relentless, urgent need to connect with their true nature. As more and more of them told me their stories, I realized they shared clusters of other characteristics, though not anything demographers record. These virtually always include the following:

- A sense of having a specific mission or purpose involving a major transformation in human experience, but being unable to articulate what this change might be.

- A strong sense that the mission, whatever it is, is getting closer in time.

- A compulsion to master certain fields, skills, or professions, not only for career advancement, but in preparation for this half-understood personal mission.

- High levels of empathy; a sense of feeling what others feel.

- An urgent desire to lessen or prevent suffering for humans, animals, or even plants.

- Loneliness stemming from a sense of difference, despite generally high levels of social activity. One woman summed up this feeling perfectly when she said, "Everybody likes me, but nobody's like me."

In addition, these people shared clusters of the attributes below. Only a few individuals possessed every single trait, but they all had a clutch of them:

- High creativity; passion for music, poetry, performance, or visual arts.

- An intense love of animals, sometimes a desire to communicate with them.

- Difficult early life, often with a history of abuse or childhood trauma.

- Intense connection to certain types of natural environment, such as the ocean, mountains, or forest.

- Resistance to orthodox religiosity, paradoxically accompanied by a strong sense of either spiritual purpose or spiritual yearning.

- Love of plants and gardening, to the point of feeling empty or depressed without the chance to be among green things and/or help them grow.

- Very high emotional sensitivity, often leading to predilections for anxiety, addiction, or eating disorders.

- Sense of intense connection with certain cultures, languages, or geographic regions.

- Disability, often brain-centered (dyslexia, retardation, autism), in oneself or a loved one. Fascination with people who have intellectual disabilities or mental illness.

- Apparently gregarious personality contrasting with deep need for periods of solitude; a sense of being drained by social contact and withdrawing to "power up" again.

- Persistent or recurring physical illness, often severe, with symptoms that fluctuated inexplicably.

- Daydreams (or night dreams) about healing damaged people, creatures, or places.

I had a lot of these traits myself, which, I assumed, was the reason other people who had them kept confiding in me. These people's inner lives and personalities were so much alike, and I had such a strange feeling they were somehow meant to work together, that I began calling them the Team. By my forties I was meeting Team members everywhere, and they were asking, "How the hell did I get here? What the hell should I do now?" with increasing frequency and almost disturbing intensity. Literally hundreds of people came to me for coaching, approached me at speaking engagements, or wrote to tell me the same story: though they don't know why, they felt they were born to be part of some very specific and beneficial change, they've been preparing for it since birth, and the time to act is getting closer.

Though I had no idea what people on the Team were expecting, I expected it too. When one woman asked what we were doing, and I said I didn't know, she replied, "Okay. Well, whatever it is, we move at dawn." We both laughed heartily as I wondered what brand of antipsychotic my peers would prescribe for me.

It was shortly after this incident that an anthropologist told me, "You know, in a premodern culture, the people you're describing would have been recognized as the tribe's healers—druids, medicine people, shamans, or whatever. You did realize that, didn't you?"

"Why, no, Professor," I said. "I did not." And I scampered off to do me some book larnin'.

FINDING A TERM FOR THE TEAM

I discovered my professor friend was right. Throughout human history, in every geographic region and cultural tradition (except modern rationalism), individuals with Team attributes were thought to have the gift—and responsibility—of connecting the natural and supernatural worlds with the express purpose of providing comfort and healing to all beings. This was not only their vocation, it was their job and their career.

Generally this wasn't a hereditary role; individuals with the telltale traits were recognized by their elders, then trained to be a . . . something. Every culture had its own word. Modern Western culture doesn't. We divide the roles of mystic, doctor, therapist, artist, herbalist, naturalist, and storyteller into separate, often inimical professions. In most other societies, there was one word, one job assignment, for somebody who was all these things at once.

I'm still struggling to find an English word for the Team that doesn't evoke images of simplistic superstition or New Age devotees who dress in wolf pelts and rechristen themselves Moonbeam Hummingbird. The word "healer" describes the Team's desired effect on the world, but as I've researched this topic in both developed and developing countries, I've encountered a lot of self-designated "healers," "gurus," and "spiritual teachers" who seem primarily devoted to the health of their own bank accounts. They certainly aren't the Team.

Every now and again, though, I've met individuals who seem to embody the whole promise of the healer's archetype. These people are walking generators of peace, hope, compassion, and restoration. The things they accomplish often seem miraculous, but they themselves are universally humble, insisting that their work is simple and pragmatic. To differentiate them from icky counterfeits, I began using the word "mender," which describes the core function of these lovely people and fits their humble approach. I'll use it often in the pages ahead. But the word I'll use most to describe the Team is "wayfinder."

FIGURING OUT HOW THE HELL WE GOT HERE AND WHAT THE HELL WE SHOULD DO NOW

The anthropologist Wade Davis coined the word "wayfinder" to describe the ancient navigators who first discovered the Pacific Islands, guiding small boats across vast stretches of open water to patches of land so small they make needles in haystacks look like anvils in breadboxes—all without modern navigation equipment. In his book *Wayfinders: Why Ancient Wisdom Matters in the Modern World*, Davis writes that Polynesian wayfinders (a few of whom are still with us) can "read" the ocean so sensitively that they recognize the refractive wave patterns of island chains hundreds of miles away by watching ocean swells break against the hull of their canoe. They use empirical observation and a dash of intuition that looks damn close to magic.

This is a perfect metaphor for the task humanity is facing right now. We must chart a course through conditions as fluid as water, in such a way that we not only stop the destruction of our own true nature, but reverse it. As we do that—and only as we do that—we will naturally begin healing the earth. I recently saw a bumper sticker that read, "Dear Humans: Save yourselves, I'll be fine. Love, Earth." Our Team of wayfinders are people who feel an internal call to heal any authentic part of the world, beginning with their own true nature. If you're a born "mender," you'll pursue this healing almost in spite of yourself. And as you find it, you'll automatically become the change you wish to see in the world, healing the true nature of the people and things around you.

YES, YOU'RE ON THE TEAM

Just the fact that you're still reading this—the fact that you picked up this book to begin with—means you're almost certainly a born wayfinder. These days, frankly, we're everywhere. This isn't just a social role, it's an archetype—a role or pattern of behavior intrinsic to all human psyches. Humans, for the most part, have the capacity to embody almost any archetype that happens to be needed in a specific situation. For example, if you've ever been in danger, you might have called on your "hero" archetype, finding the courage and grit you needed to prevail. If you've cared for a baby, a pet, or a sick loved one, you may have drawn on your "gentle parent" archetype to provide the necessary nurturing. And when you see someone or something wandering toward his or her or its own destruction, it awakens your healing-wayfinder archetype. Right now, wherever you look, some form of true nature—people, animals, places, relationships—is crying out to be mended. As a result, people everywhere are feeling the pull to express the archetype of the healer, the wayfinder.

If you suspect (or know) that you're on the Team, don't make the mistake of thinking you need to go back to school, to get more formal training or degrees. Few schools teach what you need to reclaim your true nature. You need to learn what a wayfinder would have taught in an ancient tribe. You need to know what Merlin taught Arthur. In short, you need magic.

THE MENDER'S METHODS

Speaking of Arthurs, the science fiction writer Arthur C. Clarke once wrote, "Any sufficiently advanced technology is indistinguishable from magic." As the Team got more and more of my attention, I began to seriously study the methods used by wayfinders. I learned all I could about them from books, experts, and people who still practice the ancient ways. These methods included ways of understanding the physical world, connecting and communicating with other beings, anticipating the future, and bringing comfort or healing to any situation. Often, they were viewed as outright magic by the societies where the wayfinders were trained. But the menders themselves tended to see their activities as pragmatic skills that could be empirically learned and evaluated. I called them the "technologies of magic." Whenever possible, I actually tried the technologies of magic I learned about in my research. Probably because I was bad at this (especially at the beginning), many of the "magical" techniques I tried just seemed weird, or at best ineffective. But to my astonishment, some of them worked.

By "worked," I mean that, when I performed some of the "magic" procedures from various traditions, I got reliable results in the three-dimensional world. This book will tell you much more about that. Here I want to add that the more I learned and used mender skills, the more I began to heal. Physically, my fibromyalgia—which had me in excruciating pain, bedridden for twelve years, and for which there is no known cure—went away. Psychologically, I became more happy, peaceful, resilient, and loving. Professionally, the business I never really meant to create kept growing. My life filled with more wonderful people than I'd ever imagined, and they seemed to benefit from my own path of self-healing.

This is how wayfinding works: you begin practicing certain skills just to feel better, but this seems to benefit other things too, until quite unintentionally you end up working to mend things you thought were far beyond your small scope. Whatever way you find through the wild new world (and your way may be nothing like mine), you join the Team that's ultimately working to make astonishing changes, in their own lives and in countless complex situations.

So, you may be wondering, what *are* these "technologies of magic"? What the hell should I do now?

I thought you'd never ask.

THE FOUR TECHNOLOGIES OF MAGIC

If you expect wayfinder ways to be all voodoo spells and wacky rituals, I should let you down easy right now. The true technologies of magic don't look all that impressive. (At least not from the outside. From the inside, they'll blow your mind.) The exercises in this book are distillations of skills that I found, with slight variations, in many mender traditions. Originally they were done by people of different labels, who used different languages, in different physical settings, and often wearing different fancy hats. (I'm not sure why, but menders of all cultures seem partial to excellent hats.) None of these surface details is necessary for using the technologies. This book will offer you the core skills of real magic, without much decoration. There aren't as many as you'd think. Every credible wayfinder tradition I've studied uses just four basic techniques, shaped by their separate cultural traditions, to chart a course through the wild new world. I call these skills Wordlessness, Oneness, Imagination, and Forming. Here's a brief preview of what this book will teach you about them.

Wordlessness shifts consciousness out of the verbal part of the brain and into the more creative, intuitive, and sensory brain regions. Which is more powerful? Well, the verbal region processes about forty bits of information per second. The nonverbal processes about eleven million bits per second. You do the math.

Oneness allows you to sense the interconnection between your consciousness and that of beings that are apparently unconnected to you. Science now confirms that we are highly interconnected. We are basically energy vibrating at different frequencies, unbounded and overlapping.

Once the technologies of Wordlessness and Oneness are active, **Imagination** becomes their supportive servant. Used in a state of nonverbal connection with the world around you, it will help you achieve a level of problem solving that feels like pure fun and looks like pure genius.

Finally, **Forming** creates in physical reality the situations, objects, and events you've imagined. For example, if you've used the first three methods to imagine a perfect relationship, career, or home, Forming is the stage where you actually meet your soulmate, launch your business, or buy the new house. There are two ways to make things happen at the stage of Forming: by moving things around with physical processes alone, or by adding physical action to the other three skills. Forming in this second way is so much more effective than simply slogging through various physical processes that it makes a wayfinder appear to be doing magic.

You may notice that the first two skills, Wordlessness and Oneness, aren't actions but states of consciousness. Our culture gives such things little value; we're all about doing, doing, doing. Imagination and Forming will probably feel more familiar to you, more concrete. *However, if they aren't used from within the state of consciousness achieved through Wordlessness and Oneness, Imagination and Forming have very little power.*

Many people ask if they can just skip the first two technologies, or start with the second two and work backward. The answer is—how can I express this—NO. For wayfinders, skillful being must precede all doing. But since the wayfinding state of consciousness is blissful in itself, it's well worth the strangeness of learning what Taoists call "doing without doing."

As long as I'm in caveat mode, one more thing: You're culturally conditioned to assume you can understand processes by reading about them. That won't work here. One reason our culture lost its magic is that we learn almost exclusively through language, which wipes out Wordlessness and renders the other technologies of magic powerless. You must actually *try* the exercises in this book if you want to understand them. Even so, only some of them will really rock your socks. Every mender has a unique profile, and someone else's favorite technique may leave you cold. But no skill can work if you don't actually try it. There's knowing, and then there's *knowing*. To find your way in the wild new world, you have to, you know, *know*.

CUMULATIVE WAYFINDER MAGIC

If you do jump in and try these exercises, especially if you practice them for a while, all kinds of interesting things will happen. You'll feel compelled to take a bus you've never ridden, and meet your new best friend. You'll contemplate the trip you've always longed to take, and within a few days someone will invite you to accompany her or him on just that journey. A new career will create itself around you like a living thing. These events will chart a way through the wild new world that I can't possibly predict, but they'll all have one common effect: they'll heal you. As you practice, the fractures in your true nature will begin to knit. Then you'll notice you're developing the strength, the insight, and the desire to heal other beings as well. Without even meaning to, simply by finding your own way, you'll become a wayfinder writ large.

This is even truer because our culture, while abandoning the technologies of magic, has developed what I call "magical technologies." I realize this sounds almost exactly like "technologies of magic," and in a way, I want to blur the distinction between the two. Magical technologies are machines that so defy our expectations of normalcy they almost seem unreal. Again, I don't really believe in magic; I just think it's pretty magical that during the past ten minutes I visually inspected my daughter's dorm in Japan, purchased and began reading a novel, sent a message to several hundred people, and checked tomorrow's weather forecast, all using a device so small it regularly gets lost in my purse. Because of such machines, the potential span of influence for a wayfinder today is far greater than anything possible in ancient times. If today's menders master the technologies of magic, they can spread their influence through magical technologies, potentially reaching billions of people instead of a few villagers. Through magical technologies, any healing occurring in our separate lives can flow immediately to our families, friends, communities, perhaps our entire species. If enough people start mending their true nature in the incredibly interconnected world we're creating, the cumulative effect really could begin healing the true nature of, well, everything.

This is the thought that pops into my mind as I creep sideways, my left ear filling with leaves, my nose filling with the urine-and-cilantro scent of rhinoceros, one millisecond after my true nature whispers *Nature can heal.*

Oh my God, I think. The Team is here to save the world.

Oh. That.

The mother rhino swings left, then right, a spiked wrecking ball on legs. The calf turns, noses the air, makes a short, toddling charge toward us, trips over a log, and tumbles onto his side. The mother snorts anxiously. The danger in the air crackles like electric voltage.

Beside me, Boyd begins murmuring what sounds like a lullaby. "There, there, little one," he croons to the baby rhino, which could easily roll a minivan by itself. "Go back to your mum, now. Go see your mum."

I can feel a deep calm emanating from Boyd—not the energy that, in my opinion, is called for in the present situation. But the baby rhino suddenly relaxes, as I've seen horses relax when Koelle approaches them. If I understood how skilled Boyd is at the technologies of magic, including communicating with animals, I'd feel utterly safe. But I don't understand—not yet—so my pulse keeps pounding as the calf struggles to his feet and follows Boyd's suggestion, trotting back to stand in his mother's comforting shadow. She exhales, relaxes her ears, and guides him away from us.

"Are you all right?" Solly asks me as we head off in the opposite direction.

"That," I said, my heart filled with a new vision of the Team mission, plus enough adrenaline to kill a squadron of Hell's Angels, "is the world's biggest understatement."

So here I am, five years after that day at Londolozi when I let go of my life as I'd known it and found my true nature waiting. I'm hoping that this book can lead you to a moment when you meet your own rhinoceros. Maybe the book itself can be a rhinoceros in your path, a strange lumpish thing, but one that gets up in your face, jolts you out of your usual thoughts, and demands, in the words of the poet Mary Oliver, "Tell me, what is it you plan to do with your one wild and precious life?"

All I ask, as you read this book, is that you listen for the real answer to that question. Not the answer that comes from the "you" most people see, with those uncomfortable clothes and that weary, polite social face, but the one from your true nature: the little mud-spattered princess, the gap-toothed superhero with the dishcloth cape up there in his favorite tree. If that pure self doesn't want to be a wayfinder, doesn't want to learn magic and help save the world, okay. Stop reading now; you'll get no hard feelings from me.

They look taller in person.

But if the truest part of you feels the way I did looking at that rhinoceros—as if a beautiful, impossible, almost forgotten dream is coming to life before your eyes—keep reading. Finding your way from this point through the wild new world of your own future, you'll often wonder, "How the hell did I get here?" and "What the hell should I do now?" But as the iron cages of your life dissolve and magic arises to replace them, I'm betting you'll realize that the wayfinder's journey has been your heart's real destination all along.

PART I

THE FIRST TECHNOLOGY OF MAGIC

WORDLESSNESS

ONENESS

IMAGINATION

FORMING

CHAPTER ONE

___

QUICK WAYS TO WAYFINDING
(STILLNESS, TORMENT, AND DELIGHT)

It's five o'clock on a typical morning at Londolozi. Several guests have met in the predawn darkness to pile into an open Land Rover and head out for a photo-safari "game drive." The vibe in the vehicle is jubilant: part adventure, part cocktail party. The guests introduce themselves, chat about families, jobs, previous vacations, and the animals they hope to see. They pepper the ranger with questions: What's that tree called? Why is that bird purple? Is it always this cold in the morning? Is that elephant dung over there? The ranger answers with encyclopedic knowledge and enthusiastic good humor, adding to the celebratory feel.

The man sitting on a chair welded to the very front of the Land Rover is behaving very differently from everyone else. He's a tracker from the Shangaan tribe whose English name is Richard. He's polite, but rarely speaks or even looks at the guests. In fact he doesn't seem to be doing anything in particular, just gazing expressionlessly around him at the ground, the sky, then the ground again. Every now and again Richard raises his hand, and the ranger turns off the Land Rover. As the tourists grow restless, Richard appears to do even less than usual; he just sits there looking around. Then he mutters a few words in Shangaan, pointing into the bush.

"Hold on, please," says the ranger to the guests, and drives straight into thick scrub. For twenty minutes the Land Rover barrels through tall grass, over largish saplings, across deep sandy washes, and into dense thorn bushes. The guests jolt and joke. Just as the sun turns the landscape a luminous golden green, Richard points to a clump of brush near an abandoned termite mound. There, almost invisible in the brush where their mother has hidden them, sit two leopard cubs, their fuzzy ears and bright, curious eyes just visible above the grass.

The guests squeal with delight. Cameras click furiously. Questions fly thick and fast: How old are the cubs? Why isn't the mother there? Are they male, female, one of each? How big will they get? Are they hungry? Do they eat meat, or are they still nursing? Why do they have spots? Why don't lions have spots? Why do zebras have stripes?

As the ranger supplies all the requested information, Richard sits silently with that daydreamy expression. In the flurry of inquiries about leopards, no one asks an arguably more interesting question about him. How in God's name did he find two tiny, silent, camouflaged animals three miles from any road, in dense brush? The answer could be a very long one, detailing all the tiny cues, hunches, and educated guesses that lead a master tracker to the thing he's hunting. But the most basic reason Richard can wayfind with almost miraculous skill is that he's a master of the first technology of magic, a state of awareness I call Wordlessness.

This brain state is the most important skill for any wayfinder in any culture and any situation. I spend a lot of time talking about the reasons for my clients' emotional swings and their life choices, but I've learned there are two ways to make such a choice: from a place of verbal thought, which has very little effect because it isn't rooted in their deepest perceptions, and from a place of Wordlessness, which makes every thought and action much, much more powerful. If you know how to drop into Wordlessness, you'll be so aware of your situation and your own responses to it that you'll go straight toward your best life, no matter how obscure it may seem or how many obstacles lie before you. At a time when social change is so rapid and the pressures on each person so unpredictable, Wordlessness is a skill you truly need to find your way.

In addition to helping you reach your objective, Wordlessness is a destination in itself, a core aspect of your true nature. It connects your consciousness with the deep peace and presence that is the essential *you.* Deep Wordlessness eliminates virtually all of the fear, anger, or regret that bedevils most humans most of the time. That's why it's taught by the wisdom traditions of virtually every culture—except our own. It's the opposite of what you were probably taught during your own education. But this chapter will begin to help you reclaim it.

THE CULTURE OF WORDS

During the Age of Exploration, adventurers from various European nations traveled the globe, planting their flags and often trouncing local opposition with powerful weapons. The scientific method that helped develop these weapons also gave their owners a sense of intellectual superiority. European explorers routinely described indigenous populations as dim-witted, unmotivated, and backward. This prejudice still resonates, as scholars "discover" things about the world that indigenous people have known since prehistory. Scholars are beginning to admit that indigenous peoples' local knowledge is extensive and worth learning. But our culture still maintains one of its most deeply held beliefs: that "real" learning is spoken, read, and written, that real knowledge consists of words.

It's a pretty safe bet that your education, dear reader, consisted of sitting in airless rooms listening to lectures, reading books, and taking tests in which you interpreted verbal or numeric questions and tried to give exactly the answers your teachers already knew. If you couldn't do this, you were shamed and punished, or perhaps diagnosed with a learning disability and medicated to the point where you could focus exclusively on words and numbers. If you did this well, you were praised and rewarded. If you spent too much time outside playing, you experienced punishment and failure. Screening out everything but words, you were taught, is the way to create a good life, to find your way in the world.

Compare this to how Richard grew up learning in the wilderness. Out in the African bush—the environment in which all humans evolved, the context of our literal true nature—any child who riveted attention on a tiny page full of black squiggles would be cat food in about fifteen minutes. Richard learned to track in the same way that all children evolved to learn everything: by paying attention to the adults in his community while moving continuously through a natural environment, observing the whole interconnected ecosystem with all five senses.

Richard is, in fact, an intellectual of staggering virtuosity. Every detail of his environment is significant, meaningful, and informative to him. He can tell from a scratch in the ground and the grunt of a hyena exactly where lions are hunting nearby. The flight pattern of a tiny bird tells him the position of a buffalo half a mile away, because that particular species of bird likes to eat ticks off the large herbivore's back. A guinea fowl alarm call says "Predator!," and since the call is coming from low brush, Richard knows that the bird is probably facing a snake, which could potentially attack one of the flock. In his mind Richard can see both the snake and the bird, visualizing with astonishing accuracy what each is doing right now.

In other words, as Richard sits at the front of the Land Rover, he's doing on land what Polynesian wayfinders do at sea: he's thinking with his whole brain—the eleven-million-bits-per-second nonverbal part, rather than the forty-bits-per-second verbal region. He doesn't participate in the guests' chatter, despite his excellent English, because his job is to navigate through the wilderness, and he can't do that if his brain is locked up in words. To find our way in any complex world, we need an awareness beyond language, the wayfinding state of our true nature. And we need it not only to make our way through external environments, but to navigate the inner workings of our own psyche.

FINDING THE WAY INTO THE HEART

In his autobiography the psychologist Carl Jung, one of the great wayfinders of inner life, described a conversation he had with a Native American chief named Mountain Lake, whom he regarded as a kindred spirit. "I was able to talk with him as I have rarely been able to talk with a European," Jung recalled. Perhaps because of their mutual respect, Mountain Lake gave Jung a very frank account of the way his people saw Europeans, the flip side of the white men's "natives are slow and stupid" story.

"Their eyes have a staring expression," the chief said. "They are always seeking something. What are they seeking? The whites always want something. They are always uneasy and restless. We do not know what they want. We do not understand them. We think that they are all mad." Jung asked Chief Mountain Lake to elaborate: Why, exactly, did white people seem so insane to the Indians?

"They say they think with their heads," responded Mountain Lake.

"Why of course," said Jung. "What do you think with?"

"We think here," said Chief Mountain Lake, and he pointed to his heart.

This is the key to Wordlessness, according to wayfinders from all times and places—and it's not just metaphorical. To navigate the wild world, you need to move your basic perceptual and analytical thinking out of your head and into the whole inner space of the body. This is how you begin to find your way through a terrible loss, a fulfilling career, a complicated relationship, or a broken heart, as well as through the ocean or the African bush. But most people don't seem to know this. Just as the guests in the Land Rover miss details of the environment because they're busy talking, we cover up the directional cues of our physical and emotional experience with verbal thinking.

Menders of all times and places have taught that silencing the thoughts in our heads and opening to the experience of the body and emotions is the basis of all healing. It's the only means by which we can reclaim our true nature or feel the subtle cues telling us how to find our way through life. Every Team member must heal inwardly by responding to this inner knowing before moving on to guide the healing of other things. Yet most of us still think more like European rationalists than like Chief Mountain Lake and Richard the tracker.

Tell me this: Right now, this very moment, what are you feeling? What physical sensations? What emotions? Now think about your plans for later today, or tomorrow. How do the feelings in your body change? What about your emotions? Next, picture a person in your life. How does that person's energy affect your inner senses? What do you feel emotionally in that person's company?

The majority of my clients can't answer these questions when we begin working together. They don't have a clue what's happening inside them in different situations or in their relationships with others. When I ask them, they respond with a concept.

"What do you feel when you're with your grandmother?"

"That she's had a hard life and I should treat her well."

"What do you feel about your job?"

"That I have to pay the rent."

"What do you feel about your son leaving for college?"

"That he's building a solid future."

Such answers have nothing to do with feelings; they're all verbal *thoughts*. They're socially grounded and socially acceptable; they make sure we won't rock any boats. Lord knows what would happen if you actually realized, for example, that you feel tense and angry around your grandmother, that your gut churns every time you hit the office, or that you're drowning in empty-nest grief as your son moves away. These feelings might take you off the smooth, paved roads of behavior you find normal and appropriate, but they are also your guides through life, the signals that tell you where to find what your soul is seeking.

WOUNDED INTO WORDLESSNESS

Sometimes it takes a radical event to reawaken you to the inner voice that's always telling you what decisions to make, what to embrace and what to avoid, how to steer through various inner and outer situations. This happened to Jill Bolte Taylor, a neuroanatomist at Harvard Medical School, when, at the age of thirty-seven, she had a massive stroke that wiped out the speech center in the left hemisphere of her brain. An expert in neurology, she was able to observe her own horrific experience with clinical precision, but it took her eight long years of grueling effort to rebuild her verbal functions so that she could describe the event in words. Immediately after the stroke she didn't even recognize her own mother, or know what the word "mother" meant.

This would have been tragic if it hadn't been so illuminating. You see, as Taylor lost her ability to think verbally, she gained the experience of a human mind freed from language. And that, it turned out, was worth having.

"I felt enormous and expansive," Taylor recounted later, in a TED talk you should watch (Google "Jill Bolte Taylor TED talk"). "My spirit soared free like a great whale gliding through the sea of silent euphoria." Before her stroke, Taylor "knew" herself to be "a single solid individual separate from the energy flow around [her] and separate from [others]." But when her verbal brain shut down, she found herself knowing, with equal if not greater conviction, that she lived in a universally interconnected universe in which "we are perfect. We are whole. And we are beautiful."

This is precisely the kind of thing we hear from menders of all cultures: Wordlessness allows us to see our true nature, and to heal from the violence of a thought system that cuts us apart, destroying our compassion for ourselves and others. Native American medicine people call Wordlessness "the Great Silence." The Buddhist term is often translated as "emptiness," and in Zen it is the "uncarved block." A medieval Christian mystic describes full awareness without language as "the cloud of unknowing." The Judeo-Christian-Muslim scripture referred to it as pure Being, the great "I Am." All say that it is a blissful and absorbing experience, a place where concepts dissolve, and everything is love.

UNLEARNING TO BE BRILLIANT

To master Wordlessness, heal your true nature, and become a wayfinder, you must unlearn almost everything you were taught in school about what it means to be intelligent. The sharp focus you were told to sustain is actually a limiting, stressful, narrow attention field—something animals only use in the moment of "fight or flight." Dropping into Wordlessness moves the brain into its "rest and relax" state. This affects the whole body, releasing a flood of hormones that helps repair and heal your body, relaxes your muscles, and puts you into a deep stillness, with expressionless face and soft eyes. Because you're paying attention to so much nonverbal sensory data, you may not respond verbally to comments or questions from other people when you're wordlessly "in the moment."

In our culture, gazing into the middle distance, ignoring language, and reacting only to genuine social interactions, physical feelings, and emotions is interpreted as laziness or stupidity. This is one reason we're so plagued by unhappiness and illness. Yet when you try to drop into Wordlessness, you may find that *not* paying attention to words is a delicate, sophisticated, and, at first, difficult skill. You won't be good at it without a lot of practice. I don't mean mere repetition, but something psychologists call "deep practice."

DEEP-PRACTICING WORDLESSNESS

Scientists have recently discovered that we physically restructure our brains when we learn new skills, especially when we use a learning process known as "deep practice." Deep practice is more than simply repeating something over and over. In deep practice, we aim for a precise experience, at first "getting it" only in brief flashes, then repeating the effort until we can perform the skill reliably. Wayfinders of all cultures deep-practice dropping into Wordlessness whenever they need to orient themselves, to figure out what they should do next or which direction to go.

You'll find several methods of dropping into Wordlessness in this chapter. Remember, *you can't learn them by reading about them.* Trying to understand Wordlessness by reading is like trying to understand skydiving by drawing parachutes. Please, actually *try* the exercises. In fact deep-practice them. You'll know they're working when you begin feeling flickers of peace, calm, and safety. You'll become more aware of subtle clues informing you about your surroundings, about other people's feelings and intentions. You'll want to make choices according to your own perceptions rather than whatever people are telling you. You don't have to start acting differently— not all at once—but you'll begin to figure out how you *wish* you could act. Persist long enough, and you'll be able to stretch the moments of total clarity into minutes, and eventually hours. If you want to be a true wayfinder, the time will come when you remain in a Wordless state most of the time.

TECHNIQUES FOR DROPPING INTO WORDLESSNESS: THE PATHS OF STILLNESS

Let's start with the best-known ways of reaching Wordlessness, which I call the paths of stillness. They involve—follow the logic closely here— sitting still. Meditation, which was regarded as bizarre by most Americans during my childhood, is now something many of us feel we should be doing, the way we feel we should stop eating sugar and organize our shopping receipts. If you love to meditate, good for you! Keep it up! But if meditation holds the same appeal for you as water-soluble medical fiber, try one of the techniques below. They're very simple, which shouldn't be confused with being easy. Persist at deep-practicing these techniques until you feel flickers of softness, expansion, and peace. Then practice holding that sensation longer and longer.

Path of Stillness: Feeling the Insides of Your Hands
Spiritual teacher Eckhart Tolle, author of *The Power of Now,* offered this technique to a listener who asked for a pragmatic technique for becoming fully present in the moment. It's similar to strategies from many wayfinding traditions, and probably works by activating both sides of the brain.

1. Close your eyes and hold up one hand so that it's not touching anything but air.

2. Ask your thinking mind, "Without opening my eyes, how can I know that my hand exists?"

3. Feel your mind's attention go inside the body to answer the question, activating a nonverbal part of the brain.

4. Now hold up both hands (eyes closed, remember) and feel the inside of both at the same time. Your awareness will slide out of left-hemisphere verbal thinking into both-hemispheres Wordlessness. You won't articulate this until it's over, and that's okay. The point is to feel it.

Path of Stillness: Pulling Your Senses into "Open Focus"

This method was discovered by a Princeton researcher, Les Fehmi, as he was playing around with new brain-observation technologies (for details, read his book, *The Open Focus Brain,* or visit his website). Fehmi's method parallels many exercises from wayfinder traditions of other times and cultures. Because he uses the idiom of modern science, many of my clients find it less suspicious than similar techniques espoused by people with unfamiliar hairstyles from faraway lands.

1. Sit, stand, or lie still and focus your eyes sharply on an object in front of you.

2. *Without moving your eyes,* broaden your attention until it registers everything in your field of vision, including the original object of focus.

3. Now, still without moving your eyes at all, make the object the foreground of your attention, and everything else the background.

4. Next, make the object the background, everything else the foreground.

5. Focus on everything in your visual field at once while repeating this yoga slogan: "Floor to ceiling, wall to wall, all things equal."

6. If you want to kick it up a notch, repeat this question: "Can I imagine the space inside the distance between my eyes?" Fehmi found that this question pulls the brain straight into a "synchronous alpha" wave pattern, a deeply relaxed, Wordless state.

Path of Stillness: Follow Your Own Bloodstream
This method, which one of my teachers learned from the tracker Tom
Brown Jr., is supposedly an Apache technique for putting the mind in
a state of Sacred Silence. It's my personal favorite way of dropping into
Wordlessness.

1. Take a few deep, full breaths.

2. Exhale completely, and pause before inhaling.

3. In the space before you need to breathe in again, focus your
   attention on your heart until you can feel it beating. This may
   take up to a minute.

4. Take another breath and exhale. Along with your heartbeat, find
   the sensation of your pulse moving through your hands, feet,
   scalp, entire body.

5. Stay focused on the feeling of your entire circulatory system as it
   channels your lifeblood to your head and extremities. See if you
   can feel it moving through your organs as well.

6. Perform some simple task—walking, washing the dishes, making your bed—while continuing to feel your heartbeat and overall pulse. You'll find the activity becomes strangely blissful.

WORDLESSNESS IN MOTION

Feeling your bloodstream while you walk around is a level of Wordlessness
that can challenge many meditators, who associate deep awareness with sitting peacefully on a cushion in their favorite yoga studio. Fully reclaiming
your true nature means sustaining a Wordless connection to your environment and inner condition no matter what's going on. This means replac-
ing thoughts about events with authentic sensations that track whatever's
occurring in the present moment. Because thinking is the most familiar
state of being for most of us, dropping thought and feeling our sensations
and emotions may be frightening, even painful. But in the end, it's far less

painful than typical human behavior, which is to become lost in thoughts and unavailable to anything real.

One universal teaching from wayfinders is that we suffer more from our thoughts about events than from the events themselves. Detaching from our verbal thoughts eliminates almost all our psychological suffering. As Wordlessness arises, fears about the future and regrets or anger about past events slips away, because past and future don't exist except as stories in our minds. This, according to the psychoneuroimmunologist Robert Sapolsky, is why wild animals don't get stress-related illnesses. They react with fight-or-flight responses when circumstances call for it, but then return very quickly to a baseline state of relaxation.

I learned how different this was from my own method of navigating life one day at Londolozi, when I was out roaming the bush with Boyd and Koelle. We noticed three giraffes staring fixedly at something we couldn't see. They looked horrified, their bodies rigid and their huge eyes wide. When we drew nearer to them, we saw why. On the bank of the river a lion was slowly and laboriously killing a baby giraffe. The huge cat braced like a wrestler in a clinch, his muscles taut and rippling, his jaws clamped on the windpipe of the desperately kicking baby, waiting for it to suffocate.

It was a long wait.

I felt a spasm of empathy, then went completely numb. Boyd, who probably noticed that I'd turned a pale shade of green, whispered, "Not your pain." When that didn't help, he added, "His pride has nine cubs. They have to eat." Boyd was trying to counteract my story ("This is God-awful!") with a more benevolent one ("This is the circle of life"). It didn't work.

For the rest of that day I felt strangely distracted. The joy and fascination I usually experience in nature were gone; in fact every feeling was gone. I remained lost in my own internal fogbank until I was headed home, trudging through London's Heathrow Airport. I'd bought a safari hat for my son, and to avoid squashing it, I was wearing it as I traveled. As I cleared security, which involved every form of examination except a colonoscopy (the machine must have been broken that day), the African hat fell backward off my head and the loose drawstring caught on my neck, pressing my windpipe ever so lightly.

That slight pressure acted as an associative trigger. Suddenly I became the baby giraffe, its neck clenched in the jaws of the lion, panicked, kicking, fighting, dying. The urge to run exploded inside me. For the next twenty minutes London travelers were treated to the sight of a crazed woman hurtling through Heathrow in cowboy boots and an African-tracker hat, weeping. I doubt anyone mistook me for British.

After a few laps around the terminal, the need to run suddenly vanished. I found my way to my departure gate and sat down in a quiet corner, panting.

Then something even *worse* happened.

This time I wasn't the baby giraffe; I was its mother and the other adults, watching it die. I succeeded in keeping relatively quiet—no more than two or three dozen people were looking around for my psych-ward attendants—but the horror and grief coursing through me felt as though they were turning me inside out.

And then it was over.

I. Mean. *Over.*

I slowly sat up and looked around the airport, feeling as if I'd just been born. Everything about me and around me seemed tender and fresh, dazzlingly beautiful. The sights, sounds, and smells I'd experienced in Africa (but had been unable to internalize) finally landed in my consciousness in a huge, soft swell of gratitude. I was absolutely and completely at peace.

And so, I realized, were the giraffes.

It was over for them too.

THE CURSE OF LANGUAGE

These days, when Jill Bolte Taylor finds herself feeling any sort of unpleasant emotional reaction to a situation, she says she simply checks her watch and waits ninety seconds. That's how long it takes for her body—and yours—to process the hormonal reactions associated with fear, anger, or grief. If you experience them without resistance, the emotions then disappear, though they may return again, but only in ninety-second waves. Taylor learned this experientially when she was still unable to think in language. Instead of pushing away or holding onto experiences through mental storytelling, she simply felt the negative emotion until it went away, leaving her back in euphoria.

If giraffes had our capacity for language, those three adult animals who watched the baby die might have done what I did: become so overwhelmed by the awfulness of Nature Red in Tooth and Claw that they blocked out their emotional reaction to the event while it was happening, while paradoxically attaching their entire psychology to the story of the attack. Language would have let them torture themselves with thoughts about what this terrible experience meant, for them, for other giraffes, for the fate of every prey animal. It could have been their 9/11.

"We're not safe!" verbally capable giraffes would have told each other. "Listen, from now on, we sleep in shifts. When you're awake, you can graze, but for God's sake don't enjoy it—stay alert! Also, we should try to kill lion cubs whenever we can. Bobbette! Stop browsing and pay attention, damn it! Have you already forgotten what happened to Li'l Jasper?"

Li'l Jasper's mother, Florine, may have been so inconsolable she'd have thrown herself to the crocodiles in the river where her child perished. Jasper's older siblings, wracked by the memory of their brother's death *and* their mother's suicide, would have spent their lives getting smashed on fermented marula fruit and abusing their spouses. And so it would have gone, generation after generation, until giraffes developed life coaching and began cleaning the language-based pain from their brains.

But giraffes don't live this way. Their attention is not in verbal thought, it's in sense perception, in the present moment. Giraffes don't get ulcers because they experience life as it happens: lion, horror, pain, death, grief, relaxation, beauty, peace, peace, peace, peace, peace. Humans, on the other hand, often live for decades in moderate to severe stress responses, triggered by memories of past pain and projections of future disaster: lion, horror, pain, death; memory of lion, horror, pain, and death; fear of future horror, pain, death; impotent rage at mortality as a concept; protective numbness; underlying despair, despair, despair, despair, despair.

After working with hundreds of clients who've learned to separate themselves from their negative stories, I've seen with my own eyes that difficult circumstances offer opportunities to drop more deeply into a Wordless perception, where we find more peace and inner strength. That's why so many movies are made about heroes learning to be better people by going through hell, climbing mountains or fighting bloody battles or thrashing themselves through some sports-related training program that turns them into geysers of blood, sweat, and tears. That's why many cultures train their healers and visionaries by deliberately putting them through some sort of physical trial.

DROPPING INTO WORDLESSNESS
THROUGH THE PATHS OF TORMENT

The key to making painful experiences paths to Wordlessness is to *surrender all resistance to physical suffering you can't avoid.* This means allowing yourself to pay full attention to your own physical or emotional pain, without trying to avoid the feeling, or thinking that things must or should be different. That nonresistance is what allows the suffering to pass quickly; even as it's occurring, it's less torturous without verbal thought. I don't suggest you deliberately seek pain, but life being what it is, you'll probably experience some painful things in the upcoming days or weeks. If you use them as paths to Wordlessness, they may actually become gifts.

Path of Torment: Fatigue
You'll almost certainly get tired this very day. Every day, in fact. Instead of fighting it, use it. Physical work, sleep deprivation, long periods of boredom—all can help you into Wordlessness. Fatigue can grind the sharp edges off your intentions, swings moods around like a shillelagh, and ultimately—here's the key—leave you so tired you just can't think. The next time you're worn out, don't tell yourself to pep up. Do what your body and brain want: surrender to the weariness. Breathe into it. The most likely result is that you'll relax and fall asleep—exactly what an animal or baby would do. Being able to feel Wordless fatigue makes you more capable of resting deeply in whatever time you've got, allowing you to stay more rested physically and much calmer emotionally.

Path of Torment: Hunger
One thing I've noticed about clients who have weight problems is that their addiction to overeating is mental, not physical. It's fueled by high anxiety, which is caused by attachment to mental stories. If you run into occasional life circumstances where you don't get a chance to eat until you're very hungry, don't tell yourself it shouldn't be happening: surrender to what you're feeling. Study your own low energy, your stomach cramps, your fantasies of pancakes as if you're an observer from Mars. You'll find that you become less frantic to get food and less compulsive about eating it.

Path of Torment: Exposure
My dear friend Max, at age fifteen, spent four days and nights alone, without shelter, tools, or food, in a ten-foot-diameter circle in the wilderness. He emerged more clear-eyed and centered. He was also under the careful observation of an extensively trained wilderness survival expert. DO NOT DO THIS WITHOUT EXPERT HELP. But if you accidentally end up without creature comforts, stuck in an airport, stalled car, or stuffy waiting room, surrender your mind's resistance to what is happening even as you work to improve your situation. There are two ways to be adrift in the wilderness, a big city, a foreign country, a highway detour: in panic and resistance, or accepting the situation. The path that drops you into Wordlessness will keep you calm and help you act more wisely on your own behalf.

Path of Torment: Illness
I hope you never get sick, but most members of the Team are intimate with illness. The mender's archetype often comes with an extremely sensitive neural apparatus, high anxiety, intense empathy, and insomnia. Perhaps this contributes to the illnesses that anthropologists call "shaman sicknesses," which are usually chronic, painful, and stress-related. If you're a born wayfinder, you may have anything from migraines to irritable bowel syndrome to lupus. Do everything you can to feel better. Use every technique or medication your doctor prescribes. But also treat sickness as an opportunity to reach a very deep level of Wordlessness, where pain is a mentally and emotionally neutral phenomenon, like a cloud in the sky, and you are not "in pain" but in the Sacred Silence. Without struggling against your pain, try the practices I mentioned above: feeling into your hands, your breath, your circulatory system. Watch how pain can change, becoming far more tolerable, when the brain isn't focused on verbal thinking.

DROPPING INTO WORDLESSNESS THROUGH THE PATHS OF DELIGHT

Whew! I'm so glad *that's* over! Any suffering is an opening into Wordlessness if used appropriately, but I much prefer experiences on the other extreme of the enjoyment spectrum. I call these the paths of delight. Unlike ordeals, delightful experiences often aren't inevitable. When they do happen, humans have an odd tendency to resist them by staying in our mental stories. We seek pleasures obsessively because our mind-stories say that happiness depends on them, but those very mind-stories and the habit of thinking verbally keep us from actually enjoying the pleasures that arrive. As the poet Howard Nemerov says, "We think about sex obsessively except during the act, when our minds tend to wander."

To use a pleasurable experience as a path to Wordlessness, *hold full attention in the physical experience of the moment.* Again, the simple strategies of feeling the inside of your own body or putting your eyes in "soft focus" can transform your experience in wonderful ways. If mental stories arise, focus on the delightful experience by using your verbal mind to silently name the physical and emotional feelings: "softness," "sweetness," "comfort," "excitement," "affection," "gratitude," and so on. This pulls attention away from narratives and allows you to let go of your mind.

Here are a few paths to Wordless delight you can use right now. I suggest you try them several times this very day.

Path of Delight: Finding the Sweetness
Most people pay closer attention to discomfort and anxiety than they do to comfort and calm. Both are available to you in most "normal" situations. Choosing to flood your attention into the pleasurable aspects of a situation— with sensation, not Pollyanna stories—can turn an ordinary day exquisite. This method borrows from "open focus" brain research, opening the aperture of your nonverbal mind to more and more aspects of enjoyment.

1. Right now, find something in your present environment that is visually beautiful. Put your full attention on it.

2. Without moving your eyes, listen to the sounds around you, and then listen to something deeper: the silence in which the sounds are taking place.

3. Find a spot on your body that feels comfortable. It may be just one toe. While still watching beauty and listening to silence, fully feel the comfort in that toe.

4. Breathe in slowly, feeling the sensation of your lungs filling with air and nourishing your bloodstream. If you can smell anything fragrant or delicious, focus on that scent.

5. Practice focusing your attention on all these pleasurable things at once. Feel the calm that arises as this process drops you out of language.

Path of Delight: Sense-Drenching

When people have a few idle minutes in a relatively comfortable place, they tend to spend them worrying. Instead try dropping into Wordlessness by fully experiencing good things stored in your memory. This is just like the previous exercise, but it can draw on many more images, in any situation.

1. Start by imagining the taste of your favorite food or beverage: fine wine, caviar, Ding-Dongs, whatever.

2. Add a memory of a favorite scent that's unrelated to the taste: mint, perfume, the ocean, your baby's hair.

3. Without dropping the memory of the taste or the smell, add a delicious tactile sensation; petting a puppy, snuggling into flannel sheets, hugging your beloved.

4. While still holding the taste, smell, and tactile memories, add the memory of sounds you love: laughter, your favorite music, the rushing of the surf, wind in the pines, birdsong.

5. Throw in a specific remembered sight; a beautiful landscape, a rainbow, a favorite painting, a loved one's face.

6. As you hold all these sense memories, you'll have too much activity in your brain to continue thinking verbally. Try to vividly reexperience *all these sensory experiences at once.* You'll have to stop reading to do this. In fact you'll have to stop thinking. And that's a very good thing.

Path of Delight: Sharing Happiness

Once you can drop deeply into a delightful experience, you can magnify the joy of the experience by giving it to someone else. There's nothing more selfishly delicious than watching someone enjoy an experience you know they'll love. Once you've found a path of delight, invite someone you adore to share it. Then focus not only on your own sensory experience, but on the experience of generosity and communion. Be fully present, observing with all your senses, as your son gets his first glimpse of the ocean, your best friend tastes the new dessert you've discovered, or your spouse relaxes on the fabulous new mattress you've just purchased.

Path of Delight: Connecting with Nature

Nature exists in a state of continuous Wordlessness. Mountains, seas, and forests bring us into their deep presence with their sheer immensity; animals live in a state of consciousness without words that invites us to join them. Any experience of nature is conducive to Wordlessness, but encounters with wild animals are particularly powerful. As the naturalist Craig Childs describes it, "You want to ask questions now . . . but you can't. You can't get a word out. You just stare for as long as you can because suddenly it will all be over, you will get your name back and life will begin again. . . . [Later] the experiences are translated, now made of words, like trying to build the sky out of sticks."

Take any opportunity you can to connect with the natural world. Wayfinders from all cultures, from Jesus heading out into the wilderness for forty days to the Buddha leaving his palace for the forests, have relied on the natural world as their anchor into the Wordless realm. A stroll on the beach or an hour watching the birds in your own backyard may not seem like the answer to your many problems. But by dropping into Wordlessness, you'll arrive at the state of mind that allows all wayfinders to find the answers they're seeking, the way a tracker finds an animal in nature. More important, the very state of Wordlessness delivers you immediately to your ultimate goal: peace of mind and body, gratitude of the present moment, joy in living.

WHAT WE HEAR WHEN THE STORIES STOP

I suggest you deep-practice at least one of the exercises in this chapter at least twice a day, for as little as five minutes each time. You may begin to savor stillness so much you extend these practice sessions until you're meditating for an hour or checking into Wordlessness at every traffic light.

If you do this, Wordlessness will begin subtly changing your inner life, and through it, your outer life as well. As for me, the more I coach, the less I talk. I've learned that my clients can't think their way out of problems caused by thinking. If I can get them to experience Wordlessness for even a few minutes, their anxiety drops, their creativity increases, and they become natural wayfinders, even in the most challenging life circumstances.

At five o'clock on a not so typical morning at Londolozi, a group of guests are climbing into Land Rovers, but they're not like most safari-goers. Each one has a strong streak of Team, and they've come here with me—lucky, lucky me—to learn the ways of the wayfinders. They'll spend this game drive in silence, focusing on their physical and emotional sensations in every moment. I've also asked them to hold in their minds a problem that's been dogging them, a situation they really need to resolve during this seminar in the African bush.

From the beginning, this game drive is unusual. The Shangaan tracker, and everyone in the vehicle, looks relaxed, with soft eyes and quiet faces, breathing very deeply. Occasionally they point at things that most safari guests ignore: the light on the dew, a golden spider web, the clouds. Perhaps because they're so highly attentive to nature, nature also seems highly attuned to them. Shy animals that would ordinarily hide from humans—dwarf mongooses, a jackal, impala—stand calmly still as the Land Rover passes within feet of them. The birds and monkeys watch us without their usual alarm calls.

We see an unusual number of babies on our silent drive. A mother elephant nurses a calf so tiny he can still run under her body. A little zebra, fuzzier than its elders, gallops along with the Land Rover for a while. A lioness lets us watch her cubs tussle from a few yards away. When we reach a hyena den, several pups too young to know what we are come up and sniff the vehicle, their huge eyes, black noses, and big round ears making them look like children's toys.

After four hours of Wordless communion with nature, we return to camp. It's time to do some life coaching, dammit, to address the problems I asked the guests to hold in their minds. But as it turns out, no one managed to hold onto the problem. I knew they wouldn't. By gently pushing them into Wordlessness, I saved myself a world of useless talking. Though they are no longer clinging to their problems, all these Team members feel more capable of solving them. Some of them are surprised to realize they've come to their solutions while they weren't thinking: Robert sees how he can delegate a project at work; Connie has decided to pull her children out of a prestigious private school where they've been miserable; and Suzanne realized that instead of doing major renovations on her creaky old house, she wants to sell it.

But these concrete plans are byproducts of a deeper solution: the reclamation of each person's calm, present, vastly resourceful true nature. As the poet David Whyte wrote, "What you can plan is too small for you to live. What you can live wholeheartedly will make enough plans." We'll talk more about planning in future sections of this book. For now, it's enough to know that dropping into Wordlessness is like logging on to the universal web of pure intelligence, discovering the energy that has allowed menders to find their way through complex areas of both the widest world and the deepest self for as long as humans have existed. As you learn to gain access to this energy, your own true nature, and nature itself, will conspire to calm and assist you. As the thirteenth-century wayfinder and poet Rumi wrote, you will "close the language door and open the love window." From there, you can see your way to anything.

Martha Beck

She also looked taller in person.

CHAPTER TWO

TINY RELATIVES AND THE PATH
OF SACRED PLAY

I'm on my way from my cottage at Londolozi to the central camp when I catch sight of several vervet monkeys bouncing around in the grass. Closer inspection reveals that the monkeys are gathered around a placid-looking female nyala, a lovely antelope that looks something like a striped deer. All the monkeys are juveniles, ranging in age from babies the size of kittens to half-grown adolescents the size of . . . bigger kittens.

As I tiptoe nearer to the vervets, I can see they're playing an almost organized game, which might be called something like DUDE, I TOUCHED THE BIG ANIMAL! Proportionally this activity is to them what running up and touching an elephant would be to a human. Some of the little ones are just watching, but the bravest monkeys move hesitantly toward the nyala, dance backward when their courage fails, then nerve themselves to try again, until they can reach out one hand and poke the antelope's leg. At that point they dash around in exultation for a few minutes, accepting the admiration and envy of their peers. The nyala just keeps munching leaves, sighing occasionally.

The first time I ever heard a rustle in the underbrush and glanced over to see a monkey's face was both joyful and unnerving. I'm used to seeing birds and squirrels and chipmunks, which are delightful but (no offense) not exactly rocket scientists. By contrast, when you meet a monkey's eyes, you can immediately tell it's *thinking*. You can almost see the mental gears clicking away behind that little humanoid face. Monkeys are so very much like us, sharing about 93 percent of our DNA, that watching the game of DUDE, I TOUCHED THE BIG ANIMAL! I feel as if I've stumbled into a community of Lilliputians.

As I move forward to get a better view, stepping slowly and stopping often so as not to scare them, the little monkeys finally notice me. The bravest, biggest juvenile looks at me for a long moment. Then he looks at the nyala. Then he looks back at me again.

Suddenly I sense that DUDE, I TOUCHED THE BIG ANIMAL! is about to be kicked up a level.

Sure enough, the troop leader stops edging up to the antelope and begins moving closer to me. Within seconds the other kids—I mean vervets—realize what's up. They all abandon the nyala, like five-year-olds suddenly riveted on a new screen for a video game. Five or six of the most adventurous begin to approach me, looking scared but determined.

For a minute or two I'm thrilled. To have wild things walk right up to me is like stepping into a Disney cartoon—and, just like my rhinoceros, it's real! But when the monkeys get within about three feet of me, it starts to feel a little *too* real. Sure, they only come up to my knees, but they can jump really high, and they outnumber me. Plus, that almost-human vibe is getting slightly alarming. I suddenly remember a story about an old woman who was attacked and eaten by her own ten miniature poodles. I recall that movie with Dustin Hoffman where one monkey bite kills a human, via an infection that threatens to wipe out humanity. "Whoa!" I say, and do a little jazz-hands thing in the air.

The baby monkeys bounce backward as if yanked by unseen bungee cords. For a moment, they comfort each other, chirping and squealing as they get their heart rates down and their fear under control. But then, goading one another on, they advance again.

"Hah-hah!" I say, trying to sound confident and light-hearted. The monkeys are getting downright brazen. The look in their eyes reminded me of women waiting for the doors to open on Super Sale Saturday day at Walmart. They creep forward slowly but steadily.

"Aaagh!" I blurt, rather too loudly. Bigger jazz-hands this time.

They jump back, but only a foot or so. Almost immediately they resume forward progress. I can feel my heart rate speed up.

"Boo!" I shout, waving my jazz-hands high in the air.

This time the little monkeys don't jump back. Nor do they attack. Instead, as if by arrangement, they stand up, raise their arms, and wave their hands above their heads.

Tiny jazz-hands!

I burst out laughing, my nervousness suddenly drowned out by astonished delight. Something has changed for the monkeys. They've registered the fact that I'm not just a big animal they can use as a dare, like the nyala. Just as I've been keenly aware that they're nearly human, they seemed to have realized I am nearly simian. I've graduated from being the object of the game to being a full-fledged participant.

For the next ten minutes or so, I mimic the monkeys' moves while they mimic mine, until it's hard to remember who is leading whom. "Humans love playing with other animals," says Diane Ackerman in her wonderful book *Deep Play*, "and sometimes this leads to a purity of exchange almost magical in its intensity." I can only hope that my playtime with the vervets is as magical for them as it is for me. We have more and more fun, until eventually we all get up the nerve to let them touch the hem of my pants, an event so exciting I think we all pee a little.

To the people who must maintain Londolozi's elegant ambiance and top-rated cuisine, monkeys are an annoyance—they'd as soon steal your toast as look at you, and their droppings are both copious and malodorous. But I've always loved the vervets: the babies with their tiny faces, the adult males with their impressively bright turquoise testicles (yes, literally blue balls). Playing with the monkey nursery plunges me as deep into Word-lessness as I've ever been, their minds are so very like human children's, but without one syllable of language. By the time we hear an adult vervet piping an alarm and the babies head for the treetops, I've almost forgotten the tense and ordered way I usually think.

PLAY YOUR WAY TO WORDLESS ACTION

As a baby, your brain was wordless and wide open, able to learn on all cylinders and master virtually any skill. By returning to Wordlessness through the exercises in chapter 1, you began reclaiming the parts of your true nature that came as standard equipment with your existence as a human. Now you need to continue reclaiming that original nature by doing what you did as you gained some control of your infant body: play.

Some of my clients become frustrated when I begin coaching them by telling them not to think, then ask them to play around. "What are we working on?" they sometimes ask. "When do we start solving my problems?" If that's how you're feeling, rest assured that finding ways to Wordlessness is prepping your entire consciousness to act as an automatic wayfinder, which will plot your course through life better than any set of goals and plans ever could.

Remember the scenes in *The Karate Kid* when Mr. Miyagi insists on teaching his protégé how to wax cars and sand floors? Through these apparently unrelated activities, the student internalizes the action and power he needs to learn martial arts. Stick with me, here. Wax on, wax off. Your ability to remain Wordless while performing complex tasks can be developed only by playing. The skill set of a wayfinder, which requires rapid learning and responsiveness in any situation life may bring you, can't be fully learned in any other way. To thrive in our wild new world, you'd be well advised to play until you can't think.

THE IMPORTANCE OF NEVER GROWING UP

In virtually every mammal and bird species, play is the way individuals learn how to find their way through the world. (I'm excluding human serial killers, who, whatever their differences, share one characteristic: they never play, not even as children.) By the time they are adults most animals play much less than their young, having learned enough basic skills to survive. This is partially true of human adults; as a mom I identified completely with a mother leopard I once watched grow so tired of being pounced by her two cubs that she finally sat on one of them. Only his tail was visible, lashing around from under her rump, making it look as if she'd grown an extra appendage.

The playful behavior of young animals is driven by a genetically governed trait called "neoteny," from the Greek *neo,* meaning "new," and *tenein,* meaning "to stretch." Neoteny is what makes young creatures stretch beyond their capacity; to touch a nyala, or even a human, just to see whether they can. That stretching, that enlarging of ability and confidence, is the underlying motivation of all true play. As Chip and Dan Heath point out in their book *Switch,* "Play doesn't have a script, it *broadens* the kinds of things we consider doing. We become willing to fool around, to explore or invent new activities . . . building resources and skills." The neoteny of young animals not only makes their play innocent and cute; it allows their brains to learn at astonishing speed.

And here we encounter perhaps the coolest thing about being human: we never outgrow our neoteny. However long we live, our true nature retains the features that wilder apes have only as babies: relatively flat faces, small nose, small teeth. The anthropologist Lee Berger, who discovered the richest deposit of "missing link" hominid bones in scientific history, told me that the egalitarianism of a human-like species can be judged by fang size. Baboons, who are brutally hierarchical, have huge canine teeth, while our canines aren't any bigger than our molars. Like humans and unlike any other apes, small-toothed, peace-loving bonobos bare their teeth in friendship rather than aggression, peeling back their lips in a bright smile that says, "Look! I still have baby teeth! I couldn't rip out your throat with my jaws even if I wanted to! But I don't even want to! Hah-hah!"

An ancient Sioux story says that the Creator had enough survival gifts for every animal except humans. So we got only one thing: the capacity to learn. Scientifically speaking, it's our unusually prolonged neoteny that gives our brains the capacity to absorb information and create ideas continuously no matter how long we live. My vervet friends will lose this characteristic as they become adults. As neoteny and its accompanying playfulness disappears they'll stop being so quick on the uptake. Rapid learning goes with play like pie goes with ice cream.

So despite our pathetically infantile teeth, claws, skeletons, and musculature, we dominate other species the way Peter Pan dominated Captain Hook: simply by refusing to grow up. We've proliferated and thrived because we never stop playing, and the way to cope with the increasing complexity of the wild new world is to play more. Yet most of us adult humans tell ourselves that playing is "leisure time" activity, not to be confused with "productive work" nor taken to excess. This will have to change as we adopt a new, Earth-healing consciousness. In fact I think we'd be far better off if we did virtually nothing but play. When I train coaches, I suggest that they eliminate the word "work" from their vocabulary and substitute "play" instead. What I'm doing now is wordplay. I try to play hard, and sometimes I play long hours. Some people would say I play too much, but what can I say—it plays for me.

Not only is this a much more interesting way to live than work, work, working; it also awakens the right hemisphere of the brain and drops us into Wordlessness. Then whatever we create, from a business meeting to a blueprint to a peanut butter sandwich, is imbued with magic.

DEEP PLAY, DEEP PRACTICE

We've already discussed the phenomenon of deep practice, the continuous, ever-evolving effort to master some skill beyond our ability. Some forms of play are pure frothy fun, like rolling in the snow or jumping on the bed. But if you scroll through your memories of truly wonderful play, you'll notice that "deep play" involves mastering something difficult. When my two youngest children were three and five, they put a two-step stool near a sofa, climbed to the stubby summit, and leaped across to the cushions. Then, without any adult prompting, they began moving the stool back, three or four inches at a time, demanding more and more leaping capacity. My monkey friends switched from touching a nyala to touching a human for the same reason: challenge!

By contrast, when I ask adults to find pictures of play or relaxation in the pages of magazines, they typically—I mean, like 95 percent of the time—cut out images of people lying inertly on some sort of low-slung beach furniture, getting plastered on margaritas. News flash: this is not play. It's just evidence of two sad things about modern life: (1) most of us are desperately sleep-deprived, and (2) we've largely abandoned our playful, imaginative true nature to media clichés.

Real play is actually a wildly creative application of deep practice. It means picking something hard and doing it at a level that's almost too difficult. I spend a lot of time pushing clients (and myself) to this edge. At first, it isn't fun—remember, even people who feel driven to deep practice don't say they're having fun before they've mastered something. This is why, despite our tendency to neoteny, most humans resist learning anything substantially new once they reach the age of about twenty-three. At that point they can basically negotiate the world, so why keep learning?

You know the answer if you've ever persevered in playing a new game until your brain actually finished rewiring itself. That's the moment you suddenly spoke in the new language without thinking, used the new computer technology effortlessly, climbed the rock face you thought you'd never master. The rush of joy that comes at that moment is hard to match. "DUDE!" you think, "I TOUCHED THE BIG GOAL!" If you push yourself far enough, it's like touching the face of God.

Neuroscientists have found that this "edge of impossibility" is where the brain produces its maximum doses of feel-good hormones like dopamine. It's where we find what Mihaly Csikszentmihalyi famously labeled "flow," and where Ellen Langer found the intensely restorative, age-reversing quality of "mindfulness." It pushes us to such intense concentration that we enter the present moment, put down thought, and enter

Wordlessness—even if we're telling a story. The language of play is in the fascinating lilt of all great stories, the healing stories told in every traditional culture. They're the stories that entertain and entrance, just as a wonderful game can. This is why, as Diane Ackerman notes, the wayfinders of every culture "court deep play with a sensuous rigor bordering on mania." To figure out our own best course through life and to serve the world as our heart's desire, all Team members must learn to play like we mean it.

MYSTICAL MOVEMENT

When a troubled member of a traditional society went to the tribe's healer, the healer didn't open the discussion with questions like "How long have you been experiencing spleen discomfort?" or "What, exactly, is your deductible?" Instead he or she asked when the person stopped feeling spontaneous joy, stopped singing, stopped dreaming. In other words, wayfinders need to know when the sick, stuck, depressed, or failing patient stopped playing. Any confident traditional healer with access to modern medicine will gladly recommend a splint or antibiotics for someone with a broken leg or an infection, but for the soul sickness and stress-related illnesses that so bedevil many of us, wayfinders know that playing to the point of enchantment is necessary medicine.

Another common feature of many cultures is the use of what I call the "four D's" to put people in contact with the wild wisdom of their true nature. The four D's are drumming, dancing, drinking (or drugging), and dreaming. When the time comes for a sacred ceremony in a traditional society, the tribe's mystics dress in formal outfits, then spend hours singing, chanting, telling stories, performing ancient dances, using psychoactive chemical compounds, and reporting on whatever visions come to them, awake or asleep.

In modern cultures, people congregate in dark clubs to get drunk or high and gyrate wildly to deafening music. It's as if we're desperately seeking our true nature by megadosing ourselves with the four D's. Without the wisdom or guidance of experienced wayfinders, this substitute for play often becomes unhealthy or even destructive. But when used according to the dictates of our true nature, play can heal our bodies and minds in ways that seem almost magical.

THE RHYTHM OF WORDLESSNESS

I relearned the power of play when I'd been chronically ill, in continuous pain, for about twelve years. I'd been diagnosed with several autoimmune diseases, none of which modern medical science understands very well. They're all supposed to be progressive and incurable. Yet I no longer have symptoms, except for minor flare-ups when I forget to follow my life's real purpose. I've learned through much experimentation that, when I'm in pain, the way back to health is either deep rest or deep play. If it's rest I need, I must follow it with play to stay healthy. Once, shortly after I'd been diagnosed with a painful condition called interstitial cystitis, a nurse told me, "You should avoid stress, but remember: when you want to dance, lying down is stress, and dancing is stress release."

This means that I've adopted many ways of singing, dancing, dreaming, and telling stories. For me, this doesn't involve club hopping; I hate large crowds and deafening live bands, and alcohol simply puts me to sleep. I have my own preferred ways of having deep fun, and you have yours. To fulfill your Team mission, you must determine your own "play profiles" and then get busy playing. A lot.

BRAIN PLAY, WORDLESSNESS, AND THE DIVINE

Any unusual action that demands full concentration and learning (which describes all forms of deep play) shifts our brains into the all-out engagement that drops us out of language and into the greater wisdom of the nonverbal mind. The neurologists Andrew Newberg and Eugene D'Aquili, among the first scientists to investigate the neurology of mystical experience, found that moments of transcendent joy and inspiration were associated with activity in a part of the brain that controls the sense of our body's boundary, separating our awareness into what feels like "self" and "other." This region of the brain happens to be contiguous with the part that allows us to merge with another person emotionally and physically, a process we call "falling in love." They hypothesized that mystical moments can be induced by behaviors that are ritualized, rhythmic, and unusual.

We see this in young animals playing and in adult animals who are seeking mates and forming pair-bonds. Storks and birds of paradise dance for their mates. Wolves, whales, and mice (yes, mice!) sing to one another when they're falling in love. And of course, lovers play like children, calling each other "baby," making mixed-tape music for each other, and telling the stories of their past lives and their future dreams. Play, at any age, helps "close the language door and open the love window."

DROPPING INTO WORDLESSNESS
THROUGH THE PATHS OF SACRED PLAY

As you use any deep play, including the exercises below, you'll drop into Wordlessness and a number of things will happen in your brain and body. Your sense perception and intuition will become much more acute, making everything seem vivid and vibrant. Anxiety, with its "fight, flight, or freeze" imperatives and its flood of stress hormones, will diminish. Your parasympathetic "rest and relax" nervous system will take over, generating hormones that help you heal and rejuvenate.

The Path of Sacred Song
Almost any way of making music can take us into Wordlessness—including, paradoxically, songs with words—as long as the sound and feel of music-making, not thoughts made of language, fill our attention. Singing or chanting anything, from *om* to a prayer to the braided melodies of Gregorian monks to "(I Can't Get No) Satisfaction," is one of the most reliable paths to Wordlessness. Wayfinders of every culture sing their way into their true nature. Even better is playing an instrument, which often takes so much brain focus that words fall away. Today, when you have time alone in the car or the kitchen, sing your favorite song. If possible, put on a recording or the radio and sing along. Don't try to sound good, and don't hold back. Sing as if no one can hear you.

The Path of Sacred Dance
I once had a client who was a professional athlete, an extremely energetic, emotionally sensitive, and verbal Team member. He used to alleviate stress by going to clubs and dancing for six or seven hours at a time, alone. Asking this guy to sit Zen sesshins would have been a crime against nature. He found Wordlessness in all-out action. If you love to dance, you should

do the same. Find or play music with a strong drumbeat, then either do a dance you've learned or just let your body follow the rhythm.

I myself am no dancer, so I'm thrilled to know that *any* action you love can be "your dance." The game of DUDE, I TOUCHED THE BIG ANIMAL! that I played with my vervet friends definitely counts. Skiing is my next-favorite play-dance. Running can work beautifully. So can cycling, rowing, skating, driving, even working out at the gym. And let's not forget yoga, one of the most ancient and powerful paths to Wordlessness. Anything that dissolves verbal attention into pure movement can be a sacred dance. Today, for at least five or ten minutes, move in any rhythmic, repetitive way you like. Put on a Grateful Dead album and pretend to play the drums or air guitar. Go out walking or jogging and find an effortless rhythm. Jazzercise. You'll know you're doing sacred dance when you realize that for a few moments or minutes, you weren't thinking in words.

Paint Your Visions

Betty Edwards published her wonderful book, *Drawing on the Right Side of the Brain,* the very year I took my first college art class. I later became a teaching fellow for that same class, helping people enter Wordlessness in order to create compelling images. These days I reverse the process, helping people make images in order to enter Wordlessness. The powerful right-hemisphere brain dynamics that occur when we create visual images are the reason Tibetan monks and Navajo medicine men make sand paintings and medieval priests spent such enormous amounts of time creating sumptuously illuminated manuscripts. The main point isn't the physical product, but the brain state you must reach and hold to make it.

If you like to draw, get some paint, some crayons, some colored sand, or any other medium that delights your eyes and hands. Use them, as best you can, to express your vision of beauty or meaning. If you love computers, get a graphics package and use it. Contrary to our culture's conventional wisdom, you'll actually achieve a much deeper state of Wordlessness if you try very hard to achieve exactly the effect you want. The challenge of drawing representationally is "deeper" practice than simply doodling, and as such it leads more quickly to the drop-in to Wordlessness that is the point of the exercise. As you really work to get a visual effect, or squint at your work to evaluate it, your brain will slip out of its verbal mode and become much more intelligent.

Tell Sacred Stories

The right words can take you into Wordlessness if they're used, like art or music, to convey *physical and emotional sensations,* not just information. Poetry, literature, and the active story-swapping we do in person can be as rhythmic as dance, as melodic as song, as visually evocative as a painting. In his book *Coyote Medicine,* Lewis Mehl-Madrona, a Stanford-educated physician and Cherokee medicine man, alternates between expository writing about medicine and the ancient healing stories of his ancestors. The two types of prose have a dramatically different effect; the exposition is interesting and informative, but the stories are hypnotic, lilting, enchanting. Ironically, it's in Wordlessness that we find the basis even for the verbal ingenuity of true storytelling, the kind that makes us want to listen forever.

Sometime today, tell a story to someone you love. Recount an adventure you had in traffic or a joke you read on the Internet. Do this not merely to communicate, but to entertain and hold attention. Your subtle nonverbal mind will have to tune into your listener, paying attention to sensory cues your conscious mind can't even perceive. Even as you're using words, you'll find your way into Wordlessness.

THE SILENCE OF SACRED PLAY

All types of sacred play rouse the Wordless right hemisphere of the brain. My observation of many, many clients is that as they access Wordlessness more often (for example, by using one of the exercises in chapter 1 once or twice a day) their lives begin to change, first in small ways, then in large ones. They begin choosing activities and behaving in ways that bring more interesting, playful energy into their work and relationships. Eventually everything they do begins to feel like play.

My ultimate goal for you is that you get so connected to your true nature that whenever you aren't resting, you're playing. But start small, and go easy. Choose one or more favorite exercises from this chapter and use them whenever you feel bored, stale, and sick of work. Stop working as soon as you notice these feelings. At the very next gap in your schedule—maybe a five-minute bathroom break, maybe a whole weekend—play the best possible game you can. Go outside and move. Call your favorite buddies. Start singing. Get laughing. Return to your true nature.

The more often you do this, the better you'll get at accessing the non-verbal intelligence on which all the sacred work of wayfinding depends. If you're frustrated, wishing I'd get around to telling you how to re-create your career or find the love you deserve, please realize that these hoped-for events really will happen to you much more rapidly if you can learn to drop into a Wordless state. To play wordlessly is to be, as T. S. Eliot said, "still and still moving," and when we can do that, we begin finding our way to our right lives without even realizing that's what we're doing. I learn that all over again dancing in the grass with a dozen of my smallest relatives. How lucky you and I are that unlike our monkey cousins, we get to stay "little," absorbed with the Wordless state of sacred play, no matter how big we get.

Kelly Eide

They're cute, but make no mistake: they want your toast.

CHAPTER THREE

MESSAGES FROM THE EVERYWHEN
(THE PATH OF PARADOX)

"That which knows doesn't speak, that which speaks doesn't know." So begins chapter 56 of the *Tao Te Ching,* my favorite book, the reason I don't regret thousands of agonizing hours studying Mandarin, a language for which I have the aptitude of a garden slug. The line can also be translated as "Those who know don't speak, those who speak don't know," but the original Chinese is more cryptic. It leaves open not just the possibility that humans may be divided between people who know and people who don't, but also that within each individual there is a foolish element that speaks without knowing, and a deep true nature that knows without speaking. It also implies that humans, who use words so extensively, may know less than other entities—animals, plants, rocks, rivers—that don't.

The *Tao Te Ching*'s author, the ancient wayfinder Lao Tzu, packed all of that and more into eight syllables. Not a wordy dude, but the words he did use mattered. For example, there's his name, which can be translated as "Old Child." I've often wondered if one reason I love Lao Tzu so much is that I have an old child in my own family. The author Anne Lamott once wrote that she suspected people with Down syndrome of being spies for God, and living with my son Adam has done nothing to disabuse me of that notion. In his twenties, Adam has less language than many preschoolers, yet from the time he was born, he has seemed to know things that only wayfinders know. It was Adam who, long before my epiphany on the Day of the Rhinoceros, tried to tell me that one day I'd go to Africa and become obsessed with helping a Team of menders save the world.

He didn't say that in so many words, of course. In fact, when Adam began helping me find my way into a wild new world, he hadn't spoken any words at all, not so much as "Mama" or "Dada." In the manner of guilt-ridden mothers everywhere, I thought I might be to blame for this. You see, Adam's Down syndrome was diagnosed three months before he was born. I was devastated, but far too bonded to my baby to end the pregnancy. Instead I tried to prepare myself for his condition by reading material that made Edgar Allan Poe look like a stand-up comic: horrifying statistic after horrifying statistic about conditions that might affect my unborn child. I fretted about each ghastly possibility, but in my heart of hearts I knew Adam would be fine, high functioning even. The one fear I could never shake was the impression that he'd never really speak.

Adam started speech therapy when he was six hours old. Every day, wracked with guilt about my own precognition, I poked different tastes and textures into his tiny mouth, making him exercise his speech muscles by pursing his lips (upon receiving a drop of lemon juice), wrinkling his nose (pickles), chomping vigorously (Popsicles), or sticking out his tongue (cotton swabs). Later we moved on to verbalization, hour after hour of supposed mimicry that was actually an endless monologue: me talking, Adam regarding me in bemused monkish silence. By fifteen months, the age his older sister began teaching herself to read, Adam had never even tried to imitate the language I was dutifully trying to push into his brain. One day, after another bout of useless speech therapy, he fell asleep on my bed and I lay down beside him.

"What can you do in this world without knowing how to talk?" I asked him. It was a rhetorical question (rhetoric being my strong suit, if not his). "What can you possibly do that will make your life worthwhile?"

Then I fell immediately into a deep sleep, which was somewhat odd, since I rarely nap. Things got even odder when I began to dream—and in the dream, woke up. I was still in my bedroom. Adam was still beside me. Everything looked normal, not at all dreamlike. Then Adam opened his eyes and looked into mine, and suddenly I was inundated by a flood of information, as if a storm surge had broken all the levees in my brain. I dreamed a bewilderingly vast array of images, almost all involving wild animals, each distinct and separate, but all occurring simultaneously. It felt as if the entire massive sphere of the planet was speaking to me, in images far too multifaceted for my verbal mind to track.

When I finally woke up, astonished to find Adam still snoozing innocently beside me, my very bones were buzzing with a strange energy. The feeling, and the images from the dream, took weeks to abate. I confided in one friend, telling her, "It's like, this will sound so weird, but it's like Adam is here for, for the *planet*. It's like some sort of Earth Day celebration that never ends." My friend looked at me as if wondering if my medication should be administered by tranquilizer dart, then gently suggested that I keep these thoughts to myself. I did. But every few months I'd have another of what I came to call my Adam-in-Africa dreams. To get rid of the buzzing energy they caused, I wrote them down and sometimes drew the images I'd seen.

As Adam grew up, the dreams gradually abated. I'd almost forgotten about them many years later, when Adam was thirteen and the book I wrote about him became a bestseller in South Africa. We took time from my book tour there to go to Londolozi for the first time. On our first drive through the African bush, I turned to see a bull elephant emerging from behind a copse of boxwood, eclipsing the setting sun. I gave a little gasp, and my teeth started the subtle, vibrating chatter I remembered from Adam's early childhood. I'd drawn precisely that image in my journal after that very first high-voltage dream.

Ever since then I've been running into the real-life versions of my Adam-in-Africa dreams, but he won't tell me what they're all about. I've asked him several times. He always just smiles at me like an old child, one who still can't think in words very well, but seems to know things I can barely imagine.

LOGGING ON TO WORDLESSNESS

I've spent two chapters telling you how to drop into Wordlessness, for your health and happiness and to ground your wayfinding skills. Now, assuming you've at least experimented with some techniques to reach this nonverbal brain state, I'll tell you the whole reason I've come to focus so much on Wordlessness for Team members: I believe (and many, many cultural traditions suggest) that accessing the intelligence of your nonverbal mind is like logging on to some sort of Energy Internet, a connection that gives you access not only to your own entire intelligence, but to something much bigger.

Jung called this Wordless Web the "collective unconscious," which "consists of pre-existent forms, the archetypes." For Freud, they are "archaic remnants," mental images that don't come from the thinker's own life and "which seem to be aboriginal, innate, and inherited shapes of the human mind." Every human culture contains the concept of such a universally connected consciousness. Most words used to label it are translated into English as "spirit," but my favorite comes from Aboriginal Australians: the "Everywhen."

In the Everywhen (so thousands of cultures have taught) human way-finders can travel freely through all time and space, gathering information, communicating with far-distant people and other creatures, previewing future experiences, and learning essential information for navigating through life. Perhaps this universal belief in a metaphysical world is evidence of something real, though it could be simply a manifestation of the enormous potential of the human brain. After all, neurologists tell us that there are more potential neuron connections in your brain than there are *atoms in the universe.* Whatever it is, the Everywhen is worth visiting.

If you've been practicing the drop-ins to Wordlessness I've recommended so far, you may have begun experiencing moments of heightened awareness, odd flashes of nonverbal insight, a sense of knowing what to do without knowing how you know it, or strange, significant dreams of your own. Hundreds of clients who have practiced Wordlessness told me they began to receive help, information, and even material objects just when they needed them, seemingly out of the blue. At this point I'm ready to say right out loud that if you expand your capacity for Wordlessness, small miracles will begin to happen to you too. Large miracles will follow. Eventually the things you now call miracles will feel normal to you. Because to the part of you that lives permanently in the Wordless Web, they are.

THE PARADOX OF WORDLESS WORDS

The job of the wayfinder, whether an ancient oracle or a modern scientific theorist, is to reach beyond current human knowledge into the realm of the unimagined and bring back something true and useful. For menders, sages, shamans, medicine men, artists, and the holy people of all cultures, this means expressing in words the things that can only be experienced in Wordlessness. Obviously this is a paradoxical task. It's why Lao Tzu began the *Tao Te Ching* by saying, "The Way that can be spoken of is not the true Way," and then spent a whole book to speak of the Way nonetheless. To do this the Old Child threw himself into paradox. Paradoxes are statements that seem to refute themselves, such as "This statement is a lie." If this is true, it must be false, but if it's false, it's true. Pondering paradoxical statements is a way to confuse the verbal brain into abandoning language altogether, because language is the source of a conflict that's impossible to solve.

Pay attention to most wise people, and you'll find their speech is full of paradoxes. This is as true of scientists as it is of mystics. For example, the psychologist Abraham Maslow (of Maslow's hierarchy fame) insisted on debunking "the antirational, the antiempirical, the antiscientific." But on the very same page he wrote, "To be looking everywhere for miracles is to me a sure sign of ignorance that *everything* is miraculous."

You'll find this paradox—a rational belief in miracles—in many way-finder members of our culture. Your own thinking, especially your own most personal and profound experience, may be full of such ironies. You may believe in an absolutely random universe yet feel guided by something unseen. You may be passionately religious but uneasy with anything that isn't empirically demonstrable. Paradoxes haunt the lives of born way-finders, driving them to seek resolutions to the apparent contradictions in their lives, enticing them into the world that is beyond words and can therefore contain paradox without contradiction. Every time you encounter a paradox in your own thoughts, you've found a door into the experience of Wordlessness, the place where magic becomes possible.

This chapter is not meant to help you free your mind from paradox by teaching any "absolute truths" (such as the dogmatic versions of reality taught by some religions), but to turn your usual belief in absolute truths upside down. By seeing that the things we believe to be true may also be false, we force the verbal brain to relinquish its obsessive belief that it knows the "right way," or "how things should be." This throws us out of our preconceptions and into pure perception and observation, into a state of open-mindedness. It's the most difficult but also the most powerful way for a highly verbal Team member to enter the Everywhen, the source of all the information you need to reclaim your true nature.

WORDS THAT LEAD TO WORDLESSNESS

In mathematics a paradoxical puzzle is called a "strange loop." It sends the mind pinging and ponging from one incompatible condition to the other, giving it no place to rest. Sometimes, just to get some peace, a mind caught in a strange loop finally lets go of the mental system that created the paradox—in our case, language—and finds itself in a new, open place. As the Sufi mystic poet Rumi said, "Out beyond ideas of right-doing and wrong-doing, there is a field. I'll meet you there."

One of the most consistent themes among all human wisdom traditions is the teaching "The truth shall set you free." But Westerners tend to believe that the truth is a mental or verbal story, a set of facts laid out in words. Eastern wayfinders and many other indigenous cultures, on the other hand, go to great lengths reminding students that "the finger that points to the moon is not the moon," that words are merely vehicles to carry us toward the *experience* of truth. The words themselves are not truth. They are the products of a dualistic mind-set that's necessary for language but meaningless in the nondualist Everywhen. Truth itself is something you *live,* not something you think. Even if you had never actually tasted honey, you could write a Ph.D. dissertation on it. But as Eckhart Tolle says, you wouldn't know how it tastes, which is the most powerful reason you might want to have honey in your life. You wouldn't know its essence.

The same goes for the experiences we call "happiness," "enlightenment," "knowledge," "goodness," "love," and every other worthwhile state of being. Talking about them isn't enough to experience them; in fact, it often becomes a barrier to real experience by convincing us we know something truly when we really only know it verbally. To avoid this mind trap, cultivate the ability to identify, or even create, paradoxes in your everyday thinking. In other words, *whenever you find yourself believing a statement is true, identify ways that its opposite could also be true.*

If this sounds like a mind pretzel, it is. For verbal thinkers, sustaining awareness of two mutually exclusive "truths" creates brain blisters like no other form of deep practice. The verbal mind thinks that if something is true, the opposite *can't* be true. But the world beyond words isn't divided into opposites; the varieties of actual experience are infinite. When the mind lets go of language, neither a statement nor its opposite are "truth"; because both are true, the mind must let go of dualistic, verbal thinking and enter a reality where no thought is adequate to contain truth. Awareness expands like helium rushing from a burst balloon, released from the captivity of language. As the mystic Marguerite Porete wrote in the early fourteenth century:

> *Love draws me so high . . .*
> *That I have no intent,*
> *Thought is no longer of worth to me.*
> *Nor work, nor speech.*

In our time, this release from language happened spontaneously to Byron Katie, a master of paradox whose method I love and use every day. After a lifetime of intense psychological suffering, Katie woke up one morning absolutely aware that no language-based thought was truth. She felt euphoric, interconnected with everything, just as Jill Bolte Taylor did when her verbal brain went "off-line." But Katie was still able to speak. Like a Zen monk seeing the answer to one of the paradoxical word-puzzles called "koans," she found herself laughing at the strangeness of believing any thought could be real. The first thing she saw that morning was a cockroach crawling on her foot. And without words to tell her this was a bad thing, she found herself beyond delighted: "To separate that wholeness, to see anything as outside itself [myself] wasn't true. The foot was there, yet it wasn't a separate thing, and to call it a foot, or an anything, felt absurd. And the laughter kept pouring out of me. I saw that *cockroach* and *foot* are names for joy, that there are a thousand names for joy, and yet there is no name for what appears as real now."

Few people ever experience such a profound breakthrough, one that separates perception from thought once and for all. But any would-be-wayfinder can learn to think in a way that begins creating bursts of insight and eventually creates a well-worn path to Wordlessness, the realm of joy and genius beyond thought. Here are a few techniques for opening your mind to the Wordless Web, using language to dissolve itself.

Pathway of Paradox: Find a Way to Believe the Opposite of Everything You Believe

Right now, make a list of five thoughts that hang around your brain, bothering you. It works best if these thoughts cause you great worry, anger, or sadness.

TABLE 1. FIVE MISERABLE THOUGHTS I OFTEN THINK

1. _____

2. _____

3. _____

4.
_____

5.
_____

Now comes the hard part: think of a way the opposite of each thought could also be true. Your verbal mind will reject the very possibility that this could happen. Your job as a wayfinder is to pick apart your own words until you find a way it could.

For example, my client Eric constantly broods, "I'm getting older." This sounds eminently true to most of us. But could the opposite thought, "I'm getting younger," also be true? Upon reflection, Eric acknowledges that he *feels* younger as the years go by, that he's embracing joy and play in a way he never did as a boy. Maybe Eric was an "old soul" when he was born and has been getting younger ever since.

Another of my clients, Beth, monotonously tortures herself with the thought "I'm fat." The opposite thought, "I'm not fat," doesn't strike her as remotely true. But after all, what *is* Beth? She is not just her body, since its atoms are fully replaced every seven years, whereas her consciousness has retained its identity since she weighed seven pounds. Is *Beth* fat? No. She's not any single physical form; she's her essential being.

If you're like most people, you're probably ready to smack me right about now. Eric and Beth are both *right,* you may be thinking—empirically *right,* despite all your semantic hair-splitting. That kind of talk is just plain nonsense!

Which is exactly my point.

The embrace of verbal paradox eventually shows us that *all* fixation on words-as-truth is "just plain nonsense." The point of this exercise isn't to replace your beliefs with their opposites, but to show you that language is an arbitrary system of sounds, not The Truth. Truth is never any statement. It's an *experience,* one that can come only from full presence in the infinite variety of the Wordless Web.

In Table 2, write a statement that directly opposes each of the troubling thoughts you listed in Table 1. This may cause your mind to go completely blank or make your head feel as if it's going to explode. That's a good sign that you're creating new neural tracks, a way of thinking that's not the dualistic, words-as-truth mind-set you got from your social training.

TABLE 2. THE EQUALLY TRUE OPPOSITES
OF MY FIVE MISERABLE THOUGHTS

1. _____

2. _____

3. _____

4. _____

5. _____

Pathway of Paradox: Babble

Acceptance and commitment therapy, a new and highly effective form of clinical psychology, is based on the recognition that almost all psychological pain comes not from experiences, but from the words in our heads with which we describe those experiences. To get patients into the Wordless world, ACT's founder, Steven Hayes, recommends repeating a word like "milk" over and over for forty-nine seconds. At that point the patient's mind stops associating the sound with a nutritious liquid and experiences it as a meaningless noise. This disassociation between words and reality allows patients to let go of verbal stories that have been tormenting them.

Try this if it appeals to you: repeat the word "milk" until it means nothing to you, then proceed to more emotionally loaded words that often trouble you, words like "failure" or "bankruptcy" or "chilblains." The idea is to rob these words of their sting so that you can deal calmly with life's realities, free from the additional burden of terror arising from your internal narrative.

Pathway of Paradox: Think about Koans

Zen masters plant paradoxical questions called "koans" in their students' minds, then send them off to muddle their way to an answer. Here are some classics from a tradition called the Gateless Gate. If this is a path you want to try, fill your mind with one of these koans when it would otherwise be engaged with thoughts about your struggles at work, your fear of becoming a bag lady, or your no-good freeloader of a brother-in-law.

- Does a dog have a soul? If you say yes or no, you lose your soul.

- A man is hanging by his teeth from a tree on a cliff. Someone asks him a question. If he doesn't answer, he falls and dies. If he does answer, he falls and dies. What should he do?

- When you do not think good and when you do not think not-good, what is your true self?

- It is not necessary for speech to come from the tongue.

- Nansen saw the monks of the eastern and western halls fighting over a cat. He seized the cat and told the monks, "If any of you say a good word, you can save the cat."

    No one answered. So Nansen boldly cut the cat in two pieces.

    That evening Joshu returned, and Nansen told him about this. Joshu removed his sandals and, placing them on his head, walked out.

    Nansen said, "If you had been there, you could have saved the cat."

    Explain.

There's no "right" answer to these riddles—or certainly none that I know of. You have to go to a Zen master to see if your answer to any particular koan is on the mark. If it is, the master may smack you with a board or put cabbage in your ears or something. Zen methods of opening students' minds are similar to "trickster" teachings in many cultures. In African folklore, the rabbit (that would be Br'er Rabbit to Americans) always ends up on the horns of a dilemma; in Native American medicine wisdom, the coyote finds himself attacking his own tail. Wayfinders of all places put student menders in mental double binds specifically so that they'll end up in self-tormenting paradoxes that sever their connection to words.

Students in all these traditions often feel as if they're losing their minds—because, of course, they are. If you feel crazy frustrated as you contemplate a koan, either a formal question or a seemingly insoluble problem in your own life, consider it a good sign. Be patient, do your other

Wordlessness exercises, and this temporary insanity can suddenly give way to something more sane than you've ever experienced. You won't be able to express this feeling. You'll just have to enjoy it. Rumi described this process of bafflement and breakthrough seven centuries ago: "Be helpless, dumbfounded," he wrote, "unable to say yes or no. Then a stretcher will come down from grace and gather us up."

Path of Paradox: The Words of Mystical Wayfinders

Speaking of Rumi, I think there's a reason that as the Team prepares to save the world, his ancient Persian words have become wildly popular with modern Western readers. Before you find your way onto the Wordless Web, you may find yourself strangely drawn to the words of wayfinders who got there before you. Once you begin experiencing a few moments at a time of true Wordlessness, these people will begin to feel like your best friends. As the Persian poet Hafiz wrote, "Even from the distance of a millennium, I can lean the flame in my heart into your life." The work of the great wayfinders will take you as far into the Mystery as language can go. Spend time with it, looking for a resonant ring in an apparent contradiction.

For example, my pal Lao Tzu reeled off strings of paradoxical statements: "The path into the light seems dark, the path forward seems to go back, the direct path seems long, . . . the greatest love seems indifferent, the greatest wisdom seems childish." The Bible is filled with similar koans, like the Old Testament concept of the "still voice" of God and St. Paul's self-description, "When I am weak, then I am strong." Christian mystics have been obsessed with riding paradox into spirit all the way to the present day. The twentieth-century monk Thomas Merton wrote, "I, Nothingness, am thine All." None of this makes any immediate sense, of course. But these paradoxical statements feel significant. They are taking us to the edge of truth and pushing us off the false, solid ground of the mind. Then miracles begin to happen.

TURNAROUNDS FROM THE EVERYWHEN

One afternoon at Londolozi, I'm coaching a group of clients on the veranda of a gigantic tree house. My friends the vervets keep sneaking down from the canopy to steal our biscuits and fruit, reminding us of the anxious, scheming little primates within us that Zen masters call "monkey mind."

One of the guests, a dazzling South African woman named Sal, says she's "stuck," because despite a life filled with love and achievement, she still isn't over the death of her son Rowan, who drowned as a toddler. Beneath her elegant composure, Sal's grief is an open wound. She despises herself for this. (South Africans discourage signs of "weakness," such as wincing when they must dig shrapnel out of their own abdomens with kitchen utensils.) With a set jaw, she tells the group, "I must let go of a little boy who never really lived."

It's obvious how this mental story weighs on Sal, dragging her down, paralyzing her ability to feel joy and lightness. I suspect she could benefit by softening that rock-solid South African stiff upper lip and letting herself grieve, so I decide to try nudging her into more self-acceptance by doing an exercise that involves lightly pressing her hand as she recites variations of her tormenting thought.

As I walk over to touch Sal's hand, I compose what Byron Katie might call a "turnaround" for Sal's tormenting thought, "I must let go of a little boy who never really lived." The turnaround I have in mind is simple: "I must *not* let go of a little boy who never really lived." That's the plan. But that's not what I say. In fact, I don't think *I* say anything.

As I touch Sal a completely unexpected sentence comes from my mouth. I hear my own voice, as if from a short distance: "Try saying this, Sal: *A little boy who never really died must not let go of me.*"

Suddenly my knees buckle, and I'm sitting on the sofa next to Sal with my arms around her—except that it isn't me. It's Rowan. In the heartbeat before I spoke, a deal was struck in the Wordless world: I felt an overwhelmingly positive and loving presence asking if Rowan could borrow my body for a minute, and I answered yes, of course. Then my own personality moved to the copilot seat of my body, giving Rowan the controls.

Mind you, nothing like this has ever happened to me before. I am not, and do not plan to become, some sort of life-coaching medium (now there's a very short-running reality show waiting to happen). But at this moment, out in a place where Wordlessness blankets the landscape like dew, Rowan's arrival seems completely normal to me. Nor am I worried that the other clients present will think my behavior weird or excessive. We're all so sense-drenched in the beauty of the wilderness, so meditative, so altered by sacred play, that we've long since dropped deeply into Wordlessness. In that state we can all feel Rowan as obviously as we can feel the wind. He is a huge, exquisite, incredibly affectionate energy. It never occurs to me that the guests might not realize he's the one holding his mother, not me. Sure enough, when we discussed the incident later, they all say that the way I experienced the event was their interpretation, as well.

THE GIFT PARADOX

Access to the Wordless Web brings with it a huge sense of absolute safety and calm, the most important things a wayfinder needs for navigating the intricacies of life. My experience with Sal and Rowan remind me of one of my favorite comments on duality versus reality, from Eckhart Tolle. "The opposite of life is not death," he says. "The opposite of death is birth. Life has no opposite."

Later that same evening, out in the bush, our group happens upon a leopard who's just caught an impala. When I see the antelope kicking, I think, "Oh, lord, here we go: it's the baby giraffe all over again. It's going to take me weeks to deal with this." But with Sal beside me, I decide I'm brave enough not to contract from the reality of death, as I did at young Jasper's violent passing (see chapter 1). Instead of shutting down, I use the breath-to-heart technique to get my mind clear of stories and log onto the Wordless Web. This is the way Koelle has taught me to calm a frightened horse. (If you don't think *that's* an empirically testable skill, I invite you to come on out to Arizona and experience it.) I do my best to project calm through the Energy Internet to the impala.

To my own surprise, I feel a very strong connection with the antelope, the way I'd feel a connection to you if we were having an interesting, intense conversation. Scientists now know that our brains contain "mirror neurons" that light up when we watch someone else having an experience, almost as though we're going through the experience ourselves. Maybe I'm imagining things, or maybe my mirror neurons are telling me the truth. Either way, the impressions feel crystal clear: the impala's always Wordless awareness is filled with shock and confusion, but absolutely none of the thought-based fears that make my own mortality so frightening to me. I'm struck by the lack of resistant ideas, like "This shouldn't be happening!" or "I'm not ready to die!" or "My loved ones will be devastated!" There's just awareness of the strangeness of the situation and disorientation.

Then it feels for all the world as though the impala senses my compassion for it. The animal seems very relieved to find someone caring about it, joining with it. I project all the calm and peace I can. Then I feel a gentle *whoosh,* an incredibly sweet sensation of delicious, liberating expansion. At that moment, Sal and I say in unison, "It's dead." Sal has been doing exactly the same thing I was, and we feel the same sensations simultaneously. The impala's body goes slack, and the leopard takes off as though shot from a cannon, leaping into a tree as a hyena gallops up, hoping to steal the kill. The whole scene is definitely raw nature, but from a Wordless place it feels neither evil nor wrong. There's nothing of the salacious viciousness with which humans sometimes hunt. There is only the dance of form, life passing from one physical configuration of molecules to another, like waves trading energy at sea.

Dropping back into language, I can clearly see that the leopard killed the impala. Then I immediately find truth in the opposite statement: I could just as easily say the leopard "lived" the impala, taking its stored physical energy into her own body. Holding these opposites in my verbal mind, I feel language create a strange loop, pushing me beyond paradoxical belief structures and putting me smack-dab back into Wordlessness.

USING PARADOX WHEN TIMES ARE TOUGHEST

These experiences stood me in good stead when my friend Jayne was diagnosed with terminal cancer. As I sat at her bedside, I held in my own mind the things I'd learned from menders like Ben Okri, who wrote, "Fear not, for death is not the real terror. But life—magically—is." I recalled the mystic's experienced reality that death is not an absolute but a mystery, and that life has no opposite. Each time I freed myself from verbal thoughts about my friend's illness and death, I found myself in a place of Wordless calm that Jayne said brought her peace, though I was just sitting there in silence. The only thing necessary at the truest moments of life is to find that place, so that, like Hafiz, we can tell one another, "Troubled? Then stay with me, for I am not."

When Jayne and I did speak, she liked hearing the words of paradoxical wayfinders, though they made no logical sense to her. As she slipped slowly away, I'd sit beside her and just hold these thoughts in my mind. I'd quote Tolle silently: "Death is the stripping away of all that is not you. The secret of life is to 'die before you die'—and find that there is no death." Though I hadn't even spoken aloud, Jayne would whisper, "Oh, that feels good." As we tune into the body's most basic trials—birth, illness, death—we hear the comfort of paradoxical words resonating through wordless space.

OFF THE HORNS OF THE "DUALEMME"

As you sit with paradox during the hard times in your own life, you'll see that finding your way through the wild world begins with knowing that nothing deeply real or true has an opposite. Caught in a world of language, with its absolute dualities, we're always vulnerable to mental suffering, to sorrow, rage, and dread. In bad times we curse the fates; in good times we fear them. When a baby is born, we rejoice uneasily, checking every hour to make sure he's still breathing, terrified that he could be taken away, as Rowan was. When an impala dies, we look on in mental anguish, aware that the same fate awaits us all.

This is what Buddhism calls Samsara, the wheel of suffering. The way out of it is to puncture the veil of duality by embracing the paired opposites in which the verbal mind thinks. If you can truly absorb paradox until you spend hours or even days logged onto the Wordless Web, you'll suddenly find yourself very high up, watching the world with strangely clear vision, what the Sioux call "eagle vision." And you'll understand why the words "raptor" and "rapture" come from the same root. The Welsh wayfinder R. S. Thomas put it this way: "The silence holds with its gloved hand the wild hawk of the mind."

WAYFINDING IN BOTH WORLDS

Adam went with me to Londolozi once when he was thirteen. When he's twenty-three, we go back again. He seems pleased to be here, but he doesn't say much. As we drive out into the bush, I watch my son closely for telltale signs of recognition. My own memories have so many blended images of real experience and Adam-in-Africa dreams that I don't know which world is real—or rather, I feel that both are real and not real, a paradox that holds me in Wordlessness. Occasionally a thought occurs: Did I dream that herd of zebra more than twenty years ago? Was Adam the one who brought that dream to me, out of the Everywhen? If so, he isn't letting on now, just sitting in his usual calm Wordlessness.

The animals at Londolozi, which haven't been hunted for many decades, usually ignore people in Land Rovers the way they'd ignore a rock or a stump. But they seem unusually interested in Adam. A young lion walks up to our parked Land Rover and stares directly into my son's face from a distance of about four feet—a little close for my comfort, but not, apparently, for Adam's. Later a wild elephant comes near and stretches out its trunk toward him, investigating his scent for a long minute. Maybe Adam's extra chromosome makes him smell or look interesting to the creatures of this wild world. Or maybe they recognize him from the Everywhen.

These close encounters with enormous animals don't rattle Adam in the slightest. The one thing that surprises him into speech is a common animal, but one Americans rarely see. Rounding a shrub, we flush a flock of guinea fowl, largish birds with brown and white polka-dot feathers and naked bright blue heads.

"Hey!" says Adam in his rough, garbled voice. "I saw those in my dream!"

"Really?" I say. Adam doesn't make things up. If he says he dreamed of guinea fowl, I believe him. And they're not something he would have seen on television.

"That's scary," Adam grumbles cheerfully. "To see things from my dreams."

"Oh, ya think?" I reply, hoping my son can appreciate the irony dripping from my voice. "Aren't you the one who sent me all those whacked-out Africa dreams when you were little?"

Adam opens his mouth to respond, then closes it again. Though I poke him and tickle him and ask him again, he's done with words for that day. He just gives me his most enigmatic smile, a cross between Buddha and the Mona Lisa, his eyes gleaming with the light of the Everywhen. "I'm a spy for God," say those old-child eyes. "I could tell you what's going on here, but then I'd have to kill you." Like everything and everyone that knows, Adam doesn't speak.

One of my Adam-in-Africa dreams. (Sketched when he was one, painted when he was twenty.)

Martha Beck

PART II

THE SECOND TECHNOLOGY OF MAGIC

WORDLESSNESS

ONENESS

IMAGINATION

FORMING

CHAPTER FOUR

HORSEPLAY AND THE TECHNOLOGY OF ONENESS

If I wanted to, I could see the little palomino by looking at the top of my own shoulder, picking her up in my peripheral vision. But instead I just let my eyes drink in the scenery: the rolling California hills, dappled light falling through the clouds, a truck parked nearby. Everything, including the truck, seems equally beautiful and equally alive. At this moment the palomino is neither more nor less important to me than the sky.

To say I haven't spent my entire afternoon in this state of serene detachment is like saying that the Three Stooges were not neurosurgeons. For what feels like hours, I've been pursuing a herd of two-year-old colts in weird slow motion. I amble up to them in arcs. They wait until I get close, then nervously move to a different part of the field, whereupon I doggedly start amble-arcing toward them again. My instructors have told me that striding up to them in a straight line could scare them off for good. My goal is to serpentine, calmly but relentlessly.

Amble, arc. Arc, amble.

Oops. There they go again.

I keep thinking of that joke about the turtle who's mugged by two snails and later tells the police, "I'm sorry, I can't remember much. It all happened so fast!" Perhaps it was unwise to relinquish my afternoon and good sense to the renowned horse whisperer Monty Roberts and his protégé, Koelle Simpson. I've just met both of them (never suspecting that I'll later spend some of the best days of my life watching Koelle "whisper" zebras and elephants). Monty kindly invited me to his farm after I mentioned his horse-training method in a magazine article. He and Koelle have brought me out here to this lush pasture and are now standing by the fence calling instructions and encouragement.

"Keep arcing!" they say. "A little faster—no, not that fast! Watch out for—well, that's okay. Manure is easy to slip in. Don't worry, they haven't gone far. Just get up and start over."

My ears burn with shame. Theoretically I'm learning to behave like a strong, determined horse leader, mimicking the gestures, positioning, and energy of a "matriarch mare." (Horse herds are led by experienced females, while the stallions bring up the rear, defending against predators and competing sperm donors.) Monty told me to focus my attention on the little palomino. If I approach her with just the right actions and attitude, she'll follow me of her own free will. I've seen Monty and Koelle do this with other horses. I believe it will work. But for me, learning horse communication is like trying to yodel in Latvian while undergoing dental surgery.

"Don't worry!" shouts Koelle as the herd bolts yet again. "You're doing great!"

Amble, amble, arc, arc, amble amble, arc, arc. Buh-bye now.

Why the damn palomino, anyway? She's the jitteriest, least approachable horse in the herd. They're domestic-born but not yet trained, and to me the palomino seems almost wild. After an eternity of watching me amble, some of the other colts are so bored with me that I can walk right in between them, gently pushing them aside with my hands. But just when I get within arm's length of the palomino . . .

"That's okay!" Monty says as the filly tosses her head and runs off, accompanied by the entire herd. "Keep trying! You've almost got it!"

Yeah, I wish.

But then, about fifteen minutes later, by George, I get it.

Maybe I'm so tired I slipped into Wordlessness, though this is before I've learned to value this state. Maybe there's something in human DNA that clicks into equine communication during emergencies. ("A horse! A horse! My kingdom for a horse!") All I know is that one moment the motion of the herd seems chaotic and random, and the next, everything is meaningful. I don't need Monty and Koelle to tell me why I'm ambling in arcs; I just *feel* that the horses like it better than the straight-line approach.

A subtle but absolutely clear awareness diffuses through my internal world, like dye coloring a glass of water. It saturates my body, then flows beyond me to the palomino. The moment it touches her, I know she'll let *me* touch her too. I arc up to her, hold out a hand, see her skin shudder, gently move away, move in again. We both draw in a breath, exhale in unison. I lay my hand on her neck, brush off some dust and hay, scratch along the line of her mane. Then I arc away, walk a few yards, and stop.

No need to think.

The California hills, the clouds, the light, the truck. Everything beautiful. Everything equal.

I don't look behind me because I didn't need to; the palomino has already told me she's coming. The stream of communication connecting us feels as real to me as a signed contract. So I expect to hear the little horse's footsteps drawing near. Instead, confusingly, there's a strange rustling sound, like a cottonwood tree in the wind, or a church congregation shifting in a quiet chapel.

I feel a puff of warm, moist air on my right shoulder, and then, a moment later, the palomino's velvet nose. She's accepted me as a leader. She stands behind me radiating that sweet blend of power, guilelessness, humility, and trust that is particular to horses. My eyes fill with tears. Though I've seen "join-ups" like this before, the moment is a miracle. I can't imagine feeling anything quite so magical ever again.

Until I feel a second nose, a second puff of warmth, this time in the center of my back. And then a third, on my left upper arm.

Confused, I look at my shoulder to see, peripherally, what's going on behind me. (Turning and staring would tell the horses to run.) A warm buzz runs through my body and the hair prickles on my arms as I understand what that rustling noise was: not four hooves walking up to me, but *sixty*-four. The palomino is the matriarch mare of the herd. When she accepted me, so did all the others.

I walk forward. An entire herd of horses, of their own free will, walks with me. I turn left. They turn left. I circle right. So do they. I stop. They stop. That sweet horse energy fills my body so completely I seem to be seeing through their huge soft eyes, hearing through their fuzzy ears. The loveliness of the day blends seamlessly with their consciousness. There are infinite wonders out here in this pasture: the herd, the horse whisperers, the truck, every mouse and mosquito living in the grass, me.

And there is only One.

FINDING THE ONE

This happened in the days before I began talking out loud about the Team, before I'd read much about sacred archetypes or come to believe in the "technologies of magic." When Monty first demonstrated a join-up to me and my children, I'd paid only cursory attention to something my teenage daughter, Katie—sorry, sweetie, I mean Kat—noticed immediately. As Monty began his process by gently guiding his horse in a circle, stopping briefly at each of the four points of the compass, Kat whispered, "Mom! He's calling the quarters!"

"Calling the quarters" was what Celtic druids and other European way-finders once did to begin any sacred or magical act, including communicating with animals. Now I recognize it as a ceremony that helps menders drop out of human language, logging on to the Wordless Web, where they can communicate with distant things. In many Native American tribes, a virtually identical procedure was called "invoking the Four Directions." Monty spontaneously adopted this same pattern. (Why hadn't he decided to orient the horse by just walking it in a circle, or by turning in three directions, or five, or eight? Why the universally sacred number four?) But I didn't think much about my daughter's observation at the time. I watched Monty's work with awe, but saw it only as he explained it, in terms of behavioral biology.

Throughout my stumbling attempts at a pasture join-up, I'd been thinking, calculating, telling myself to *do it right*. It was only by accident, through the boredom of repetition, that I'd fallen into Wordlessness. So when the herd joined up with me, I was totally unprepared for the emotional enormity of the experience, for the absolute clarity with which I felt them accept me. What was that burst of incredible tenderness? Why was I almost crying? Why did I see the world so differently and feel such unity with everything around me?

The answer to all those questions is that dropping into Wordlessness while interacting with the animals had pushed me into Oneness, the subjective awareness that there is no separation between me and everything else in the universe. Entering sacred silence is the first technology of magic in all wisdom traditions. But it's just the beginning. Where Wordlessness logs you on to the big Internet of universal energy, Oneness lets you deliberately navigate that realm—to figuratively send and receive email, surf for interesting information, interact with others. Wordlessness is presence in the magical realm; Oneness is connection and communication through it.

Rationalist culture, unlike the vast majority of human societies in history, didn't teach us that we're capable of communicating without either close physical proximity or physical implements like written words or telephones. Most of us still see the world as Newton described it: a bunch of random, unrelated particles knocking each other around. Ironically, physicists have known for almost a century that solid particles are mere energetic patterns until observed by consciousness, and that energy is always communicating in stranger-than-fiction ways Einstein disparagingly called "spooky action at a distance." He was so unnerved by the implications of quantum mechanics that he resisted them until very near his death, when he commented that this had been his greatest mistake as a scientist.

Einstein was rare in changing his mind while he was still alive. Nobel Prize winner Max Planck, the founding genius of quantum mechanics, once commented, "New scientific truth usually becomes accepted, not because opponents become convinced, but because opponents die, and because the rising generation is familiar with the new truth at the outset." The Team's generation is familiar with new truths that are probably making Newton spin in his grave until acted upon by an equal and opposite force. Here's how the science journalist Lynne McTaggart summed up just a few conclusions of twentieth-century science: "Human beings and all living things are a coalescence of energy in a field of energy connected to every other thing in the world. . . . There is no 'me' and 'not-me' duality to our bodies in relation to the universe, but one underlying energy field. . . . Things once in contact remain in contact through all space and time."

THE EMERGING SCIENCE OF ONENESS

You may notice that the falling away of dualistic thought in science echoes our internal changes in perception when we escape the dualism of language. Both Wordlessness and Oneness are dramatic phenomena, but I've been describing them as inner events. I'm emphasizing their importance for finding your way in our wild new world because these states of *being* give us access to incredibly powerful ways of *doing*. Let me give you just one example of what scientists are doing, now that they more fully realize the connection between even the most distant objects.

In a laboratory at Duke University, a monkey named Aurora sits earning herself tasty drops of fruit juice by playing a video game. Every time she scores, a machine squirts a bit of juice into her mouth. But Aurora isn't moving a muscle. In fact she doesn't even have a control panel for the video game. The panel is being operated by a human-size robot, which sits at the controls picking up impulses from Aurora's brain via wires attached to her head. All Aurora has to do is *imagine* playing the game, and the robot responds exactly as if it were her own body—*faster* than her actual body can respond to commands from her brain. In fact Aurora's brain has developed a special area devoted entirely to operating the robot, as if it is literally an extension of her body. Oh, and one more thing: Aurora is doing all this in North Carolina. The robot that's playing video games under control of her brain is in Japan.

This is not science fiction. It's not a prognostication of some fantasy future. It's happening. That's why I keep using the phrase "wild new world" to talk about the current and future state of human life. The rules about what we can do and how we can do it are changing radically as science gets past the illusory separations of the physical world to the truth of Oneness.

Most Team members are fascinated by findings and experiments like these, not because they match our fantasies, but because they match our experience. Physicists talk about "quantum entanglement"; born wayfinders describe the eerie connection we feel between distant things, including one another. Experiments show that objects are affected by energetic "fields," while we chat half-seriously about a cinematic invention called "the Force." Heisenberg showed that particles solidify out of wave potential only when observed by consciousness; we have the persistent suspicion we're somehow cocreating reality.

CAVEAT MANIFESTER!

At this point I must warn you that I believe most discussions about quantum physics and our role as cocreators of physical reality are hideously overstated and anything but scientific. Physicists are only beginning to explore quantum phenomena, and their experiments concern particles so small they make atoms look positively gargantuan. New Age gurus and movies toss around the term "quantum mechanics," then vault to the assertion that scientists have "proven" we can all manifest brand-new Ferraris while sitting on our La-Z-Boys eating peanut butter from the jar. If that were true, I'd look like Halle Berry, you'd live in that Tuscan cottage by the sea, and nobody would ever die of cancer.

That said, I must admit something is going on here. Monkeys in labs aren't the only beings functioning as wireless communication devices. Our brains and bodies are interacting with everything around us, and if we know how to use Oneness, we can sense what to do much more accurately and take action in the real world much more powerfully. I've been convinced of this by countless experiences, from encounters with way-finders both in books and real life, to horse "whispering," to mangling an enormous quantity of silverware.

CUTLERY AND THE TECHNOLOGY OF ONENESS

I'm sharing dinner and conversation with Jo, a fascinating anthropologist in her eighties who's spent her whole life studying traditional cultures. We met just minutes before, but I'm already enthralled by Jo's descriptions of far-flung Siberian research sites and wayfinders she's studied in obscure societies. I want to pick her brain for every trick she's learned about the technologies of magic. When I ask her if she's ever learned any traditional magic that actually works in the physical world, I expect insights into the medicinal uses of lichens or hints on herding reindeer. But Jo is a trained field researcher, and as such, she's highly pragmatic. She talks about what's immediately observable.

"Have you ever bent a spoon?" she asks.

"A spoon?" I say. "What, you mean like Uri Geller?"

I've seen Uri Geller on TV from time to time. He made a name for himself, beginning in the 1970s, by bending metal objects with gentle finger pressure, supposedly boosted by the power of his mind. I'm not sure whether I believed Geller's claims, but over the years I've occasionally tried to bend spoons as he did. It's never worked. At all.

"Spoon bending's nothing special," says Jo. "Anyone can learn it."

I pick up my fork, a nice solid restaurant fork, hold it in both hands, and try to bend it. No way. It's as rigid as a bar of steel, perhaps because it *is* a bar of steel.

"Teach me!" I beg. I hold the fork out and smile into Jo's eyes, strengthening the person-to-person connection that enlivens any dinner conversation. Suddenly the fork folds double in my hands. It feels like a piece of soft clay.

"There you go," says Jo, and turns her attention to her salad.

"This must be a really flimsy fork," I say, and try to bend it back to its original shape. I can't. It hurts my hands.

"Wrong energy," says Jo mildly.

"What?" I'm simultaneously boggled, skeptical, and intensely curious.

"Feel inside the fork," Jo says.

At this point I'm quite concerned about ruining the restaurant's silverware, so I ignore the fact that this instruction makes no sense. I hold the fork in both hands again and drop into Wordlessness. Now that I'm paying attention, I feel something incredibly strange: the fork seems aware. It actually feels (you can do this too, and then you'll know I'm not nuts) *friendly*. As I picture it straightening, I swear I sense it *deciding* to go along with my desire. In fact the fork feels like part of my own body, as though we've become One. At the time, I don't yet know that our brains literally do morph to include the tools we use as parts of our body. All I know is that the fork turns soft and pliable again, and I easily return it to its original shape.

For the next few days I'm silverware's nemesis. I go home from that restaurant and bend every teaspoon I own, then the soup spoons, then all the forks, then a heavy-duty soup ladle. I twist a soup spoon handle into a corkscrew. I consider silverware sculpture as a possible second career. My finest hour, I believe, arrives when I bend a length of steel rebar in front of a skeptical cowboy, who, despite being six-foot-five and very strong, can't straighten it out again.

YOUR TURN

I bring up this strange preoccupation for one reason: it's a simple, empirical, testable entry point into the magic of Oneness, and you can experience it for yourself. Find a fork or spoon that's too difficult to bend with your bare hands. Then drop into Wordlessness and "feel into" the spoon. Don't strain or "focus"—this is the mistake most people make because they don't realize that soft, open focus is part of the first technology of magic. Mentally ask the spoon if it will bend for you. Send it a friendly mental image, a picture of itself in a bent configuration, so it'll know what you mean. Wait for permission—not words, but a feeling of agreement and companionship. Eventually you'll get it.

Maybe this will work the first time. Maybe it won't. What I hope is that for you, as for me and many other people to whom I've taught this little technique, there will be times when you can't bend a given piece of silverware at all, and moments when you know the implement has become One with you and it's suddenly bizarrely pliable.

Once you've felt this effect, you'll be stuck with the same question I had to ask my own spoon-bending self: "What the hell is happening here? Why does this work so well sometimes, and other times not at all? What's the 'trick'? Why do I feel affection for, and from, a *spoon*? What does this imply about my relationship with all the objects around me? About the power of my mind, and the other minds I encounter every day?"

These are the same kinds of questions that filled my mind as I led that herd of horses around the pasture in California. Throughout human history, countless wayfinders have experienced similar waves of wonder after first experiencing the astonishing subjective truth of being connected with everyone and everything else in the universe.

FROM ONENESS WITH SILVERWARE
TO ONENESS WITH EVERYTHING

The chapters in this section will teach you ways to experience and use Oneness, communicating and working with everything in your experience as if it is part of yourself, because it is. We'll start with simple things like spoons, then move on to more complex subjects and situations. Each chapter will offer you some exercises to help you use Oneness to heal your own true nature, and then communicate the sweetness of healing to everyone and everything around you. This, as you'll see later, is actually the most practical and productive thing you can do to thrive, both psychologically and logistically, in the wild new world humans are helping to create.

All wayfinder traditions include extensive training to experience Oneness. One South American shaman who was trained by a tribe deep in the forest told me he actually has to work to step out of Oneness so that he can understand the fear and neuroses of his First World patients. The many exercises you'll find in this section are just different ways of moving you, little by little, closer to this continuous true nature connection. Try each of them, and see which work best for you. Practice your favorites whenever you feel sad and alone, when you're missing a loved one who's far away or long-since deceased. Practice them when you're scared, when you want to feel the comfort of an inconceivably powerful force that loves you unconditionally.

A saying from the Ojibwa always reminds me to do this: "Sometimes I go about pitying myself, and all the time I am being carried on great winds across the sky." All the Oneness exercises, in this chapter and the few that follow, are to help you feel how safe you are, how levitated by the All. There's no program for learning them (minutes per day, units per month). There's only the suffering of your lonely human soul, which will goad you into practicing Oneness until you stop feeling lonely. Forever.

A SIMPLE GATEWAY TO ONENESS:
MENTAL-TO-METAL MIND MELDS

It's obvious, as I sit here typing on my wireless keyboard and sending and receiving emails on my wireless network, that electronic machines can communicate with one another without tangible, physical connection. We also know that our nervous systems are, to quote the neurologist and author Jeffrey Schwartz, "electrical circuits made of meat." Both our wireless devices and our brains operate by sending weak pulses of electricity to receptor molecules. I suspect this is the reason many Team members have an interesting relationship with metal objects, especially electronic devices.

For example, my friend Jenny can't wear watches; they stop as soon as she puts them on her wrist. Allan has to touch metal before he hugs his loved ones to discharge the powerful shock they'll get if he doesn't drain electricity. When a client named Madeleine experiences strong emotions, nearby televisions and lamps often turn on or off spontaneously. Judith attended a seminar in which Uri Geller bent spoons; she didn't manage to bend any silverware herself, but when she arrived home, she couldn't get in because her house keys had curled in her pocket. And many Team members, including computer scientists, have told me their computers fritz out when they get tired, emotional, or extremely mentally focused. Walt Whitman might have been slower to "sing the body electric" if he'd been working on a laptop that crashed every time he waxed rhapsodic.

MACHINE MIND-MATCHING

There's no doubt that our electronic technology is getting more and more sensitive, reaching the level where our own self-generated electricity may begin to affect it. But there's also strong experimental evidence that machines respond to human attention, even when the devices are shielded from electromagnetic influence. Random number generators (RNGs) are machines designed to spit out data, such as strings of ones and zeroes, based on the process of radioactive decay, which is as close to absolute randomness as engineers can get. The machines perform like repetitive coin tosses; over millions of "tosses" they yield virtually perfect, 50–50 randomness. Usually. But on days when events of great significance to humans are occurring, the randomness of RNGs drops bizarrely.

For example, on September 11, 2001, two hours *before* the first terrorist plane hit the World Trade Center, RNGs all around the world began generating data that were nonrandom, at a high level of statistical significance. This nonrandomness climbed throughout the fateful day and remained statistically significant until midday on September 13. Scientists at Princeton who wrote about these results noted, "We are obliged to confront the possibility that the measured correlations may be directly associated with some aspect of consciousness attendant to global events."* This may be one reason why, on the day I did my first pasture join-up and finally felt connected to that beautiful little palomino mare, I felt equally connected to the hills and the trees and even the old truck. It may be that despite remaining motionless, that truck "joined up" with my consciousness just as the horses did.

This thought occurred to me some weeks later, when I was back home, driving around Phoenix. My car had a GPS device that, once it had been switched on and programmed, would direct me around town in a silken British-accented voice my children had named Prunella. One day I stopped at a red light and began revisiting the sense of Oneness I'd experienced when I'd joined up with the horse herd. Just thinking about it put me into a deep, sweet, shimmering silence. Then a clear, rather loud voice said, from *inside my car,* "You have reached your destination."

For about three seconds I whirled my head around wildly, like a demented owl, seeking the source of the voice. My heart started up again when I recognized it as Prunella's Oxford-educated tone. Still, I stared at the GPS device in something close to fear. The machine was off. The screen was dark. Never before and never after that did Prunella speak without being switched on and laboriously programmed. I don't know whether a random spark triggered her single statement, or whether the

*Nelson, Radin, Shoup, and Bancel, "Correlations of Continuous Random Data with Major World Events," *Foundations of Physics Letters* 15, no. 6 (October 4, 2002): 537–550.

machine simply decided to say howdy in its language, as the horses had greeted me in theirs.

It seems likely to me that Oneness has something to do with quantum entanglement, though as I've said, we know little about such phenomena at a macro scale. But thousands of years of careful observation has led to a sophisticated description of Oneness as experienced by wayfinders of all mystical traditions. These ancient teachers maintained that we are communicating with everything, and everything is communicating with us, all the time.

In the Gospel of Thomas, from the Nag Hammadi manuscripts, Jesus says, "I am the light that is over all things. . . . Split a piece of wood; I am there. Lift up the stone, and you will find me there." In everything, through everything, around everything: if any being is connected in this way, then so, by definition, are all others. This is the universe that seems self-evident to people grounded in sacred silence. This is the world in which the Team may learn to connect, communicate, and coordinate. It's the world you'll call home as you begin to consciously navigate the One. You can start with the simple exercises below.

Mastering Oneness: Distort Metal

Ancient epics and stories are filled with references to sacred objects made of metal: Excalibur the Sword, the Ring of the Nibelung, the brass lamp that housed Aladdin's genie. Because metal is a good conductor of electricity, and our nervous systems use electricity, it makes sense that we'd have a certain rapport for this particular form of matter, and it for us.

The silverware-bending exercise described earlier is a handy way to begin using Oneness consciously. Find a spoon you can't easily bend, and persist in becoming Wordless and asking it to bend for you. Carry it around and play with it while you're parked at a stoplight or waiting in line. You'll find that when you can intend to bend the spoon without thinking about it in your usual, wordy way, you'll feel a strange sense of communion, and the spoon will become malleable.

Mastering Oneness: Buy and Use a Mind Flex

I have a cool little "toy" called Mind Flex, which you can buy online. (Mine was given to me by my Team friend Sonja Alar, thank you very much, and you can see me demonstrate it online if you Google "Martha Beck Mindflex" or navigating to www.youtube.com/watch?v=sKTdkZX9_ak.) The

Mind Flex includes a head strap that presses a small metal sensor onto the left side of your forehead, while extraordinarily unfashionable ear-clips pick up sensors from your earlobes. A separate small machine houses a motorized fan. The fan is controlled by electrical energy from your brain.

To play the game, you place a small Styrofoam ball atop the fan, and by activating your brain's left hemisphere (the manual suggests doing mental math) rev up the motor and cause the little ball to rise on a column of air. By turning down the electrical activity in your left hemisphere, you turn off the motor and make the ball go down. (Unfocusing your eyes and thinking about sleep are suggested. Both activities put you into Wordlessness. No coincidence there.) I believe this little toy is a forerunner of many similar machines we'll one day operate by controlling the electrical output from various regions of our heads.

Mastering Oneness: Buy and Use an emWave

This device, which you can buy online for about $200, consists of a metal box about the size of a deck of cards. It sports a cord connected to an earlobe clip. The name "emWave" stands for "electromagnetic wave," because the machine measures the synchrony of electromagnetic emanations from your brain and heart. When you're in a typical, busy, thought-fixated mental state, a red light appears on the box. If your mental chatter calms down a bit, the light turns blue and you hear a mellow "bing!" When you get really calm, your brain goes into a state called "synchronous alpha," where all your internal electromagnetic waves are simultaneously broadcasting a gentle, even, powerful frequency. At this point the light on the emWave turns green, and the "bing!" turns into an even more mellow "bong" (not the object, the sound).

Using an emWave not only shows you how your nervous system can affect objects around you, but helps train you to drop into Wordlessness. As such, it's excellent training for both the first and second technologies of magic.

By dealing with the inanimate objects listed above, you'll begin to feel the sensation on the inside of your head change when you drop into Wordlessness. You'll feel it spread through your entire body as your sensitivity increases and your focus becomes softer and more inclusive. And you'll have external, empirical evidence that the more Wordless your brain is, the more powerfully you receive and transmit communication between your own body and your environment.

ACHIEVING ONENESS BY SLEEPING AROUND

Like any kind of deep practice, learning to navigate Oneness is strangely draining, even though it's quite blissful, until your brain has developed a certain level of mastery. You'll know you're making progress when you can consistently maintain control over one of the inanimate objects listed above, and as this happens you'll also probably need extra sleep.

Scientists who study skill development have found that music students who deep-practice, as opposed to those who simply repeat exercises, develop far greater mastery, but also need more sleep as their brains change to accommodate their high level of integration with their instruments. Jill Bolte Taylor wrote that after her stroke, she needed to sleep long hours, like a baby, when her brain was working to restructure its normal neural pathways.

ONENESS IS WORTH THE WORK

The intensity, persistence, and delicacy necessary to function in Oneness is hard to overstate. It's not an ambition for the easily discouraged. But then, neither is spending your life as a mender, a healer of self, of other beings, and of complex systems. Neither is setting out to thrive in a world dominated by incredibly rapid, enormous changes. Neither is aspiring to save that world. The effort is daunting, but the rewards are inexpressible.

If you persist in "deep practicing" the skills described in this section, there will come a moment, and then many more moments, when you'll stumble into Oneness. You'll begin to receive the communication flowing toward your true nature through the true nature of all other things. The gentle message underlying every moment of conscious communion is that the world, and you yourself, are far more magical than you ever suspected. In your own place and time, you will feel the world "join up" with you. You'll get your own version of the soft footsteps coming closer, of the palomino's soul touching yours, of the sweet velvet noses against your back.

Kœlle Simpson

Oneness Rocks.

CHAPTER FIVE

MY AUNTIES, THE TREES
(ONENESS WITH THE GREEN NATION)

We are made of just two things: stardust and sunshine. Unbearably chirpy as that sounds, it's factually true. Every molecule in your body was made in the belly of a massive star that exploded, hurling all the elements we know into space. Every spark of energy that enables you to walk and think and live comes from our favorite star, the sun, as its heat radiates energy to Earth. But using sunlight to animate stardust—in other words, transforming matter and energy into a living creature—is a technology of magic no human has yet achieved. For that we rely on another kingdom of beings, a kingdom some American Indian traditions call "the green nation": plants. Wayfinders from all over the world and throughout history have cultivated (har har) a special and loving relationship with plants, a form of Oneness that's essential for healing one's self and virtually all other life.

In the grand scheme of life, plants have far more power over us than we do over them. If all humans disappeared, plants would thrive; if all plants disappeared, we'd die very promptly indeed. Every calorie we eat, as well as the oxygen we breathe, comes from plants, whether eaten directly or indirectly, through animals that get *their* calories from plants. Your cells are ultimately made of rice and alfalfa and (especially if you're American) corn. Because we are what we eat, it's impossible not to be One with the plant kingdom. It's only possible to forget that we are One. This chapter is meant to remind you of your connection to the green nation for the purposes of healing yourself, others, and a world in which humans can survive. Fully experiencing this Oneness with plants makes our connection with the entire world far more conscious and vibrant. And in some cases, with some menders, it can be powerful magic.

We'll cover two types of Oneness in this chapter: the physical connection between your body and the food or medicine created by plants, and the spiritual connection with the green nation that our culture barely acknowledges (though it's central to wisdom traditions of many cultures).

Plants don't need us to create a green revolution; we are the ones whose lives depend on it. But as you begin to consciously experience your Oneness with plants, these great beings will begin to care for you in turn.

THE GIVER OF ALL LIFE

I'm finding out just how vast and intimidating the plant kingdom can be while clambering through the mountainous jungles of Rwanda in 2010. My friends and I, following our guide, are chopping and clawing our way through the steep nettle forests as if swimming in a sea of green. A painful sea. "These plants bite," our guide told us before we started hiking. "If you are bitten, please suffer in silence." And we do. My feet don't touch soil for hours; every footstep and hand-hold lands on stinging plants that anoint my skin with burning toxins. We're wearing heavy gloves, so my hands are okay, but my wrists, shoulders, and knees, which occasionally contact the nettles even through my clothes, are burning like shame.

Around midday we stop to rest in the shade of a tree that looks at least a thousand years old. It's massive, astonishing, a vast living *Avatar*-style city upon which thousands of other plants are growing—bromeliads, mosses, creeping vines, orchids—all feeding thousands of insects, hundreds of birds, dozens of mammals. Perhaps because I have a touch of altitude sickness, or as a side effect of stinging-nettle venom, I feel as if the tree is conscious of me. It's like meeting Jesus; I have an overwhelming urge to kneel and pray. My knees are such masses of fire that I stay upright and spare myself the embarrassment, but the tree seems to sense the prayers in my breath, in every wisp of carbon dioxide coming from my lungs. It magnanimously returns each breath to me freshly filled with its own home-made oxygen.

We hike on, climbing higher and higher, our guides slashing a tunnel through the green nettle sea with machetes that are both obviously necessary and uncomfortably reminiscent of the Rwandan genocide. Chop a plant, and the plant grows back unperturbed. Chop a person, and that person dies. And we think *we're* the powerful ones?

The mountainside is so steep that although I'm just a few feet behind the guide, my eyes are level with the backs of his knees. The bruised nettles make footing slippery; it's all I can do to keep from skidding downward and backward into my friends. I focus on each step, each surge of nettle-fire in my skin, and sink so deeply into Wordlessness through the paths of dance and torment that I gradually forget why we're here. Then the guide stops. I glance up. There, amid the tangle of green, lies an absolutely enormous arm. Its coat of dense black fur makes it look even more massive. I can almost touch the callused hand resting, lazily open, directly in front of us.

Where does a six-hundred-pound mountain gorilla sleep? Anywhere he damn well pleases.

I back up a step and circle around our guide until I have a view of the whole animal, a silverback male. He's napping on a mattress he's made for himself out of stinging nettles. His toes twiddle happily in the air, and his dreaming eyes move behind closed lids. As my friends climb up to join us, the silverback gives a contented sigh and rolls over onto his stomach, mooning us with his enormous buttocks.

A few feet ahead the nettles part and several pairs of bright brown eyes peer out. Two adult females and several juvenile gorillas are studying us intently. A Rwandan porter makes a deep rumbling sound in his chest, and the females relax and go back to eating, but the babies are still intrigued. One thumps his little chest and moves to within a few feet of me, his eyes searching mine. I step back—there are rules about keeping space between humans and gorillas—but I am entirely in love. It's rare for humans to gaze Wordlessly into one another's eyes with no self-consciousness or fear. This little gorilla's eyes shine with virtually all the intelligence of a human mind but none of its verbal machinations, so that we can hold one another's gaze with no caution or pretense. It feels more intimate than a kiss.

The youngster's mother reaches out one long arm to corral him, and he goes back to work munching up greenery. "How amazing!" I think. "Gorillas are made of stinging nettle!"

As if to prove my point, the silverback rolls over, opens his eyes, and scrunches up a mouthful of spiky leaves. I've heard conservationists talk about "green" projects for years, and felt only a vague guilt about drinking water from plastic bottles. But in this moment, with my senses full of jungle, my skin burning fiercely (it will tingle for days to come), and my soul caught in the web of consciousness with the giant tree and the huge apes, the desire to re-green the Earth absolutely overwhelms me. Oneness with the plant nation feels more important than anything else humans can do. That goes double for the wayfinders, who, in all cultures, use plants to achieve their two-part sacred task: the healing of self and the healing of all else.

OF FOOD AND PHYTOCHEMICALS: HOW PHYSICAL ONENESS WITH THE GREEN NATION HEALS US

After returning from Rwanda, I met with several of "my" master coaches (born wayfinders all) to discuss new ways we could earn a living doing exactly what we damn well please. I couldn't help noticing that several of these people looked like they'd been enhanced with Photoshop. They were all glowy: their skin was clear, their eyes were radiant, and they seemed to have the continuous, resilient energy of small children. They happily chatted about the magic that had wrought this rejuvenation. Two words: green smoothies.

"I hear it's a trend on the West Coast or somewhere," said Susan, a brilliant coach who was once seriously overweight and continuously tired, and who now bikes hundreds of miles a week looking so good men drool helplessly as she zips past. "I don't know why I got into it. One day I just had a compulsion to start putting kale and spinach and other greens into a fruit smoothie, and when I drank my first one, my entire body shouted YES!" Susan had spread the word to other coaches (who, due to the nature of our work, are constantly trading tips). Now the whole posse was slamming mixed greens as if their lives depended on it.

This group of coaches had spent years practicing the technologies of magic, dropping into Wordlessness, feeling Oneness. They could all bend spoons like Uri Geller; they'd all done a bit of horse-whispering. So none of us was really surprised when, late at night after a glass or two of wine, people began confessing that the plants they were eating seemed to be volunteering for the job.

"They, um, they sort of sing to me," said one coach. "And my body sort of sings back. They're in this together." She wasn't hearing things, just trying to describe a Wordless connection, a communication between beings that relied on something deeper than her ordinary senses. She wasn't alone, either. It turned out that several people in the group were "hearing" this duet between their body and plant food.

These master coaches didn't know that in many traditions, plants are thought to "sing" their particular usefulness to healers or medicine people. In most "primitive" cultures, the mender is not only the tribe's storyteller, animal communicator, artist, and mystic, but also the resident herbalist. The shamans of the Amazon Basin say that they've learned the medicinal or psychoactive uses of some eighty thousand plant species from the plants themselves. Wade Davis, the Harvard anthropologist who coined the term "wayfinder," found that certain shamans classified six different varieties of a plant that looked identical to scientists. When he asked them why, they said, "You really don't know anything about plants, do you?" Then they explained that when the moon is full and the plants sing, the six subspecies of this particular plant sang in completely different keys. Dr. Davis might have ignored this as superstition, except that the shamans were mixing very effective medicinal compounds from various blends of these plants. They were getting highly sophisticated information somewhere, and their plant chemistry worked.

As you begin paying attention to your own wayfinder archetype, you're likely to begin connecting with the part of our brain/body that knows which plants to consume. Medicine aside, a basic need for health and healing is good nutrition, and good nutrition consists primarily of eating lots and lots of plants. Our ancient ancestors had to snarf down enormous amounts of greenery to get enough calories; this is obvious once you've watched a family of nearly human gorillas feed. That means we evolved to be at our healthiest when we get a wide range of phytochemicals—molecules formed by the green nation (*phyto* means plant). It may seem odd that eating your vegetables is a technology of magic, but it really is the best way to make life out of stardust and sunshine, and every wayfinder needs to do it.

Since humans began farming rather than browsing, the variety of plants in our diet has dropped steadily. Monocrop existence (living mainly on just one staple plant) caused potato famine in Ireland, rice-related starvation in Asia, and many famines in Africa when corn crops failed. It's also a good way to achieve chronic borderline malnutrition. Different plants contain a bewildering variety of chemicals that nourish different aspects of our physiology. Being One with plants means not just avoiding "bad" food but eating lots and lots of good food.

I'm the opposite of a health food fanatic; I've lived entire decades of my life fueled primarily by Milk Duds. But after meeting the gorilla family and seeing my smoothie-obsessed coaches go all luminous, I became a green smoothie devotee myself. I immediately noticed improvement in everything from my energy level to my eyesight. Try getting your sunlight energy and stardust matter from a variety of fresh green plants, and I believe you'll see the same improvements.

If you can't hear the produce department at your grocery store "singing" to you, here's a simple technology-of-magic method for choosing which plants to put in your green smoothies. I've also included a smoothie recipe, but ideally you'll let the Oneness between your body and the plants help you improvise the ideal blend for you.

Mastering Oneness: Let Plants Tell Your Body What It Wants

One wayfinder I know calls this technique "body-dowsing." You can use it to observe the communication between your body and various foods, especially plants. I don't know why this works, nor have I found any studies that purport to explain it. For that matter, no one knows exactly why lithium calms mania. Some things are useful because they work, even if the reason they work remains obscure.

1. Stand in flat shoes with your shoulders directly over your heels. Repeat the word "pain" several times. Don't move deliberately, but notice whether your body sways backward or forward. The sway may be very slight, or quite pronounced. This is probably because your nervous system causes your body to subtly move away from even the thought of pain. Your body may back off, or it may want to run forward. Experiment to see which way you sway.

2. Return to a neutral posture and repeat the word "calm" several times. Notice which way your body sways. Again, most people find themselves leaning slightly backward for "pain" and slightly forward for "calm," but in some people the opposite is true.

3. Once you've established your positive and negative reactions, stand in a neutral position, then pick up a vegetable or fruit and notice whether your body sways in one direction or the other. If the plant causes you to sway in your "positive" direction, buy it.

4. Eat the foods that catalyzed a positive sway. I've found that even people who don't like vegetables may have dramatic swaying responses to foods that are missing from their diets. If you're one of these people, please realize that there are dozens of ways to prepare any vegetable, and keep trying different recipes until

you find one you like. If you consume healthy food in a state of Wordlessness, you'll find that your body feels weirdly joyful as you eat. This reaction motivates me to keep eating veggies, though I like to pulverize them into a state that's roughly similar to sorbet. If you decide to take up the smoothie habit, use one fruit ingredient for every vegetable ingredient (you'll find one recipe below) and you'll find that the characteristic taste of "vegetables" disappears into the sweetness of fruit.

Mastering Oneness: Guzzle Greens

GORILLA SMOOTHIE

2 cups fruit juice
1 cup ice
handful of raw baby spinach leaves
1 tangerine
handful of mixed field greens
4 strawberries
handful of lettuce
⅓ of a banana
handful of wheat grass
½ cup blueberries
3 baby carrots

Throw all this stuff into a blender, where it will form a lovely still life of deeply saturated color. Then push the button and wait until the whole thing looks as if you already ate it, then threw up (serving suggestion). Really, it might not be pretty, but your body will *love* it. I like to drink a large smoothie for lunch every day. Other smoothie addicts I know prefer to guzzle theirs for breakfast or dinner, or a between-meals snack. In societies where greens form a large part of the diet, people tend to "graze," snacking on plants whenever they feel peckish. This is an extremely healthy habit, and if you're inclined toward it, I suggest you start grazing now.

BEYOND NUTRITION

While every human needs to be One with plants through nutrition, many members of the Team have a relationship with the green nation that goes well beyond food. Virtually all traditional menders know how to use certain phytochemicals to alter body chemistry. They use plants for everything from healing headaches to having visions.

Wayfinders from different cultures have slightly different methods for mastering plant medicines. Ancient Chinese healers conducted centuries of experiments, eating every herb they could find, noting each plant's apparent effects on their own body. In Europe midwives passed down knowledge of medicinal plants to one another. (Many women burned for witchcraft during the Dark Ages were targeted simply because they were sophisticated herbalists.) North American medicine people carried "medicine bundles" of potent herbs. And many of the drugs sold as prescriptions today were discovered by South American shamans, arguably the most plant-obsessed healers on the planet. Rain forest wayfinders developed an incredibly sophisticated mastery of phytochemicals—for example, combining exactly the right plants to create monoamine oxidase inhibitors, used in the treatment of depression.

First World science is only beginning to tap this ancient knowledge, but at least we now recognize it for the literal "big medicine" it is. An entire academic field, ethnobotany, trains scientists to interact with native tribes and healers specifically to learn medicinal uses of plants. The World Health Organization recently began encouraging all countries to adopt the use of traditional herbal medicines; doing so not only improves health at a low cost, but makes "new" medicines (actually ancient ones heretofore unrecognized by Western medicine) more likely to be "discovered."

Like most First World Team members, I first connected with phytochemicals in a desperate attempt to stay healthy. My travel bags contain a "medicine bundle" to rival a small pharmacy: insecticides, sunburn-healing aloe, remedies for headaches, nausea, vertigo, and infections both fungal and viral. Where traditional herbal healers gleaned medicine from fields and forests, I buy mine at drugstores and health food centers. But the sources of virtually all these healing potions are plants. I carry them because I have what may be a "shaman sickness," the aforementioned fibromyalgia and its various attending illnesses. Over the decades my symptoms goaded me into trying dozens of prescription and over-the-counter medications, from mugwort tea to Percocet. Since you may have a wayfinder's chronic sickness yourself, I think this is worth a bit more discussion.

MOTIVATION TO STUDY PHYTOCHEMICALS: THE BLESSED CURSE OF "SHAMAN SICKNESS"

"My two cousins are *sangoma,*" a Shangaan friend named True told me one day. "I'm going back to my village tomorrow to attend my older sister's initiation ceremony."

True is one of the smartest men I've ever met. Like all trackers, he's a consummate scientist. He speaks five languages fluently and is a voracious reader.

"Both my cousins got sick when they were quite young," he said. "They were exhausted, couldn't get out of bed for months. My family tried all the traditional medicine we knew, but it didn't work. So we took them to hospitals in Johannesburg, and that didn't work either. They had to begin training as *sangoma* before they got better."

True sounded regretful. The life of a *sangoma,* a Shangaan mender, isn't an easy one. It requires a great deal of hard work and sacrifice, and he clearly wished his cousins had been spared from Team membership. I wanted to sympathize, but I was too fascinated to feel really bad. True's cousins fit into a classic pattern by which medicine people are identified all over the world: a seemingly normal person develops baffling chronic illness, tries every treatment known, but doesn't heal. At that point the tribe begins to suspect a "shaman sickness." The patient begins training to become a mystic, artist, and healer, and the symptoms lessen or disappear—but the person feels better only so long as he or she continues acting as a *sangoma.* Leaving the path of the wayfinder means getting sick again.

As I've mentioned, many Team members I know, most of them First World intellectuals who've never heard of a shaman sickness, fall into this archetypal pattern as perfectly as my Shangaan friends. Sarah developed Chronic Fatigue Syndrome after an automobile accident when she was thirty. She became too ill to work at her job as a management consultant and spent almost a year in a weary, bedridden fog. Then she received a gift certificate for a massage that changed her life.

"As soon as the therapist touched my head," she said later, "I felt a sort of flame running through all my nerves, right down to my toes." After the massage, she felt like her old self for several hours. "I went back the next week," she told me, "and that was when I realized I had to learn to do whatever that massage therapist was doing." She entered training to become a master of Reiki, a Japanese healing art. Her illness began to retreat. Now she's once again working full time, in her own consulting business, but says, "If I stop doing Reiki, I get sick again."

Mark had a similar history. "I was an athlete in college," he told me at the fibromyalgia conference where we met, "but when I was twenty-six, I developed horrific chronic pain. They diagnosed me five years later. By then I'd found that meditation and yoga helped my symptoms. When I started *teaching* yoga as a healing art, things improved really rapidly. Now I'm an athlete again, but mainly I'm a healer."

"I was almost leveled by cluster headaches and fatigue," said Julie, who runs a care and rescue center for dogs. "There were some miserable years in there, while I tried to live a 'normal' life. Then I realized that, for me, 'normal' means being around a lot of animals, outside, almost all the time. When I started living by my passion for helping people and animals find each other, the symptoms went away."

As I've listened to hundreds of similar stories, I've wondered if the sensitive wiring that gives wayfinders high levels of intuition can also cause burnout, leading to chronic stress-related illness. If you're a sickly sort, and you notice that your illness comes on more strongly when you stray from your heart's desires, try this: conditionally accept membership in the Team. Experimentally commit to reclaiming your true nature as a wayfinder. See if your symptoms improve.

I don't want to give you false hope—even assuming a shaman sickness is a real phenomenon, not every illness qualifies, and many wayfinders never get completely better—but as I've said, my own "incurable" conditions (fibromyalgia, interstitial cystitis, granuloma annulare) have virtually disappeared, although they recur when I do anything that isn't on track for my true nature. This could be a placebo reaction to my beliefs about the existence and nature of the Team—except that I stumbled onto the concept of shaman sickness while trying to figure out why my symptoms went away: my knowledge of the phenomenon came *after* I'd experienced the cure, not vice versa.

However, the placebo effect may well explain why I had a powerful experience of being healed during a South American—style sacred ceremony. (That said, isn't the placebo effect—people healing from symptoms simply because they believe they're being healed—a technology of magic in itself?) It was an astonishing experience of Oneness with the green nation, and also helped convince me that the archetype of the mender may be fully as magical as many ancient peoples believed.

HEALING ADVENTURES WITH RAIN FOREST PLANTS

This adventure occurs at a time and place that shall remain nameless, because I have no idea whether it is actually legal in the country where it's taking place. I've been invited to join a small group of people—some friends, some strangers—who've engaged a South American shaman to officiate over an "ayahuasca journey." Ayahuasca is a powerful hallucinogen brewed from two unrelated and inconspicuous rain forest plants. Though each plant is inert by itself, their chemical mixture has extraordinary affects on humans. Once, in college, I saw a documentary about ayahuasca journeys. The grainy film showed a bunch of smallish men wearing red mud in their hair. They drank a nasty-looking liquid, threw up, and then lay around a hut for hours and hours.

I didn't get it. I've never done recreational drugs—being on so many prescribed ones made that seem superfluous—and I couldn't imagine any kind of high that would make vomiting worthwhile. But according to the mud-haired men, their special brew allowed the spirits of the rain forest plants to teach them wisdom and peace. Whatever.

Decades of illness later, I'm excited when a friend invites me to such a ceremony. It not only matches my newfound interest in traditional healers, but elicits a reaction from my body that's basically, "Oh, yes!" By this I mean that when I think about attending I feel physically energized—a sensation I know and respect. To a wayfinder, the body is a kind of tracking device, always helping us find our way. Stay in the horrible job, and you get psoriasis. Join the crazy family argument, and your back goes out. Deny a love, a dream, any inner truth, and your gut goes into spasm. I know that when my body says no to something and I still do it, or when my body says yes and I don't do it, I get sick. And I'm sick of being sick. So I say, yes, I'll attend the ceremony.

A few days before the event, surfing the Internet, I stumble upon a list of several drugs that should never, under any circumstances, be taken within a blue moon of consuming ayahuasca. Just days before, I've actually taken one of these drugs—a compound so obscure it's rarely given to people, though my beagle was on it during his later years. If I drink the ayahuasca anytime soon, it could land me in the hospital. (That's why *I recommend that you do not ingest anything stronger than tap water* on your wayfinder's quest. In fact tap water can be really harsh. I'd filter it, if I were you.)

I'm quite shaken by this near miss, and also a bit crestfallen. If I'm so tapped into Oneness, sending and receiving ineffable signals from the green nation, why did I feel such a positive reaction to the ceremony, only to find—too late to do anything about it—that there's no way I should join the "journey"? I decide to go anyway, just to observe. As the group gathers and barf buckets are handed out, I become increasingly glad I've decided not to participate. I explain my predicament to the South American shaman, who surprises me by being one of those people who emanates a sense of pure peace. I'd expected to feel some sort of culture clash—I've never even been to South America—but everything about this gentle, gray-haired man (no mud in evidence) makes me deeply comfortable.

At sunset the dozen or so "journeyers" sit in a circle, and the medicine man gives each person a carefully measured dose of liquid. Then we all just sit there. It's a bit anticlimactic, if you want to know the truth. I begin to meditate as the medicine man hums songs in a language that sounds a million years old. His voice is ethereal, beautiful. Strangely there are moments when I think everyone else is singing along with him, in harmony. I wonder how my friends learned those strange songs. Then people started throwing up, and I grow increasingly pleased that I haven't taken the plant extracts.

THE UNEXPECTED AUNTIES

The shaman begins walking around the circle of silent people, stopping to whisper a few questions to each individual. By now it's pitch dark, so I can't see what he's doing, but I can smell an extraordinarily fragrant smoke, and sometimes I hear the shaman blowing through his pursed lips. Then he reaches me and whispers a few questions. Is there anything in my body or life that needs healing? Anything at all? He speaks so gently, with such love in his whispered voice, that my eyes fill with tears.

"Well," I say, "I had a lot of pain all over my body for a long time, and sometimes I'm afraid it will come back."

The shaman nods and begins muttering in that strange, ancient-sounding language as he moves his hands in the air near my body. He inhales smoke from a pipe, then blows it over my head, down my back, along my arms and legs. Next comes a dose of flower-scented water, delivered in much the same way; he holds a little liquid in his mouth, then blows its fragrance over my body. I find the whole process fascinating. Then the shaman moves on, and I go back to meditating.

My right hand twitches.

Huh, I think.

My left hand twitches.

Interesting.

My right hand begins twitching again—more than that, it starts *vibrating*. Part of me wants to tense up and hold it still, but what the hell, I think. It's dark and no one's watching. If everybody else can throw up more or less in public, I can vibrate.

As soon as I make this decision, the vibration ripples up my arms, into my torso, down my legs. My muscles, from the tiniest to the biggest, begin to shiver in a way I could never replicate deliberately. The medicine man's singing seems louder, and now I definitely hear other voices singing along. Then I realize the voices couldn't be coming from the people in the room. For one thing, they're all using that unfamiliar language, and for another, all the voices are female. Suddenly I hear this alto chorus speak to me in English.

You see? they say. *We came for you, anyway.*

Remember, I haven't taken anything.

You've had enough pain on your journey, sing the trees.

Wait—how do I know they're trees? I don't garden, can't even keep a houseplant alive. Trees?

More nausea would be wrong for you, they sing. *We wanted you to experience only healing.*

I begin to weep from wonder and confusion as every little muscle along my spine quivers, first the one at the base of my neck, then the next one down, then the next. One of my feet begins tapping in rhythm with the chanting, and the other starts a bewilderingly complex syncopated rhythm. The quivering continues, without my deliberately moving a muscle, for over four hours. Sometimes I feel like a contestant in the World Wrestling Federation, getting tossed from side to side by giants. Then the shivering will become subtle and localized. But however intense it happens to be at any given moment, it is *delicious*. It feels *amazing*. Each muscle experiences a level of bliss as deep and intense as the pain I endured for all those years.

There's no way a few breaths of tobacco could do all this, I think, or every smoking section on Earth would be full of people thrashing around like Linda Blair in *The Exorcist*. I relax more and more, marveling that my body can quake so violently without the slightest effort or intention. I'm being *dandled*, the way you'd bounce a baby to help her calm down. The tree spirits—I've given up resisting my bizarre certainty that they are tree spirits—begin to laugh with delight as I relax. *Oh, you little monkeys*, they coo. *You're just ADORABLE!*

Dandle, dandle, dandle. Bliss, bliss, bliss.

About three hours in, a worry crosses my mind: I have a writing deadline. I become concerned I won't be able to make it after this strange night. As I begin to tense up, the trees say, very clearly, *Have we taught you nothing?* Then they burst into peals of laughter, chuck my cheeks, tickle my toes. They are the most adoring aunties you could possibly imagine.

I have to say, it leaves me wondering what happens when you actually drink the stuff.

THE STRANGE SCIENCE OF PLANTS

This experience left me shaken, in every sense of the word. For one thing, it forced me to consider that the South American shaman's belief in Oneness with plants may be an actual phenomenon, not just a quaint superstition. It also sent me back to a book I read when I was a kid, *The Secret Life of Plants*, by Peter Tompkins and Christopher Bird. The book caused quite a sensation; some readers roundly denounced the authors, and others happily embraced them. As with every other idea in this book, I suggest you try out their ideas to see how they resonate with you.

Tompkins and Bird claimed that plants aren't mere objects, but beings. They claimed that plants connected to polygraph machines react to many stimuli the way a conscious creature would. For example, readouts show sharp disruptions in electrical conductivity in plants that "observe" attacks on animals or other plants. "Kirlian" photographs, which translate the electrical output of an object into visible images, show that some leaves that have been chopped in half reveal a pattern of electrical voltage that not only shows the existing plant matter, but also a perfect halo-image of the missing parts. Furthermore the authors claimed to have discovered that talking kindly to plants can make them healthier and more robust.

I was twelve when I read *The Secret Life of Plants,* and even at that age, I remember wondering why the two authors were so fixated on vegetation that they would risk their reputations by making wild claims about "the physical, emotional, and spiritual relations between plants and man." Looking back now, I'm guessing Tompkins and Bird were simply members of the Team, the sort who have a particular passion for the green nation, trying to teach the rest of us the intense experience of Oneness with plants that I finally felt on the Gorilla Mountain.

PLANT PEOPLE

If you're a plant person, this is all obvious to you. I meet plant people everywhere these days, and their love for greenery seems to be getting more and more intense. For example, Sheri is so obsessed with her plants that she keeps photos of individual shrubs on her cell phone, along with pictures of her grandchildren. As she shows them to me, she strokes the screen with her finger, whispering sweet nothings to what I see as your basic bushes.

When Mary talks about gardening, she becomes too *verklempt* to speak. "I don't know why talking about rose bushes and chrysanthemums makes me so emotional," she apologizes, wiping away tears. "It makes no sense. I just, I just love them *so much!*"

Another client, Tom, describes his fantasy dream home as having "a huge gardens all over the property." A gardens? His use of the plural is a classic Freudian slip, so I call his attention to it. Tom also tears up as he says, "I see gardens all over the world." Then he has to stop talking, because it would make him weep outright, impugning his masculinity.

When I have a chance to meet the famous, radiant, and delightful Team member Elizabeth Gilbert, author of the blockbuster bestseller *Eat, Pray, Love,* she tells me her interest in travel, so passionately expressed in that book, has, for now at least, been eclipsed by a profound love of gardening.

To show how far this can go, consider Wangari Muta Maathai, the first woman in either East or Central Africa to earn a doctorate degree. While serving on the National Council of Women in 1976, Maathai had the bright idea of enlisting African women to plant trees. Through what eventually became the Green Belt Movement, she has helped plant more than 20 million trees (and, incidentally, won the Nobel Peace Prize).

The beautiful Hebrew text, the Talmud, tells us, "Every blade of grass has its angel that bends over it and whispers 'Grow, grow.'" Throughout history, many born wayfinders seem to have felt and aligned with such angels. If you're a plant person, you probably already have a practice that reinforces your Oneness with the green nation. If not, it's time to try the technologies of magic listed below. Again, please actually *do* at least some of these activities—you won't know how they may affect you if all you do is read about them.

CAVEAT PHYTOPHILE

One of the paths wayfinders in modern Western culture often follow in an effort to achieve Oneness is the use of "magical" plants, from marijuana to cocaine, to alter mood or consciousness. Mostly this is a sad and dangerous effort to reconnect with the careful plant magic of our ancestors. In traditional contexts like the South American ceremony I attended, psychoactive plant chemicals aren't guzzled for recreation, but used with enormous care, precision, and solemnity. Randomly gulping psilocybin mushrooms or peyote buttons is more likely to be sickening than enlightening, and can lead to addiction, allergic reactions, even death. The plant nation, as my tree aunties reminded me, has a lot of power to influence our bodies and minds. Approach it with respect. Are we clear? Excellent. Then try these techniques for enhancing your Oneness with the green nation.

Mastering Oneness: Look at Growing Things
This simple practice, which even I can happily achieve on my very worst days, is more powerful than most people imagine. A 1984 study at Texas A&M University found that surgery patients who had a view of trees had significantly shorter recoveries than those who looked out at bricks and mortar. In a 1999 Swedish study, postoperative patients whose rooms contained landscape paintings healed more quickly, with less pain and anxiety, than a control group. (A third group who looked at abstract art actually felt worse, mentally and physically, than anyone else.) If you can't keep plants

in your living and working environments, use images: paintings, posters, computer screen-savers with images of green growing things. Just looking at a postcard of a verdant scene can enhance our health.

Mastering Oneness: Garden, Inside or Out
People with a natural yen for the plant nation report enormously increased feelings of health and well-being when they take time to garden. Hospitals and nursing homes record health benefits for patients who are allowed to grow even a single flower in a pot. If you want to maximize the benefit you can get from gardening, keep a vegetable patch, a tomato plant, or a windowsill herb garden, and eat what you grow.

Here's an odd but intriguing idea I heard from a Russian wayfinder: put vegetable seeds in your mouth until the seeds are saturated with your saliva, then plant them and eat what grows. My source believes this gives the plants a map of the gardener's DNA and allows the plants to modify themselves specifically to keep that particular person healthy. I mean, why the hell not?

Mastering Oneness: Plant Trees Anywhere and Everywhere You Can
Enough said.

Mastering Oneness: Join a Gardening Co-op
People in many large cities are now able to "pre-buy" produce from local farms: after paying, say, $800 for a year's worth of fruits, vegetables, and other foods (such as meat and dairy products) they receive regular deliveries of fresh, local food. This not only creates economic incentives for "green" farmers and merchants, but ensures that the customers get really fresh food that hasn't been chemically processed or frozen.

Mastering Oneness: Talk to the Trees (and Other Plants)
I like to experiment with the idea that plants are sensitive to the events, beings, and energies around them. Try growing a plant in an environment that doesn't change much (such as an interior room with constant lighting and temperature), and then introduce different stimuli for periods of time to see if it changes the growth rate and/or health of that plant. For example, every day for a month, play your favorite music to your plants, noting whether changes in the plants corresponds to your experimental period.

Mastering Oneness: Take Medicine with Awareness

If you're on medication, always thank any plants who synthesized the chemicals that are changing your body. This act of thanksgiving, if you believe my South American friends, makes all plants more interested in helping and healing you.

GOING GREEN

Wayfinders from many times and places suggest that as you practice these methods—and anything else that helps bring your attention to our inherent Oneness with the green nation—you'll make your body a more sensitive and robust transmitter through the Energy Internet. Go further into any plant practice that makes you feel healthier, more alert, more intuitive. You may well find yourself living mainly on green smoothies, planting a forest, or somehow knowing exactly what mixture of phytochemicals will fix a sick friend's body. Your stardust will grow healthier, your sunshine brighter. And one night, out under a full moon in a rain forest, you may hear the great, growing denizens of the green nation silently singing you home.

Martha Beck

Gorillas in the midst of the green nation.

CHAPTER SIX

GETTING FAMILIAR WITH FAMILIARS (ANIMALS AS GATEWAYS TO ONENESS)

It's been a long trip from America, and my body has no idea what time it is. My watch says it's almost three in the afternoon, time for tea at Londolozi. Tomorrow Boyd, his sister Bronwyn, Koelle, and I will start coaching our yearly retreat for Team members, and I'm reading up on our guests and fine-tuning our schedule. When I hear Boyd come to the door of the Varty guest cottage I'm still focused on my computer.

"Hey, Boydie," I greet him without looking up, still tapping away at the keyboard. "I'm almost done here."

Boyd says nothing. I can hear him standing on the other side of the screen, shifting his weight from foot to foot, rustling the shrubbery. He's very patient. He still hasn't spoken when I look up five minutes later—into the dark, soft eyes of a kudu, a tall dove-gray antelope with long spiraling horns and a bold splash of white across his face, as if he got a little sloppy while whitewashing a fence.

Imagine being wakened from a peaceful sleep by having cold water splashed in your face. Now reverse that: imagine being lost in a tense, worried, cold trance, and being dashed in the face with peace. That's what I feel. I put my laptop aside, moving slowly so I won't startle the kudu, and my weariness seems to fall away with it. The antelope stops browsing for a moment, then takes one delicate step closer to the door screen that separates us. He's perhaps five feet away from me, perfectly aware of my presence, completely untroubled. He reminds me of how Mary Oliver describes deer, as "soft-lipped angels."

A few yards beyond the kudu, on the Vartys' front yard, two little bushbuck, much smaller than the kudu, with white spots on their soft flanks, are also nibbling the foliage. A family of warthogs munches grass nearby, genuflecting to reach tender shoots of grass. Sharp cracks in the brush beyond the garden tell me there are elephants browsing there. As I search for them with my eyes, I notice a hyena lying peacefully under a tree, just where a hippopotamus was standing last night when I arrived.

As I take in this scene, the stress of my "normal" life seeps away, replaced by the Wordless peace of the animals. After Nelson Mandela was released from twenty-seven years of imprisonment, he often came here, to Londolozi, to relax. I understand why. There's no place I know that can heal the wounds of a human life, a human soul's true nature, more power-fully than this healed land. There could have been no better environment for Mandela to gather his mighty wayfinder powers and mend one of the most fractured countries on Earth.

As I've said, the Vartys refer to their mission in life as "restoring Eden." Most places created by humans are shaped by our loss of innocence. This place is all about the hope that innocence can be regained—not just by people who have the energy, vision, and resources to repair swathes of wil-derness, but by every single human with the heart of a mender. The most powerful emissaries of this vision tell their story without words; they are soft-lipped and four-legged, clothed in feather or fins. I always think I'm coming to Londolozi to help humanity reclaim true nature for the sake of the animals. But on each visit, I'm humbled by a million gentle reminders that animals must help us to reclaim the true nature of humanity.

FAMILIAR FACES

"Most people have forgotten how to live with living creatures, with living systems," wrote the great naturalist and wayfinder Konrad Lorenz. "And that, in turn, is the reason why man, whenever he comes into contact with nature, threatens to kill the natural system in which and from which he lives." Our culture tends to accept this, however sorrowfully, as inevitable. Every wildlife program on TV, every biology class, every book I see in the United States reminds me that nature is dwindling, animals disappearing. When it's gone, all these sad stories report, nature is gone for good.

Not necessarily.

Menders, healers, wayfinders throughout human history have lived to restore Eden—the pure, healthy, balanced innocence that is the true nature of each person, each beast, each landscape or bowl of sea. Now, after half a lifetime of pessimism, I believe we may just be able to accomplish this great restoration. But to do any healing work, menders have always needed "familiars," a word that used to mean "a spirit embodied in an animal and held to attend and serve or guard a person." Your true nature probably requires you to commune with animals in a deeper way than your socialization has ever encouraged or even allowed.

In Europe during the Dark Ages, as religious Inquisitors busily welded *What Would Jesus Do?* shackles onto the people who believed even shreds of more ancient religions, the animal familiar was demonized. The village healer's cat or owl, once seen as a holy helper, was recast as a minion of evil. This is ridiculous. Only humans—the Inquisitors are a fine example—ever get up in the morning with the goal of causing other beings to suffer. Animals may be wired to fight for dominance or kill for food, but deliberate evil is the special province of human beings.

That said, I can understand why religious fundamentalists are afraid of the mender's relationship with animals. It unsettles any dogmatic idealist because it's a truly magical phenomenon, one that threatens our belief in the absolute supremacy of humans, of the human way of thinking, of a world without miracles. Animals dwell in Wordlessness perpetually and operate through Oneness easily. They transmit information, peace, and healing with regularity that is almost totally overlooked by modern societies.

THE HEALING OF BEASTS

In his book *The New Work of Dogs,* Jon Katz describes how "man's best friend," once relied on for everything from transportation to hunting to herding, is now primarily a source of emotional comfort that can help people with cancer, social ineptitude, or a failed marriage rebuild their lives. Dogs, cats, and birds are now routinely invited into places where animals were once forbidden—hospitals, prisons, elder care centers—because science has confirmed that the presence of these animals lowers high blood pressure, catalyzes floods of restorative hormones, and helps people who seem beyond love to love again in spite of everything.

I've worked with many clients whose emotional lives were so out of balance that the only peaceful relationship they had left was an emotional bond with an animal. This is especially true of the Team, who seem acutely to need contact with beasts, and who are often physically and emotionally exhausted by their own energetic sensitivity. I believe that such pain is broadcast through the Wordless Web, and that animals, aware that every being's suffering belongs to all aspects of the One, respond to that pain with comfort. Give them a chance, and they will come to our rescue.

This was true of my client Janice, a veteran from Iraq who returned home with shrapnel in her leg and continuous fear in her psyche. One day a stray kitten wandered onto her porch. "One of the first happy thoughts I'd had in a year was that I could rescue her," says Janice now. "Instead she rescued me." Each evening, as Rocky the cat purrs on her lap, Janice feels the pain in her leg and her heart dissipate.

Another Teammate, Brian, began emerging from depression after a friend moved overseas and left him in custody of a Vietnamese pot-bellied pig named Russell. "How weird is that?" Brian says. "I paid for years of therapy, and the therapist that finally helped me is a *pig!*" But it makes perfect sense when you see them together; Russell's affection for Brian is a palpable sensation, a bond that makes Oneness and its healing power impossible to miss.

On the first day of a workshop we're running together, Koelle explains to our clients the horses are always broadcasting energy and receiving broadcasts of energy from us. Most of the clients roll their eyes; others look baffled. But by the end of the first day, they can all see the communication between human and horse so obviously they're advising their friends, "Soften your vibe, dude! Listen to the horse!" Once, a woman who'd been hiding her grief about a divorce went into the enclosure to learn how she could "ask" a horse to walk or run in chosen directions. Though she tried to get the horse to move away from her, he refused to leave. Instead he moved his huge side next to hers and turned his head, embracing her between his flank and neck in something Koelle called a "horse hug." For fifteen minutes this great, patient beast enveloped the grieving woman in an embrace of pure kindness, as she leaned against him and wept away the sharpest edge of her suffering.

Ellen Rogers is an author whose son Ned was paralyzed in an accident. In her book *Kasey to the Rescue: The Remarkable Story of a Monkey and a Miracle*, Ellen describes his terrible injuries and the animal that helped him deal with them. After his accident, not only was Ned immobilized, but he was also in horrible, constant nerve pain. One of the few bright spots in this dreadful scenario arrived in the form of a service animal, a capuchin monkey named Kasey who'd been trained to help disabled humans.

For some time, Kasey, apparently resenting being torn from the people who'd raised her, wasn't particularly friendly toward anyone, including Ned. Then one day Ned's pain became intolerable. "We'd tried everything, in the hospital and at home," Rogers writes. "Medication, massage, hot packs, cold packs—nothing seemed to help. I was beside myself as I helplessly watched my son suffer.

"Mom," he called out. "I'm on fire! Mom, please do something!"

I didn't know what I could do, but in that moment I looked to Kasey like I've never looked at another creature before. What did she see? Hope? Desperation? Somehow that dear little monkey understood just what was needed. As soon as I took her out of her cage, she clambered up on Ned's chair and wrapped her tail around his neck. With a deep, guttural "hoo-hoo" that was more like a whisper, she carefully positioned herself on Ned's chest, right over his heart. Both of them were very, very still. And then; I don't know; the anguish that had been so visible in Ned's face, his contorted expression, suddenly disappeared. His pain was beginning to recede.

Ned later told his mother, "It's amazing, Mom. . . . Kasey comforts and relaxes me like no drug."

Some animals appear to be interested in helping us not only through this life, but into whatever comes next. Oscar is a nursing home cat, a feline curmudgeon who avoids humans . . . unless they're about to die. Then he becomes deeply attached to them. After noticing that Oscar had cuddled up to more than fifty people just before they passed away, a doctor published an article about him in the *New England Journal of Medicine* that was picked up by the media.

"If kept outside the room of a dying patient," one reporter wrote, "Oscar will scratch on the door trying to get in." Then he stays until death do him part. "It's not like he dawdles," said a doctor. "He'll slip out for two minutes, grab some kibble and then he's back at the patient's side. It's like he's literally on a vigil." I can't help but wonder if Oscar has ever been seen holding his tiny paws over the nose and mouth of a patient, but everyone else believes he's sensing some sort of physical or psychic vibe that tells him a human's end is near.

These animals aren't just following the genetic programming related to long life and reproduction. They seem to be spontaneously interested in humans, in offering us relief from suffering. Without language, they hear messages on the Wordless Web: Alert! Alert! Part of the One Great Self, a human caught in the illusion of isolation, is suffering! And as part of the same One being, they naturally respond, sending comfort to humans in ways we don't yet understand. "It is not just that animals make the world more scenic or picturesque," says Gary Kowalski. "The lives of animals are woven into our very being—closer than our own breathing—and our souls will suffer when they are gone."

Animals can work similar magic on menders who aren't damaged as obviously as Ned, whose emotional or physical pain is hidden under polite, appropriate social behavior. You may well be one of these people. If so, learning to commune with animals through Oneness is perhaps the best thing you can do to reclaim your true nature and find your way to happiness, creativity, and every other form of thriving.

PUTTING ON KING SOLOMON'S RING

An ancient mender's tale that has survived for millennia is the story of the biblical King Solomon, who had a ring that let him speak with animals. This legend is deeply enticing to born wayfinders. We can feel Oneness in connection with things like spoons and plants, but these friends don't, as a rule, get out much. Connection with animals is even more deeply rewarding. If you don't have an animal familiar already, you may want to adopt one someday. But you'll reclaim your true nature even faster if you do what humans at Londolozi, and many ancient cultures, have always done: go into the animals' environment and let them connect with you. Here's a basic technique that, if practiced regularly, will establish your presence on the Wordless Web of all animals; like Facebook, it will allow you to communicate with friends of all kinds. It's very simple, but it must be done with persistence. I often challenge Team clients to do it every day for thirty days. I've never seen anyone complete this challenge without becoming more peaceful, luminous, and healthy.

Oneness-with-Animals Technique: Establish and Use a Sit Spot

1. Choose a spot from which you can observe some bit of nature, whether that's the Amazon River or Central Park. I use a mes-

quite tree in my yard, where I've positioned a bird feeder just to spice things up.

2. Every day at the same time, go to this spot, sit down, and sink into Wordlessness. Maintain this mind-set for twenty to thirty minutes, gently returning to Wordlessness when you find yourself thinking, worrying, or planning.

3 With all your senses softly focused, notice everything happening around you, especially the way animals and birds change their behavior as you sit. It usually takes about twenty minutes of stillness before wild animals relax with a human on site. (This happens more quickly the more we can stay Wordless.)

4. Watch and feel how the many animals around you—songbirds, chipmunks, housecats, pigeons—go about their lives. Join them in their peace. Allow them to include you in their fields of energy.

The longer you persist at this practice, the more you'll feel the Oneness of animals restoring Eden within you. Sometimes this will be as subtle as the passing of one ant. At other times you'll feel yourself wearing King Solomon's ring. My friend Lynn, after visiting her "sit spot" regularly for many months, was once visited by a deer that actually grazed her body with its nose, gently curious about this creature who looked and smelled human, yet blended with Oneness so completely that the animals felt no threat from her, only kindness.

Simply sitting in nature will eventually bring you this kind of experience, and you will feel a bit of your true nature coming back to life, your inner Eden reclaiming a bit of its original innocence, a bit of your power to thrive and serve the world returning to your spirit.

WALKING IN ONENESS WITH ANIMALS

We begin training in Wordlessness by sitting still, and then bring in action. Doing this in nature will teach you that you can connect with animals not only in stillness, but in motion. The spiritual teacher Eckhart Tolle has said that when we humans walk through a wild place with our verbal minds fully engaged, we frighten animals, who recognize our obsessive thinking as a form of insanity. When we can move Wordlessly, on the other hand, we feel what it is to become One with the web of life that chirps and grazes and hunts all around us.

I learned the technique below from Team members Michael and Lynn Trotta, who have spent decades training with Native American wayfinders in various forms of woodlore, from "bird language" to animal tracking. They showed me how to do something called "fox-walking" that can tune you into Oneness so deeply a walk through your local park becomes a journey into the mystical realm of animals.

Oneness-with-Animals Technique: Fox-walk through Nature

In his book *Born to Run,* Christopher McDougall argues that our feet were meant to walk without the surrounding structure of a shoe, and that going shod is actually detrimental to our body mechanics. For example, he points out that the more cushioned a running shoe, the more injuries are associated with it. Direct physical connection with the Earth is a fascinating way to enhance your sense of Oneness, especially your connection to animals. As you try this technique, notice how differently animals react to you, and how much more sensitive you are to their presence.

1. Go to a place with at least some vestige of the natural world: a patch of woods near your home, a park, an abandoned quarry.

2. Take off your shoes and socks.

3. Put all your weight on your left foot, reach out with your right, and feel the ground with the ball of your foot, testing it for sharp objects.

4. When you find a spot you can step on safely, transfer your weight to your right foot. Then step forward, in the same exploratory way, with your left.

5. As this action becomes familiar, speed it up. You'll find you can actually move very quickly, with more balance and agility, than you can with your shoes on.

6. Drop into Wordlessness as you walk. Open your focus to include not only sights, sounds, and smells, but the feeling of your feet on the earth. Let yourself sense not only what's in front of you, but in what some Native American traditions call the "seven directions": before, behind, to the left and right, above, below, and within you. Imagine yourself at the center of a sphere of perception. You'll have to breathe easily and deeply, and completely let go of sharp, verbal thinking, to sense this sphere. Deep practice will allow this to happen more easily.

7. Beginning by imagining a sphere of awareness just bigger than your body, gradually listen, look, smell, and "feel" outward. Imagine the sphere or your attention growing. Continue until you feel yourself as the center of a sphere about thirty yards in diameter.

8. As you walk, listen to the birds and any other animals present. Enlarge your attention even more, noticing the difference between the way animals sound and behave near you, the way they sound and behave at the outside periphery of your thirty-yard sphere, and the way they sound and behave far away. Typically the nearby birds and animals are silent, those on the periphery of your energy circle give shrill alarm calls, and those farther off sustain a gentle, relaxed, continuous murmur.

9. Still walking, picture the circle of your energy getting softer, quieter, and smaller. Then make it large again. Shrink and expand it a few times, paying close attention to the behavior of the birds and animals. As you do this, the circle of silence among the animals will shrink or grow along with your "energy circle." If you persist, eventually you'll find that you can change the ring of alarm calls and silence deliberately.

10. See if you can fox-walk softly enough so that birds stop alarm-calling as you pass nearby, even within a few steps of them. Shrink the circle of your energy to nothing, imagining that you've put on an "invisibility cloak" like Harry Potter's. This will require deep

Wordlessness, and you'll feel an overpowering sense of becoming One with everything around you.

The day Michael and Lynn gave me my first fox-walking lesson, after I'd practiced for several hours and was padding through the Sonoran Desert preserve near my home, an actual fox walked right out in front of me. She looked at me exactly the way my dogs do when I've called them. "Well, you've been thinking 'fox' all day," she seemed to say, "so here I am." The next morning I fox-walked within about twenty feet of three deer, who glanced at me nervously with their huge, gentle eyes, but didn't run until I began thinking, "Wow! I'm doing this right!," which knocked me out of Wordlessness.

As I headed off to bed that night, after a whole day of sensing Oneness, I passed within arm's length of a large shrub when suddenly it grunted, as if I'd dropped an ice cube down its shirt while it was watching television. The "shrub" was a javelina, a kind of peccary resembling a small wild boar that lives in the Arizona deserts. I hadn't noticed it, and it hadn't been disturbed by me, until we were practically close-dancing. The javelina trotted off a few feet, then stopped. We gazed at each other through the darkness, surprised but not frightened, one manifestation of the single Great Self contemplating another. We had a moment.

LEARNING MAGIC FROM OUR FAMILIARS

"We need another and a wiser and perhaps a more mystical concept of animals," wrote the naturalist, author, and wayfinder Henry Beston in 1926. "In a world older and more complete than ours they move finished and complete, gifted with extensions of the senses we have lost or never attained, living by voices we shall never hear." This is the mournful wisdom the shaman-born members of shamanless cultures generally feel about their connection to animals. But I now believe that we can create a wild new world, not just "an older and more complete" one, in which animals help us hear the voices to which we've only temporarily gone deaf.

Long ago, in one of my Adam-in-Africa dreams, my son—then a one-year-old baby, but in the dream a young adult—showed me a bit of language written on a parchment sheet in glittering, radiant script. It was one of those times when the Wordless Web sent a verbal message, but one so strange I had no idea what it meant. I awoke from that dream with images of beasts and birds flooding my mind, but also with these words, which felt like Adam's:

The earth cries like a child,
and the blood of the animals is the blood of innocence.
But you, having lost your innocence,
cannot hear the cries
or the blood as it beats in your own ears.

It is to answer those cries
that I have come
as I have come.

For years my whole body buzzed with electricity every time I remembered this dream. Was it a message from my subconscious mind? From the great collective mind Jung called the "archetypal unconscious"? From a little boy with Down syndrome? From the whole intricate interconnection of life on my home planet? It felt like all of the above, and it didn't seem meant just for me. It left me with "a more mystical concept of animals" that I believe is inviting all humans to join the Team of visionaries who sense the web of life as their own beings.

Now we're in the realm of flat-out magic, or what, as Arthur C. Clarke wrote, is "a sufficiently advanced technology [that it] is indistinguishable from magic." Animals use the first and second technologies of magic continuously, staying logged on to Wordlessness and getting memos through Oneness. For example, when a massive tsunami rolled from Indonesia to Asia and Africa on December 26, 2004, almost 230,000 people died—the worst natural disaster in recorded history. Surprisingly not many animals were caught in the floods. Many moved inland well before any humans knew what was about to happen. *National Geographic News* reported that in Sumatra, Sri Lanka, and Thailand "elephants screamed and ran for higher ground, dogs refused to go outdoors, flamingos abandoned their low-lying breeding areas, and zoo animals rushed into their shelters and could not be enticed to come back out" (http://news.nationalgeographic.com/news/2005/01/0104_050104_tsunami_animals.html).

Experts disagree over the reason for this prudent retreat: most scientists believe that either the animals have the ability to sense ground shifts more subtle than those humans notice, or there was an interspecies chain reaction: the fish notified the birds, who told the four-footed animals, who headed uphill, screaming *"Tidal wave! Run!"* to oblivious human beings. Some scientists are willing to speculate that the animals sensed an oncoming disaster through the same kind of "field consciousness," or connected awareness, that seems to be at work when random-number generators react to significant events in human affairs (see chapter 4). Whatever explanation suits you best, the animals were getting messages from something: each other, the Earth, the Force beloved of *Star Wars'* Jedi Knights.

Similar phenomena tend to occur before strictly terrestrial earthquakes, according to sources from the ancient Greeks to the modern Chinese. In the United States, the geologist Jim Berkland predicts earthquakes with a reported 80 percent accuracy by tracking sharp increases in newspaper ads reporting lost dogs and cats. He believes that the animals sense magnetic changes that signal quakes days before the actual event and bug out, perhaps looking for pet-friendly hotels. Whatever the reason, the correlation between pet disappearance and earthquakes is hugely statistically significant.

The biologist Rupert Sheldrake goes further than Berkland: he believes that animals are tuned in at a level that qualifies as a "psi phenomenon," or paranormal ability. Sheldrake conducted experiments to see whether dogs know when their owners are coming home, which you can read about in his book, entitled (I hope this doesn't spoil the ending), *Dogs That Know When Their Owners Are Coming Home.* Sheldrake brought dogs into a kind of daycare, then watched them on real-time camera. Experimenters called owners on their cell phones at random times, asking them to come get their own dogs. Frequently—far more often than would be expected by chance—the dogs would go wait by door the moment their owners *formed the intention* to come get them.

SENDING "EMAIL" TO THE ANIMALS

The poet, novelist, and journalist Anatole France wrote, "Until one has loved an animal a part of one's soul remains unawakened." The moment you love an animal, that part of your soul—the magical mending, way-finding part—wakes up. In fact, by connecting with an animal, you might have been using the second technology of magic for some time without knowing it. Communication through Oneness may be the reason you and your Dachshund let out simultaneous sighs of relaxation, or your pet lamb comes running from the pasture before she can possibly have known you're in the barn, or Oscar the cat tries to get into your bed when you're feeling profoundly unwell.

Anyone who's spent much time riding horses already knows that animals can receive and follow instructions sent through the Wordless Web. My friend Koelle has spent years learning to mimic the body language through which horses communicate with one another. For a long time she maintained a careful skepticism about believing there was anything more to "horse whispering" than gesture. Then she began experimenting with "asking" horses to move in specific ways by imagining visual images, without moving her body at all. And they cooperated.

Koelle is adept at communicating the way animals do, in part through endless deep practice, but also because a bout of meningitis stole almost all her hearing when she was only two. Because of the relative silence in which she grew up, she became preternaturally skilled at picking up visual cues. She observes and reads lips so well that most people have no idea she has any hearing loss. But though she's very articulate and an excellent conversationalist and teacher, she thinks more in visual images than in words. And this is the key to sending messages to animals through the Wordless Web.

When Koelle sets out to teach me how to ride a horse, I assume this will be a strictly physical discipline. And at first Koelle teaches it that way. She puts me on a horse named Blondie and has me urge Blondie into a trot. (Koelle believes in learning to "sit the trot," an activity that removes the skin from one's derriere like an industrial sander. I intend to wreak revenge on her as soon as I think of something cruel enough.) Next, I'm supposed to make Blondie lope by pressing my right heel against her side. But no matter how I move my legs, eventually kicking her indifferent tummy like a two-year-old abusing the family dog, Blondie just ambles peacefully along.

"Wait," Koelle says. "Stop."

I stop, or rather, persuade Blondie to stop.

"Go Wordless," Koelle tells me. "Soft-focus your eyes." She knows I've been practicing this; we talk about it a lot. So I open my attention focus and feel myself drop into Wordlessness. Koelle says, "Good. Now, picture her loping."

I hold the image in my mind. After a few seconds the hair on my arms prickles. I can feel Blondie as if she were a huge extension of my own body, the way I can feel a spoon that's willing to bend for me, but hairier.

"Excellent," says Koelle. "Now, press inward with your right foot."

I barely touch my heel to Blondie's side. She raises her front legs and pushes off, taking that first wonderful leap that moves a horse into a loping stride. I can feel the power of the picture in my head flowing into Blondie's body. I'm filled with awe, truly exhilarated, for the three seconds before I'm launched from the saddle like a corpse from a catapult, and end up clinging desperately to Blondie's mane. No, I will never be a good rider. But neither will I forget what it's like to be a centaur for a moment, One with the horse you're riding.

There have been many other occasions when I accidentally sent "email" to animals, and was stunned by their courteous responses. Once I decided to write and illustrate a children's book, marrying my interest in writing and my passion for drawing and painting. I'd just been to Cambodia, which had left my brain all lit up with stunning visual images, so I wrote a book that included Cambodian folktales. In one story, an elephant nearly steps on a rabbit. I wanted to draw this scene from the rabbit's viewpoint; I pictured the elephant rearing back, pulling up his foot and lifting his trunk with a startled expression. Unfortunately I could barely imagine what this would look like and couldn't find any photos of elephants in that position from that angle.

At about this time the circus came to Phoenix. When I took my children to see it, I chanced upon an elephant just standing around, waiting for his cue to go sit on a clown or something. I got quite close to him, crouched down near his head, and squinted up, trying my very best to imagine what he'd look like with his foot up, his trunk back, his mouth open, and his eyes staring down in surprise. I'd been picturing this for about ten seconds when, as I live and breathe, the elephant went into precisely the pose I was imagining. He held it, more patient and motionless than a paid model, while I grabbed a pen from my purse and scribbled a quick sketch.

Some time later, while reading a book about "bird language," I learn that there's only one species of parrot native to North America. It lives right where I do, in the Sonoran Desert of Arizona. I sit at my drawing table admiring an illustration of these rare birds, holding their image in my mind, wishing intensely that I could see them in real life. Just then, I hear a scratching sound from the window next to me. Oh yes, indeed. Three rare

Arizona parrots land on my window screen, not three feet from my face. They cling to the screen with their classic parrot feet—two claws fore, two aft—as I feast my eyes in thrilled disbelief.

Here's a classic wayfinder method for communicating with animals. Try your own experiments and tests before you accept that this is possible—but give it an honest attempt, some serious deep practice. Depending on how good you are at dropping into Wordlessness, results won't be long in coming. Any animal, even an unfamiliar one, can be a familiar.

Oneness-with-Animals Technique: Communicate with Your Familiar

1. In the presence of an animal, drop into Wordlessness. "Feel" the animal as if he or she is an extension of your own body.

2. Vividly picture the animal doing a specific behavior: climbing the stairs, turning around in one place, rolling over, jumping. Don't try to *make* the animal do this, just picture it, with no expectation or attachment. Notice whether your animal does the behavior. Often, initial attempts will result in the animal *beginning* to act, at which point the human gets excited and begins thinking verbally. This stops the process as far as the animal is concerned. Practice holding images while remaining calm and consistent. If you get a partial response, acknowledge it. As you learn to stay calm and consistent, the animal may complete more of the behavior you picture.

3. Take your pet out of the house while picturing different scenarios: going to the vet or kennel, riding in the car, eating, visiting a friend who has pets, playing. It's often not enough to pretend you're going to these different places, you have to actually be planning to go there. See if your animal shows signs of happiness when you initiate a trip to a favorite destination, or anxiety when you're headed to a place the animal doesn't like. See if your animal responds differently to the scenes in your mind.

4. Install a "nanny-cam" by your front door or window while you're away, and see if your cat or dog goes to wait when you form the intention to come home.

THE CALLING OF THE WILD

Once you've begun to feel the line of communication between yourself and the animals in your normal environment, you can expand your skill set by learning to "call" wild beasts, in whatever area of the world you happen to be.

I'm visiting Hawaii with my partner, Karen, when I happen to read a book about how menders from some cultures traditionally "call" wild animals. It seems pretty wacky, but my policy is not to pass judgment on anything until I've given it an honest try. So, while sitting in my hotel room, I clear my head of cynicism and commit myself to magnetizing—I cast around for something interesting on which to experiment—how about . . . some whales!

At that moment Karen, who's been watching CNN, suddenly picks up the remote and taps in a number. The widescreen TV lights up with the huge image of a whale hovering above a diver.

"Uh, Karen," I say, "why did you change the channel?"

Karen shrugs. "I thought you might like to see this."

"Why? And how did you know which channel to choose?"

Her brow furrows. "I'm not sure," she said. "I just did."

So I tell her about my whale-calling experiment, which makes her roll her eyes and sigh. I get a better reaction when I suggest that she skip a conference session the next day and go out with me on a whale-watching boat. (Like most Team members, Karen hates meetings and loves being outside.) She tells me clearly, however, that she doesn't believe we can actually summon leviathans. "Marty," she says kindly (as she often does), "you really should just be grateful for all the *normal* things in your life."

The next day, when we climb on the boat, we get a lecture clearly designed to dampen our hopes of seeing animals. "Enjoy the trip," our captain says. "It's the off-season, but we have great weather!" Translation: Ain't gonna be no whales.

Karen and I find a spot on the railing where we can feel the sea spray and bask in the tropical sunlight. This is nice, I think. I don't need to see a whale. We're chatting about whether she can fake food poisoning well enough to skip all her remaining meetings, when suddenly Karen's eyes fill with tears. She doesn't cry easily, so I'm quite alarmed.

"Are you all right?" I ask her. "What's wrong?"

And Karen whispers, *"They're coming."*

I feel a wave of electricity pass through my body, and my eyes begin tearing up as well. Five seconds later the first whale breaks the surface to starboard with a magnificent SPLOOSH! He's a stone's-throw away, his body half again as long as our little boat. SPLOOSH! Another massive form arrives on the port side. The captain begins babbling ecstatically. "Take a good look folks, we didn't expect them this time of year!"

The whales dive.

"What a sighting!" warbles the captain. "They'll be down for twenty minutes or so. We'll try to find which way they're headed and see if we can—"

SPLOOSH!

The first whale is back, doing something the thrilled captain calls "spy-hopping." With his enormous flukes beating the water beneath him, the whale raises the top third of his body right out of the water and stays that way for several seconds.

"Marty," Karen is still whispering, "he's looking us right in the eyes!"

Four whales spend the next half hour rolling, splashing, spyhopping, and otherwise cavorting around our boat. The captain, crew, and Japanese tour group who've accompanied us on the expedition nearly faint with joy. Karen and I are so overwhelmed by the sense of Oneness we can't even speak; we feel caught in an enormous field of love and gratitude. The generosity of the whales is just too big to take onboard.

Oneness-with-Animals Technique: Practice the Call of the Wild

When you're out in nature, or in the presence of an animal, try "calling" the beasts through the Wordless Web, by holding precise visual images and creating the sensation of a physically tangible connection. Here are step-by-step instructions:

1. Drop into Wordlessness.

2. Picture a bright thread of energy wrapping around your spine, from the tip of your tailbone, all the way up your back and neck, and on through the crown of your head.

3. Imagine this line of energy connecting with other living things in the neighborhood. If you want to specify one kind of animal, picture it vividly.

4. "Feel" for the connection between the animals and the line you are sending out. You may notice that the line changes shape or consistency as you do this. It may light up, draw tight and straight, or loop around. Follow it in your mind's eye until it connects with an animal.

5. Give a gentle tug on the line, and picture the animal coming to visit you. This is like sending a message. Most people raised in Western cultures believe that it isn't enough, that they must follow up with physical action or at the very least maintain focused attention. These tendencies, mental attachment to *forcing* an outcome, are known to be ineffective in every tradition of practical magic. Instead, go to the next step, as improbable and counterintuitive as it may seem.

6. Drop the image, along with all attachment to the result. Get interested in something else. Admire the view. Expect nothing. (This is almost impossible unless you're in Wordlessness, when it's automatic.)

7. Stay open to observing whatever happens. An animal may come to you immediately, or you may have to wait a while. For beginners, the animal rarely comes until you're *completely* detached from wanting it to come— in other words, when you've moved on to other activities and given up the very thought of forcing an encounter. If you drop your intention to connect and an animal wanders into your life apparently without cause, realize that this is not a coincidence. You've completed your connection through the Energy Internet by *dropping attachment,* which is like pressing "send." Again, this is absolutely counterintuitive to most Westerners. Just experiment with it until you find out through experience how powerfully the combination of picturing something and releasing all attachment draws animals (and other things) toward you.

WHEN HUMANS WEAR KING SOLOMON'S RING

Eventually the kudu grazes his way past the doorway to the Londolozi guest cottage, leaving a wake of openness that seems to quiet my very cells. I'm feeling energized but relaxed when Boyd comes to get me for tea. As we walk, the soft-lipped angel antelope watch us with their wide eyes, alert but not afraid. The hyena raises his head and sniffs the air, catching our scent. The warthogs look up briefly, then return to their peaceful grazing. All of them exist in, and broadcast, a circle of calm.

Boyd and I bask in it as we follow the path walked many times by Mandela, a great wayfinder recovering from the wounds inflicted by humans, preparing to respond not with vengeance but with a huge and powerful extension of his own healed mender spirit. This is what the animals offer us as well. After everything we've done to them, they still invite us into the consciousness of Oneness that is the source of healing for all things.

Albert Einstein said, "A human being is a part of the whole, called by us 'Universe.' . . . He experiences himself, his thoughts and feelings as something separated from the rest, a kind of optical delusion of his consciousness. This delusion is a kind of prison. . . . Our task must be to free ourselves from this prison by widening our circle of compassion to embrace all living creatures and the whole of nature." As I walk through an ecosystem that was once destroyed and then repaired, I marvel that the whole scene was created by just a few humans who gave themselves the goal of "restoring Eden."

As you practice Oneness with animals, your own innocent Eden will reawaken in your soul. Your body and mind will grow calmer, peaceful, more content. Your instincts will sharpen, enabling you to feel your way through situations and relationships of baffling complexity. This will be invaluable in helping you find your way through the wild world of human life in the twenty-first century. But more than anything, it will remind you of something you already know in the most ancient part of your being, something a German mender named Meister Eckhart wrote way back in the fourteenth century:

*When I was the stream, when I was the
forest, when I was still the field,
when I was every hoof, foot,
fin and wing . . . ,*

there was nothing
I could not
love.

Martha Beck

An angelic visitation.

CHAPTER SEVEN

YOU! YOU! YOU!
(HUMAN RELATIONSHIPS AS GATEWAYS
TO THE ONE)

I'm talking to Linky Nkuna under the marula tree, and hoping my expression looks relatively normal. Linky, beautiful and brilliant, sardonic and fierce, is not someone who seems easily disturbed, but if I showed what I'm feeling right now, it might alarm her.

The trouble is that I'm having a particularly severe episode of what I call the "You, You, You!" Phenomenon. I owe this phrase to Elizabeth Gilbert. In her Team memoir *Eat, Pray, Love,* Gilbert recounts a conversation with an Indonesian shaman, whose advice catalyzed her now famous round-the-world adventure. The shaman told Gilbert she should come stay in Bali to learn from him. Here's how Gilbert describes his reaction when she arrived:

> He leans forward, takes my shoulders in his hands and starts to shake me happily, the way a child shakes an unopened Christmas present to try to guess what's inside.
>
> "You came back! You came *back!*"
>
> "I came back! I came back!" I say.
>
> "You, you, you!"
>
> "Me, me, me!"
>
> I'm all tearful now, but trying not to show it. The depth of my relief—it's hard to explain. It takes even me by surprise. It's like . . . I'd been frog-kicking and struggling to swim . . . through the cold green water and I was almost out of oxygen and the arteries were bursting out of my neck and my cheeks were puffed with my last breath and then GASP!—I broke through to the surface and took in huge gulps of air. And I survived. That gasp, that breaking through—this is what it feels like when I hear the Indonesian medicine man say, "You came back!" My relief is exactly that big.

When I read this I was awash with relief. It was so comforting to realize I'm not the only person on Earth having inexplicably emotional reunions with dear friends I've never met before, who live all over the world and seem to have nothing in common with me.

This used to happen rarely, just once every few years. During my adolescence it almost frightened me, and I kept my private "recognition" of certain strangers to myself. When I became an adult the frequency of what I came to call Team encounters picked up to a few times a year, then every month or so. Recently it's become ridiculously common. What's more, these days I can often feel a meeting about to happen. One Teammate I know calls this "premembering." Australian wayfinders might call it a meeting in the Everywhen, the Wordless Web through which we can send and receive messages across any physical distance, either forward or backward in time. Whatever it is, lately I often meet two or three people in one week who make me want to grab them by the shoulders and shout "You! You! You!"

I'm not sure how doing this right now would come across, you know, culturally. Linky is a young Shangaan woman who grew up in a little village near Londolozi and is now working as a teacher for the Good Works Foundation, an initiative created by the people who set up Londolozi and run by a mother-daughter team named Maureen and Kate Groch (two people who made me want to shout "You! You! You!" for a solid year after I met them). The Groches offer education to the Africans who live near Londolozi and other areas of rural Africa. They are perfect examples of the way Team missions lead to unorthodox careers: both could be working at prestigious public schools, but choose to teach in some of the poorest rural backwaters on Earth. This fulfills them personally, but like all wayfinders, following their deepest passions is also allowing them to have the broadest possible positive influence on the world around them.

Helping create economic prosperity for humans is a huge part of the Team's agenda, because only when people have education, a reliable source of income, and access to health care can they curb runaway population growth and destruction of the natural biological systems. Education, especially for girls and women, is perhaps the single most important element in creating functioning, healthy societies—an idea I learned studying socioeconomic development formally throughout my time in academia, and informally ever since.

Though she's spent her life in rural Africa, Linky has as keen an understanding of Third World problems as any development scholar I've ever met. What's more, she has the same near-compulsive energy about the subject I do, the same sense of having some tiny role in a massive change that must include care of both humans and the planet on which they live. But my intense reaction to Linky isn't based on the fact that she thinks like me and my strange friends. It's not just that she's on the Team. It's more than that. *I know her.*

Now Linky is telling me, "I feel something happening in the world, and I have to be part of it." Through a huge act of will, I keep myself from bursting into tears of joy and gratitude, from jumping up and down shouting "YOU! YOU! YOU!" It's as if there's been a Linky Nkuna–shaped absence in my heart since I was born, a missing piece of my soul's puzzle, and that piece is clicking deliciously into alignment. It's as if Linky and I both agreed to connect at a certain time and place, and if either one of us hadn't made it, life would be infinitely poorer. I'm dazed with relief that somehow, despite the obstacles both of us had to overcome, Linky and I made it here, to this marula tree, to this conversation.

FRIENDSHIPS IN THE EVERYWHEN

One of the things I like about getting old and crotchety is that I've had time to gather a reasonable amount of what sociologists call "longitudinal data." That is, I can look back over many incidents in my life and see correlations between certain experiences: "Gee, every time I felt X, then Y happened." You can do the same thing, if you have enough mileage on you. For example, every time you felt a certain unease making a purchase, you later had buyer's regret; every time you felt a specific kind of nervous butterflies, something wonderful happened; every time you married a meth addict, things did not go well, and so on, and so on.

What I've realized is that every time I've felt the "You! You! You!" Phenomenon, the person I was meeting turned out to be a wayfinder. It helped immensely when I figured this out; before I articulated the concept of a world-saving Team, I just thought I was developing weird emotional fixations based on my dysfunctional childhood—though actually, the relationships that follow the "You! You! You!" Phenomenon are the most functional in my life. It always feels that we'll understand one another from the very moment we physically meet, and the "longitudinal data" of my experience overwhelmingly support that sensation.

A few of my "You! You! You!" moments have been followed by close friendships and frequent interaction. But many have been much more casual, often just a single sweet meeting. It's not as if I need to move in with every wayfinder I "recognize." It's more like we're playing on the same side in a game that requires billions of players, each in a specific role. Some people's parts of the game interact with mine closely and often, others tangentially or at a distance. But each person is absolutely necessary, uniquely important. And it's wonderful—deeply, wildly wonderful—to meet "strangers" who are up to their ears in the self-same drive to heal humans and the world.

GOOD VIBRATIONS

We English speakers often describe people we like as "having a good vibe" or "being on the same wavelength." I think this began with physicists' twentieth-century discovery that matter is really just energy, each element vibrating at a different frequency. Given that we are basically wireless electrical devices, that machines can now transmit and decode the energy emitted by our nervous systems, and that these machines routinely communicate with one another wirelessly, the "magical" belief that people can actually get on one another's wavelength no longer seems like much of a stretch.

Ancient wayfinders of virtually all cultures believed that communication between people could transcend space and time. In fact the menders of most cultures received specific training in working with the energetic connection between people: communicating at a distance, "reading" one another's feelings and mind-set, giving each other strength and support, generally sending and receiving information over the Wordless Web. When you believe that all beings are One, this isn't surprising. If you've been raised in a culture that believes in total separation between beings, you may have to get used to it. Let's start now.

HUMAN ONENESS: THE EVIDENCE FROM SCIENCE

Dean Radin is a fanatically rigorous scientist. His methodology is cutting-edge, and the experiments he cites are more carefully designed to avoid bias than most mainstream research. Radin has to be methodologically impeccable, because he studies things like ESP and other "paranormal" phenomena. As he says, "Scientists risk their careers if they express sympathy for the results of experiments that go against the current cultural norm of the scientific community, which is strongly opposed to anything that sounds like mysticism." But the fact is, many such experiments—careful, well-designed ones—exist.

For example, in one study, researchers monitored the skin resistance, pulses, and EEG patterns (neuron firing in the brain) of eleven subjects who sat in a soundproof room. In another room, a heroic and/or masochistic scientist named Charles Tart sat giving himself painful electric shocks. When the subjects were asked to guess when the shocks occurred, their guesses (thinking brain) were random, not coinciding with the shocks. However, electronic analysis of their physiological reactions showed distinct brain, pulse, and skin responses (Wordless reaction) at the moments the shocks really did occur (www.paradigm-sys.com/ctt_articles2. cfm?id=48).

Researchers at the University of Washington and Bastyr University tested emotionally bonded couples, putting one person from each couple, identified as "the receiver," into an fMRI machine. When the other partner, identified as "the sender," was exposed to a flickering light in another room, the fMRI showed increased blood flow to the visual cortex of the receiver's brain.

A particularly fascinating aspect of the remote-connection experiments is that when this linking occurs, the brain that has the most coherent wave patterns—patterns associated with calm, relaxation, and peace—seems to "pull" less coherent brains into synchrony with it, a process called "entrainment." This effect also seems to influence the heart. One researcher found that, when two people focused on one another while thinking loving thoughts, their hearts created more coherent rhythms and became highly entrained. All those clichés about "healing hearts," or "two hearts beating as one" may be literally true.

HOW IS THIS POSSIBLE?

Science gives us some tantalizing clues about what might be going on when two people connect through Oneness. Though no one really knows what consciousness is, physicists do know that it plays a role in establishing the location and velocity of particles at the quantum level. At that minute scale, "entangled" particles—bits of matter that have been in close contact with one another—communicate, over any distance, faster than the speed of light. As long as humans have lived, mystics and menders have been describing this energetic entanglement, though they observe and work with it through subtle awareness rather than particle accelerators. The consistency of their experience makes me suspect that a human consciousness may be able to feel its own role in relationship to matter, and to other aspects of consciousness.

So, if this is true, if Oneness is real, can we all start remote-viewing, sharing electroshock therapy at a distance, and entraining other people's heart rates? In a word, yes. It's not as cut-and-dried as making a phone call, but you can increase your ability to connect with other people (in ways that you can call quantum-mechanical or mystical, depending on who's listening), I've met Team members who are very good at this. This chapter describes a few of the methods they use to send and receive information via the energetic Internet and teaches you how to begin doing this more skillfully yourself.

WORKING WITH THE ONE

I once wrote a book that troubled members of a specific religion. Some of these folks, in that inimitable "What Would Jesus Do?" way, felt moved to inform me about various forms of doom and smiting they planned to visit upon my sorry hide. One day I received some sort of threat and mentioned to Koelle that I felt a bit skittish.

"Okay," she said, in the voice she used when determined to get a fussy horse to drop a phobia. "Hold out your hands like this." She extended her hands from the elbow, as if preparing to clap. "I'm going to try to push your hands together. Don't let me do it." I complied, and we had a brief struggle as she strained to mash my palms together and I tried my hardest to keep them apart. It was a stand-off.

"Okay," said Koelle. "Now do it again."

I held out my hands, and Koelle turned into Yoda the freaking Jedi Master. When she touched my hands, my muscles felt like water, and she pushed my palms together with virtually no physical effort. I stood there with my mouth hanging open, staring at my hands, for about thirty seconds. Then I said, "Teach me to do that." And she did. Since then, I've used this "trick" to put me in an energy state that communicates with and calms other people. The physical act of pushing someone's hands is just an illustration of the many ways we can affect one another. Master the hand-pushing exercise, and you can use it to silently calm others in an anxious business meeting, help your toddler cope with getting a shot, turn a potential argument into a gentle discussion. I've taught this move to thousands of people, as a way of learning to be a powerful calming connector of human hearts. I'll teach it to you right now.

Gateway to Oneness: Push-Together versus Hold-Apart

1. Have a friend hold his or her hands up as though about to clap. Tell your friend not to let you push his or her hands together.

2. Fill your mind with thoughts of struggle, effort, and domination, and have your friend do the same. Then try to push the other person's hands together. You may be able to, depending on your relative muscle strength, but it will be a struggle.

3. Drop into Wordlessness, then strengthen your presence in human Oneness by recalling memories of love and connection. Remember your baby falling asleep in your arms, or your dog nearly swooning with joy at the sight of you, or the first moment you realized you were in love. You don't have to feel affection for the person whose hands you're trying to move. In fact, don't think about that person at all.

4. While holding a vivid sense-memory of uncomplicated Oneness, just put your palms on the backs of your partner's hands and move your own hands together.

Again, it's one thing to read about this exercise, quite another to actually experience the sensation. Honestly, you've got to try it. When you're the person whose hands are pushed together, you'll find yourself weirdly unable to resist, or even unable to try to resist. It's not that you feel weak, exactly; it's that you can't remember not to go along with the other person.

If you're the person doing the pushing, the first effort feels grueling and difficult, the second ridiculously easy. Most people think the other party is faking weakness.

I suspect this works because as you drop into Wordlessness, your heart and brain begin broadcasting those strong, high-amplitude waves that entrain other people's hearts and brains. At that point you and your partner are effectively One person. Once you've felt the profound physical effect of dropping into Wordlessness and Oneness, try using it in groups of people without actually touching them. Project calm to the checkout clerk at the supermarket, and watch her face relax. Use your calming energy while waiting in line at the DMV, to see if you can cause other people's anxiety to decline, as manifested by their body language and words (hint: you can). The next time your significant other is in a bad mood, drop into deep calm, and feel your beloved drop in with you. Once you begin to get it—and with deep practice, you will—this is astonishing, entertaining, and healing magic.

In case you're wondering, your ability to change another person's state of mind by being deeply connected to Oneness will hit a stalemate if that person happens to also be totally connected to Oneness. But in real life, two people who are dwelling in Oneness never struggle. They communicate. They share. They learn to understand one another. They're on the same side, in a game that's played by remaining perpetually aware that all people are One. Struggle? Not even possible.

WHY YOU CAN'T USE YOUR ONENESS POWERS FOR EVIL

Many traditional cultures that believe in Oneness are terrified by it. They fear being zapped by the "evil eye" or spells cast by malevolent witches. Actually (as the previous exercise will show you) connecting with others through Oneness is far, far more powerful when it's calm and loving. Oneness is the very definition of empathy. When I'm fully logged on to the Energy Internet, I know—not just think but experientially *know*—that we're the same consciousness, that everything I do to you, I do to me. It takes many, many negative vibes in Oneness to equal the energy of one positive, loving impulse.

This may explain why Byron Katie, the author of my favorite technique for dropping into Wordlessness, has never been hurt by any of the people who have tried to physically attack her. Katie often works in maximum-security prisons, with mentally ill patients, and with people who live in war-torn corners of the world. Traumatized, violent criminals have run at her, screaming murderous threats. "I just see love coming toward me," she told me once. "They're just Love having a nightmare." And so far, according to what I've heard from Katie and other witnesses, everyone who's tried to attack her dissolved in tears and/or fell down. She almost always ends up holding them while they cry.

Another master of Oneness is Imaculée Ilibagiza, a Tutsi woman from Rwanda who narrowly escaped being slaughtered by Hutu assassins in that country's horrific genocide. Along with six other women, she took refuge in the home of a Hutu preacher, who hid them all in a spare bathroom about the size of an enclosed phone booth—for three months. Every day Ilibagiza heard her neighbors hunting for her, describing how they'd slaughtered her loved ones. In her book *Left to Tell*, Ilibagiza describes how she coped: by becoming such a thoroughgoing mystic that she lived entirely in Oneness, free from all fear and suffused with love.

After she finally escaped the bathroom, Ilibagiza found herself, with a few old women and children, facing a mob of machete-wielding Hutus who threatened to kill the whole group. But her Oneness skills were so rock-solid she just looked at the killers, without fear or anger, feeling—and apparently broadcasting—nothing but calm compassion. For whatever reason, the experienced and bloodthirsty killers never physically attacked. They left Ilibagiza's group unscathed.

A similar incident occurred in Myanmar (formerly Burma) in 1989, when Aung San Suu Kyi, the daughter of the country's assassinated independence hero, a follower of Gandhi's nonviolent philosophy, and winner of the Nobel Peace Prize, was confronted by a platoon of experienced soldiers from the opposition. After asking some friends to stand aside, Aung San Suu Kyi walked directly up to the rifles aimed at her. Some reports say that the order to shoot never came; others that the soldiers were told, at the last possible second, not to fire. Whatever the reason, not one trigger was pulled. When asked about her actions, Aung San Suu Kyi said, "It seemed so much simpler to provide them with a single target than to bring everyone else in." Something about that "single target," that One person deeply entrenched in compassion, apparently defused a potential slaughter.

Of course, Aung San Suu Kyi's father and her hero Gandhi were killed by crazed assassins, as were Jesus, Martin Luther King Jr., and other masters of Oneness. We'll never know how many violent attacks are defused by Oneness before they ever happen, but there are indeed many people in the world who feel no connection at all to others, and who attack other people. Part of this attack is a "broadcast" of angry or hateful emotion through the Energy Internet. And although it's no match for compassion in terms of emotional power, feeling such terrible emotions, coming at them in ways that our culture doesn't even acknowledge, can be unsettling to wayfinders who don't understand human Oneness.

A WAYFINDER WHO DOESN'T WORK IN ONENESS IS A SITTING DUCK

When dark thoughts and feelings are strongly held, they can reach through Oneness to unbalance people who are less than firmly grounded in love. Anyone who's ever flinched from someone else's unspoken rage, or felt the uneasiness of being sized up sexually by a silently predatory stranger, knows that it's possible to receive troubling messages through the Energy Internet. Some people purposely project threatening or crippling energy toward others. Many more blunder around lost in fear and pain, unaware of how loudly they broadcast their miserable vibe.

If your true nature contains a streak of the wayfinder archetype, you're especially vulnerable to other people's emotional energy. Using Oneness consciously and positively is crucial for your health and sanity. Otherwise a day at the office can leave you reeling with the crazy or fearful energy of your coworkers, a relationship with an emotional parasite can drain you right into depression, the rage of the couple in the next apartment may seem to seep right through the walls. Try the following exercise to see how vulnerable you are. It requires at least three people: one to be the "subject," one the "tester," and one or more the "influencers."

Gateway to Oneness: Feeling the Energy of Your Observers

1. Choose one person to be the test "subject."

2. Choose another person to be the "tester." Everyone else in the room will serve as "influencers."

3. Have the subject hold out one arm parallel to the ground, and try hard to keep it horizontal while the tester presses down on it. This establishes how strong the subject's arm is.

4. Repeat the arm press, only this time all the influencers will think a negative, critical, or hurtful thought about the subject. (I know, this goes against your character, but it's for the sake of science.) See if the subject's arm is as strong when these negative thoughts are in the vibe.

5. Repeat the test a third time, while all the influencers hold a loving, supportive, appreciative thought about the subject. See how arm strength is affected.

I've done this exercise with many groups, and in almost every case, the arm strength of the test subject pretty much disappears in the presence of negative thoughts and becomes weirdly strong when the group's thoughts are supportive. It can actually be quite alarming to realize how powerfully our unspoken energies are affecting each other, so follow up this exercise above with the ones below.

VIRUS PROTECTION ON THE ENERGY INTERNET

One of the main problems I've seen in Team members is that they don't even articulate the concept of sending and receiving energetic information from other people, even though they're doing it constantly. It takes only a few hours of horse-whispering for people to acknowledge that they can clearly sense the mood of a large animal; then they see that they can also "read" human energy. This simple acknowledgment is the most important thing you can do to avoid absorbing negative energy from others, whether they're deliberately attacking you or accidentally swamping you with a bad mood. Without a belief in the interpersonal energy connection, your consciousness is an unprotected wireless device, just waiting to be hacked or to take in an energetic "virus" (which you'll then transmit to others).

To set up a firewall around your energy, first experiment with suspending your disbelief and doing the following exercise.

Gateway to Oneness: Observing Interpersonal Energy

1. The next time you're in a group conversation, meeting, party, or crowd, sit back and be silent for a moment. (Your loved ones may have been waiting for you to do this for years.)

2. Breathe deeply and drop into Wordlessness.

3. Instead of focusing on what people are saying, just feel their energy.

4. Rest for each person and the group. This will allow you to feel more acutely whatever is going on inside them.

5. Peacefully label each person's mood state: "frenzied," "amorous," "guilty," "angry." Notice that you can detach from this energy just by naming it without judgment.

6. Believe your instincts.

The key to remaining aware of other people's vibes is to *stay in or return to Wordlessness.* In a Wordless state, you'll immediately perceive people's energy state. (Jill Bolte Taylor writes compellingly about how she could do this during her Wordless period.) In Wordlessness you'll also follow your instincts, because your thoughts won't talk you out of it. No animal or pre-verbal baby would pretend not to sense aversive energy, or tell itself to "act polite" or worry, "Maybe it's not them. Maybe something's wrong with *me*."

If you sense that someone's energy is unsettling or toxic, it's imperative to hold a mental position of deep connection—not connection to the difficult person, and certainly not to his or her unsettling mind, but the Wordless love you feel in nature, with a pet, with a baby. This is a radical form of deep practice. It isn't easy, especially at first, but the more you do it, the more you rewire your brain to sustain love constantly and easily. The worst-case result is that you'll be unfazed by others' dark energy. The best-case result is that your state of Wordless love will entrain the other's brain. When you refuse to leave the energy of love, you're not taking away other people's choices—they can stay violent or upset if they want—but you keep yourself safer and offer the maximum possible contribution to the other person's infinitely loving true nature as well. Try the following exercise.

Gateway to Oneness: Enlightening Dark Energy

1. Picture a circle of invisible light emanating from your body. Imagine that any dark energy attempting to reach you must pass through this light, at which point it becomes illuminated. By the time it reaches you, it only increases the radiance.

2. Project the light outward, so that your protected zone gets larger and larger. You might find yourself becoming very physically still as you do this.

3. Walk through a crowded place wearing this "illumination cloak" and notice others' reactions (or lack of reaction) to you. Some people will be drawn toward you. Others—those trapped in their own dark energy—may not even see you. If they do, they'll avoid you.

HOW TO GET TO THE RIGHT ONE

You may be one of the many Team members who recognize the "invisibility" part of the previous exercise because you learned to "disappear" energetically during an abusive or dangerous childhood. You may still be in energetically violent relationships with anyone from a romantic partner to a friend, coworker, or extended family member. This isn't uncommon for wayfinder types, but it's not how you are meant to feel or live.

The tendency of healers to be wounded early and often is the reason why, so far in this book, I've resisted calling Oneness by the more common word "love." That term triggers a tangle of just-plain-crazy associations in many people's minds. What often passes for love is more like drug addiction: a desperate, continuous attempt to make other people fill our emotional needs, an eternal clawing struggle to be rescued from what feels like solitary despair. Some people tell their lovers, with no sense of irony, "I love you so much I'll kill you if you ever try to leave me." The emotion that gives rise to such thoughts is not Oneness. It's a panicky response to a mechanistic myth of separation. It is a lie.

You can master Oneness only by accessing a state of *genuine* love, in which, as the Good Book says, there is no fear, and as Eckhart Tolle says, "there is no wanting whatsoever." That's why Oneness is the *second* technology of magic, depending on Wordlessness for its power: as long as we're trapped in stories about the bad things people have done or future fears and past regrets that pull us out of the present moment, our ability to love gets horrifically twisted. Consider the version of romantic love expressed in many popular songs, with their endlessly repeated themes:

➤ "I can't live if living is without you."

➤ "I'll be your hope, I'll be your love, be everything that you need."

➤ "I've been waiting for a girl like you . . . to make me feel alive."

➤ "How am I supposed to live without you, when all that I've been living for is gone?"

This isn't Oneness, it's a hostage situation. It's the kind of thing a parasite would sing to its host. Freud might call it "cathexis," the projection of one's emotional need onto another, but not the love that considers the other's perspective. A Buddhist would immediately recognize it as attachment, the source of all suffering. Romantic love, in particular, can turn into energetic parasitism because falling in love gives even the most emotionally isolated of us a glimpse of the Oneness that is our natural state. When the initial hormone rush fades, and we begin slipping back into the cold, violent sea that is the illusion of separation, we panic. Instead of sustaining Oneness, we grasp at the other person, often emotionally crushing him or her, like a drowning person strangling a would-be rescuer.

When I tell clients that they need complete detachment in order to love fully and freely, they look at me as though I've offered to show them my treasured collection of pen-pal letters from Stalin. To them, detachment sounds like the opposite of love: love *is* attachment. But actually, in the context of Oneness there's no need to attach to someone in order to be with him or her: we can feel our loved ones, and everyone else, and Love itself, all the time. There's no possible way we could be separated from what we are, so there's no need to entrap, extort, wheedle, manipulate, or possess the object of our affections.

Here are some paired lists of expressions of "love." The left-hand column contains thoughts that come from a belief in separation as reality. The right-hand column is grounded in a felt experience of Oneness. Which one would you rather have your spouse, your parents, or your best friend say to you?

ATTACHMENT	ONENESS
"You complete me."	"I feel whole, and I love sharing the joy of that with you."
"I need you to make me happy."	"I'm happy, and I love being with you."
"Without you, my life would be a joyless wasteland."	"My life is wonderful! Come share it with me!"
"I need to be with you all the time."	"I love being with you when you feel like being with me."
"I can't stand the thought of your focusing on anyone but me."	"I want you to have lots and lots of love in your life."
"If you leave me, I'll never forgive you."	"You can't leave me, even by dying; we're always connected wherever we are."
"You're here to heal my wounds."	"I know how to heal my own wounds, and how to love you as you heal yours."

If you'd prefer to hear the items in the first column, I can give you lots of phone numbers, many of which could lead to serious relationships, many of which could lead to restraining orders. If the second column feels better to you, your personal life and your work on the Team will contain much less *Sturm und Drang,* much more peace and joy. Enough peace and joy, in fact, to fill the universe.

•

WHAT DETACHED ONENESS FEELS LIKE

When we access nonverbal awareness for sustained periods of time, the part of the brain responsible for the feeling of being confined in a body disappears, and the sense of all things combining as one interconnected Self expands infinitely. Throughout human history, the wayfinders who've accessed this part of their true nature have tried to tell the rest of us how wonderful it is. "I know about love the way the fields know about light," wrote Rabia of Basra. "All objects in existence are wildly in love," Francis of Assisi claimed. And Teresa of Avila wrote, "I have stepped from that region of myself that did not love all the time." All over the world, the voices of the wayfinders agree that entering Oneness is falling in Love with everyone, every place, every time that ever existed or ever will exist. Aloneness, they tell us with a single voice, is illusion; the truth is all-Oneness.

The way to find this state of sustained Oneness is not to grip your loved ones more tightly, but to so saturate yourself with the experience of love that you know you'll never be without it. Below are three exercises to help you reestablish your connection with the reality of Oneness, to learn that you can access love across any span of time or space. Use these techniques when you're feeling lonely or desperate. Believe in the sense of connection you can create, and you may never again ruin a relationship, or enter a new relationship that's doomed to ruination.

Gateway to Oneness: Enjoying Your Treasures

1. Sit quietly and still your mind, or drop into Wordlessness through a path of rhythmic play (walking, playing your guitar, weeding flowers, churning butter, etc.).

2. Recall a moment in your life when you felt deeply connected to another human being. This might have been playing with a child, identifying very strongly with a character in a movie, or reading a book by an author who's right on your wavelength.

3. Focus on this moment deeply. Allow your attention to flow into it and fill it. Let the experience of connection flood your whole body.

4. Imagine that there's a golden treasure chest in the center of your head. Open the lid, and gently place your memory of connection inside. Leave it there; it will still be there when you come back.

5. Now find another memory of connection, a time a comedian made you laugh, opening a door for a stranger who seemed genuinely grateful, a kind nurse in the emergency room that night you were admitted for caffeine poisoning.

6. After letting this memory fill your attention, put it into the golden treasure chest along with your first deposit.

7. Keep adding memories of connection at least once a day. You'll start remembering and noticing them more as this process primes your attention.

8. Visit the golden treasure chest to count your treasures at times when you feel disconnected. Picture yourself opening the lid and finding all those memories there, glittering like emeralds and rubies. Play with them. Pick them up by the handful. Marvel at your own wealth.

Gateway to Oneness: Travel through Spacetime to Connect with Loved Ones

1. Imagine that the Fates have given you a chance to have the perfect conversation with someone you've loved and lost—an ex-lover, a mentor, your grandma as God made her, before the vodka. This is the conversation where your beloved says all the things your heart longs to hear: "You're perfect. You're beautiful. None of your 'failures' matters. I'm so proud of you."

2. Write down both sides of this Perfect Conversation, as if you're writing dialogue for a play. For example:

YOU: You were my first love, back in high school, but you never even noticed me.

BELOVED *(saying whatever you most yearn to hear):* I was an idiot not to see what a magnificent person you are. Now I do see, and I'm dazzled. You are amazing.

YOU: I used to cry myself to sleep, wishing I could be with you.

BELOVED: Well, that's never going to happen again, because I'm right here, and I'm never leaving.

Here's another example, using a parental figure as the Beloved:

YOU: You were so hard on me. I was just a little kid who loved you, and I lived to please you, and all you ever did was criticize me.

BELOVED: I was out of my mind. How could I not have seen what a priceless treasure you are, and how much more important it was for me to love you than to focus on my own pain? I only criticized you because I didn't see who you really are, and I didn't know who I really was, either.

3. Once you've written down every last thing you want to say, and the perfect responses from your Beloved, reread the conversation. Realize that the things you're hearing at last from your Beloved are actually profound realities, coming from the perception of your own true nature. No words are genuinely "right" or "wrong," but these are much closer to "right" than the painful alternatives you've been holding in your memory for so long.

4. Suspend your disbelief in the wonderful things your Beloved is saying. Feel the wisdom you've been trying to teach yourself, although your mind chose to see it only by fixating on other people. The ego thought these people could fill the abyss in your heart. Actually the abyss is an illusion. The sensation you get from believing you are loved and connected is real. Feel how the truth—that you are infinitely valuable and loved—makes your whole body relax.

Gateway to Oneness: Travel through Spacetime
to Connect with Your Tribe Members

1. Think of someone you respect, admire, or want to meet someday. Or you might choose someone you've never physically
met, such as a spiritual master or historical figure, as long as this
person's love would mean a great deal to you. For example:

YOU: I know if I'd had your guidance and mentorship, I'd have
felt worthy, and my life would have gone better.

GANDHI: It's true. I wish I'd been here earlier. But I'm here
now, and together we're going to be the change we wish to see in
the world. C'mere, buddy, let's shave that head of yours!

2. Again, feel the truth of your loved one's presence—the One who
has always been part of you and who could not be complete
without you, no matter how distant from one another your lives
may seem.

3. When you read or hear about the words of other wayfinders,
allow yourself to believe that they somehow felt your Being, as
you feel theirs.

SENDING GROUP "ENERGYMAIL" THROUGH ONENESS

The more you feel the truth of Oneness, the more you'll reclaim your true
nature, the more easily you'll find your way through relationships, and the
more healing you'll naturally offer the world. For example, teacher and
healer Dan Howard, whom I encourage you to Google, lives to teach people how to rest. You'll learn one of his techniques later in this book, but
you already know the most important components: dropping into Wordlessness and connecting with a sense of Oneness. Rest is not inert or powerless. It "broadcasts" through the Energy Internet very strongly. It's so
healing that many of my clients say they find it more helpful than their
medication for healing physical and emotional pain. (Don't stop taking
your meds! Just learn to rest deeply too!)

One strange result of Dan Howard's fascination with rest is that he's found he can do it transitively; in other words, he believes he can rest for other people. When he rests for me—usually without my knowing he's doing so—I really do feel calmed and energized. I learned the following exercise from Dan. He calls it "love smuggling."

Gateway to Oneness: Smuggling Love into Everything You Do

1. While in a crowded space, such as a mall, a concert, a movie theater, or a White House press briefing, drop into Wordlessness.

2. Feel the energy of the people in the space around you. When you locate someone whose energy feels jittery or unhappy, begin thinking positive and supportive thoughts "toward" that person.

3. Watch for changes in the person's behavior.

4. Once you've learned that you can calm strangers with your energy (yes, you really can!) try it in more intense and improbable situations: traffic jams, political rallies, Wall Street on a day the market dives.

5. Begin looking for people who are obviously in a difficult mood state, so that you can practice at more challenging levels. Calm the angry office assistant, your difficult child, your aging parent. Sneak love, your secret weapon of healing, into any and every situation.

6. Notice how much easier all your interactions become.

GETTING POSITIVE ENERGY TO GO VIRAL ON THE ENERGY INTERNET

Very few people realize how powerfully we influence others when we're logged on to Oneness. I don't understand it myself, but sometimes I get a hint. It helps a great deal to live in energetic connection generated by my Wordless son.

For example, one evening while communing with nature during a desert sunset walk with my dogs, it occurs to me that it's easy to feel Oneness in such ideal conditions. I wonder if I could work this technology of magic in a less idyllic setting. A perfect opportunity to try presents itself immediately: I'm scheduled to take Adam and his friend Joey, who also has Down syndrome, to a Phoenix Suns basketball game.

An NBA game isn't exactly a silent grotto where monks might go to find stillness. The arena is packed with screaming fans, flashing lights, deafening music, spilled beer. Manic cheerleaders are shooting a "gift cannon" at the audience, and Adam and Joey (who are fifteen years old physically but cognitively about eight) reach for every souvenir as it soars over their heads. Adam wants a Shaq T-shirt, and Joey wants a stuffed gorilla dressed in a Suns outfit. I watch sadly as they learn a lesson that will probably be true their whole lives: they're too short, uncoordinated, and slow to out-grab the other fans for such prizes.

This chaotic scene is just the right place to test my ability to tune in to my true nature. I settle in my seat and drop into Wordlessness, wondering if I'll be able to find even a shred of stillness in such an unlikely spot. It takes a minute or two, but then I manage it. At the moment verbal thought disappears, I feel flooded with unexpected, dazzling beauty. The game taking place on the basketball court becomes an incredibly graceful ballet, each team of five huge men moving like separate fingers of the same hand, the two giant hands tossing the ball back and forth in the bliss of deep play, the crowd swaying and surging like sea plants in the surf.

A moment later I feel an explosion of human Oneness. Every being in the enormous space seems connected to every other. The power of that connection overwhelms all our surface differences, our sense of being many separate beings. I don't see how the arena can handle the pressure; it seems as though the roof will blow off any moment from the force of so much love. To my great embarrassment, I feel tears on my cheeks. I wipe my face and look around to make sure no one's watching me. That's when I notice the crowd acting strangely.

All around me, in a huge circle, I see a ripple of action, a disturbance like the rings that extend from a stone dropped into water, but in reverse: the waves are coming toward me. It takes me several seconds to realize what's happening. From every direction, people have begun handing over the prizes they've snatched out of the air, passing them person-to-person in a spontaneous bucket line. They're offering their gifts to Joey and Adam.

I completely lose it, weeping openly as someone hands my son a Shaq

T-shirt. Joey tries to be manly, but can't help hugging and kissing his new Suns gorilla. I stand up and turn around with my hand on my heart, trying to Wordlessly thank at least a hundred strangers who have all been part of the full-circle bucket line. It feels as though, by dropping the illusion of separation, I've allowed myself to activate the loving connection inherent in all these beer-sloshing basketball fans. They responded with love as generous, gentle, and selfless as a mother tending her baby. Many of them are weeping too. Adam and Joey politely refuse the rest of the gifts, and the people around us began offering them to one another.

I don't know exactly what's happening in that basketball arena, only that it is completely magical and utterly natural. When human beings open to the experience of Oneness, groups, crowds, whole nations may respond to single loving impulses with inconceivable power. This is the power that has made us such a successful species. It may be enough power to let us mend our own true natures and the world. If my experience of the "You! You! You!" Phenomenon is any indication, the Team—which may include everyone on Earth—is taking field positions to play this most amazing of all possible games. The Team is gathering. By accessing Oneness, you can join that gathering, right now.

DÉJÀ VU: CONNECTING WITH YOUR TRIBE, EVERYWHEN

Many people randomly experience flashes of déjà vu, the sense of already having seen some new experience. What wayfinders know is that we can "already see" people we haven't met by logging on to the Wordless Web and feeling the presence of loving energies across time and space. Sitting under the marula tree, listening to my new long-lost friend Linky, I know why my love for her is already so absolute: we are Team members whose missions intersect, and we have "already seen" each other on the Everywhen our whole lives.

You can meet Teammates the same way right this minute, no matter who or where you are. If you do deep-practice this, just watch: you'll not only feel your true nature claiming its rightful place as a magical being, but you'll experience joys you can't yet imagine. You'll find your way through a wild new world of love, connecting with people you may or may not have met in the flesh. Then, when you do meet them, you'll know why you're so very relieved, why there are tears in your eyes, why the two of you want to grasp one another's shoulders, shake gently, and shout, "You! You! You!"

Bigstock Photo

This is how you're always supposed to feel.

PART III

THE THIRD TECHNOLOGY OF MAGIC

WORDLESSNESS

ONENESS

IMAGINATION

FORMING

CHAPTER EIGHT

IMAGINATION PRONKS

"You have to come to Phillipolis," says Boyd one day after we've just finished leading one of our yearly retreats in the bush. "It's the most amazing place."

"What's there?" I ask.

"Nothing," says Boyd. "That's just it. These amazing people are living nowhere, with *nothing* to support them. There's so much nothing you can feel what wants to happen there. It's magical."

Admittedly Boyd's view of Phillipolis is heavily biased by his obsession with "restoring Eden." The village lies in a vast, barren plateau in central South Africa called the Karoo. In the nineteenth century and early twentieth the land was farmed by *voortrekkers,* Dutch pioneers, until the soil was exhausted and the farmers left. The Karoo's original human inhabitants had been the Khoikhoi (culturally very similar to the people depicted in the film *The Gods Must Be Crazy*).

The Khoikhoi had lived for centuries in intimate harmony with vast herds of an antelope called the springbok, much as the plains Indians once relied on the American bison. (Springbok were named for their habit of springing straight up in the air as if they're made of flubber, a feat known as "pronking." It's amazing to watch and also, I think you'll agree, a most excellent word. Check out pronking for yourself by googling "springbok pronking" and watching the videos that show up on YouTube and other sites, or by going to www.youtube.com/watch?v=FlddKpKVXV4&feature=fvwrel.)

For thousands of years the springbok migrated back and forth across the Karoo, following the rains. They ate the tops of grass and other plants, but never the roots, so the savannah was perpetually regrowing. The ecosystem supported so many springbok that the *voortrekkers* often had to sit on their wagons for three solid days, waiting for the herds to pass by. People were trampled to death by springbok, overwhelmed by sheer numbers, even though each animal only weighs about seventy-five pounds. This huge population of herbivores provided sustenance for cheetahs, leopards, hyenas, wild dogs, and countless other predators, including a strain of snow-white lions who were held sacred by the Khoikhoi.

All that changed when imported sheep and goats got to work on the local flora. They ate plants down to the root, leaving nothing but dust, and the soil quickly eroded. The huge majority of springbok, along with the other wild animals of the Karoo, were either killed outright or died of starvation. The white lions were particularly popular hunting trophies. As if that weren't appalling enough, the Khoikhoi were also hunted *for sport*. Those who weren't shot often starved as the animals and edible plants disappeared, or were pressed into servitude on European-style farms. When the farms shut down and most of the white settlers departed, the indigenous people were left in a post-apocalyptic-looking landscape, with neither a wild ecosystem nor a human economy to support them.

It became one of the Varty family's dreams to replicate the Londolozi model of restoring land and indigenous people in the Karoo. Because the place is so empty of human inhabitants, it would be relatively easy to restore the grasslands and allow the springbok, along with dozens of other species, to resume their ancient migration. The Vartys hope to create a human economy by bringing in ecotourism, giving the Khoikhoi and the Griqua (people of mixed racial ancestry) a way to thrive financially by using their ancient methods of tracking and interacting with wild animals.

It takes almost unthinkable amounts of political and economic diplomacy to obtain permission to undertake such a huge task, but the Vartys set out to do just that. They also set out to earn the trust of the local people—no easy task in a country scarred by such a horrific past. So Boyd and Bronwyn's former tutor, the educator named Kate Groch I mentioned in the previous chapter, moved to Phillipolis. There Kate teaches pretty much anything to pretty much anyone—English, basic numeracy, adult literacy. Just as important, she learns from the local people about their history, culture, and values. The summer before I visited, she, the Vartys, and several friends from inside and outside Phillipolis built a preschool for the village, using a borrowed brick-making machine, dirt, and sweat (total cost about $150).

I've heard a lot about the "springbok migration" project since I met the Vartys, so when Boyd invites me to visit Phillipolis, I'm totally in. So are several of my friends: Koelle; my partner Karen; one of our friends who, like Karen, is an American social work professor; a business consultant and a master coach, both from Dubai; a South African rock concert organizer; and a drama therapist. One chilly July day we all piled into a rented van and headed into the Karoo.

Nine Team members in one van makes for a very jolly road trip. We drive for six hours through the blank, dusty landscape, where only termite mounds, many gouged by hungry aardvarks, break the desolation. As we near Phillipolis, Boyd gestures toward the windshield at the measureless emptiness. "Okay, everyone," he says, "imagine this whole landscape green. Covered with springbok, from horizon to horizon. Cheetahs and jackals and white lions following the herds. Millions of animals living the way they did for thousands and thousands of years."

The rest of us fall silent, staring out the windows. With Boyd narrating, we really can see the land healed. The silence in the van is almost trance-like, and not just because we're all dazed by an overdose of corn chips and Diet Coke. It's as if the ghosts of the animals that once lived on the land we're crossing—or perhaps the spirits of those that will live there in the future—have joined us. I remember reading that the Khoikhoi knew the herds were coming days before they saw any animals, when they felt the ground begin to vibrate. One of their ancient songs describes it:

> We know the springbok are coming
> through the feeling in our feet.
> Our feet feel the rustling of the feet
> of the springbok.

For our little van full of people, that moment in the middle of a vast African nowhere is when the magic kicks in. Specifically the third technology of magic: Imagination.

THE WAYFINDER'S IMAGINATION

What our little posse feels as we headed toward Phillipolis was different from an idle daydream. We are "premembering" the healing of the springbok migration. Premembering is sparked by the mind, but experienced in the body. It comes with vivid flashes of what feels like sensory memory, except that the event hasn't happened yet; we see, hear, taste, smell, and feel "what wants to happen," exactly as we'd recall an occasion that happened in the past. Something electrical affects our skin, giving us goose-flesh, and we may tear up or weep openly without really knowing why. Often the mind is baffled by these physical reactions. The body links directly to the Imagination, bypassing what we think is logical.

Normal imagination is contained within the mind, while the wayfinder's Imagination includes the mind as a portion (a tiny portion) of its vast Self. Grounded in Wordlessness and Oneness, it reaches across space and time into the Everywhen. Because the ordinary mind only pictures things based on past experience, it's locked into the personality's belief structures, hemmed in by the possible. Up to this point in history, ordinary imagination has been sufficient to track and predict change. But it's almost impossible to navigate today's world without an Imagination that can go beyond the mind's limitations—in other words, by the intelligence we access through Wordlessness and Oneness.

USING YOUR IMAGINATION (BECOMING THE MAGICIAN)

In the introduction, you may recall, I mentioned that whereas the first two technologies of magic are about achieving a certain state of being, the second two are more active: as you do them, you'll actually feel that you're *doing* them. If you've ever seen a deck of Tarot cards (an ancient, much misused prop for wayfinders) you may have seen one devoted to the archetype of the Magician. This symbolic being carries a magic wand, more properly called a caduceus, a staff with two snakes twining up toward the handle. (Sound familiar? It's still the logo of modern-day physicians.) The top of the staff reaches into the Everywhen, the Wordless Oneness of the spiritual realm. The bottom is located in the ordinary, physical world. The Magician (healer, mender) knows how to bring things from the first realm into the second. This isn't a trick. It's a healing technology.

Your caduceus is your wayfinder Imagination. To use it, you don't exactly make things up—that's a mental exercise. Instead you feel what "wants to happen" in the Everywhen. I wish I could describe this in words, but that's impossible. Some people feel it as a kind of tugging sensation, as if their perception is being pulled somewhere. Other people feel a future reality waiting to be born the way you might feel a baby kick through its mother's belly. You don't know what's there, but you know it's something, something with energetic weight and consequence. Using your Imagination is about drawing a blueprint of the things you want to create, things that haven't existed in precisely that form ever before.

This, like the Magician archetype, isn't a fuzzy woo-woo item. It's a muscular, active practice of creation. The exercises in this section won't ask you to dream up some version of Puff the Magic Dragon. On the contrary, they'll require that you go deeply into Wordless Oneness, find *what wants to be real,* then work like a detective, like a doctor, like an architect, like an engineer, to conjure that thing into three dimensions.

Wordlessness logs you onto the Energy Internet. Oneness sends you a message about what you might do with your life. Using your wayfinder Imagination is building a new website based on that message. It means working with the laws of nature *and* the laws of what we now call the "supernatural" to transform the life you have now into a life perfectly suited to your true nature. Roll up your sleeves, friend. Learning to use your wayfinder's Imagination is good, hard, life-changing play.

IMAGINING THE WAY FORWARD

When the ethnobotanist Wade Davis traveled on a voyage with a traditionally trained Hawaiian wayfinder, he was impressed by the navigator's vast empirical knowledge of waves, clouds, sea life, and stars. But, Davis said, "it was one thing to know what to look for, these clues and signs and indications; it was quite another to pull it all together and confront in the moment the ever-changing power and reality of the sea."

To do this, Polynesian wayfinders needed more information than they could access consciously. As they calculated the positions of the hundreds of stars they knew on sight, their nonverbal minds—the Wordless part of their brains—were also reaching into their immense stores of information and sending up messages about where to guide their canoes across heaving, unexplored ocean. And that often looked like magic.

Here's a story Davis heard from a wayfinder named Nainoa, whose canoe, the *Hokule'a,* is still sailing today—without modern navigation equipment:

> At one point, close to their goal, Nainoa snapped awake in a daze and realized that with the overcast skies and the sea fog, he had no idea where they were. He had lost the continuity of mind and memory essential

to survival at sea. He masked his fear from the crew and in despair remembered [his teacher's] words. *Can you see the image of the island in your mind?* He became calm, and realized that he had already found the island. It was the *Hokule'a,* and he had everything he needed onboard the sacred canoe. Suddenly, the sky brightened and a beam of warm light appeared on his shoulder. The clouds cleared and he followed that beam directly to the island Rapa Nui.

Thinking and acting like this is the only way I know to find your way through the wild new world of the twenty-first century. Mystics and medicine people have always functioned in much this manner, because the metaphysical realm they travel has always been as uncharted and changeable as the sea. Ordinary imagination wanders aimlessly, but wayfinder Imagination extends consciousness through all the knowledge our senses can give us and on into the sight of the mind—perhaps into the bubbling, random froth of quantum foam, where consciousness crystallizes matter from wave energy.

Whether navigating across the Pacific or through the chaos of modern civilization, wayfinders use the same process described by Nainoa: dropping into calm (Wordlessness), realizing that they have already found the destination in the Everywhen (Oneness). Then they feel their way toward the physical destination they have Imagined. As they do so, literally everything begins guiding them with moments of validation and illumination, like the beam of light warming Nainoa's shoulder. To onlookers, it seems that the wayfinder is magnetically pulling in what she has envisioned; as Davis writes, "The metaphor is that the *Hokule'a* never moves. It simply waits, the axis mundi [center axis] of the world, as the islands rise out of the sea to greet her."

HUMANITY'S WAYFINDERS

This is standard operating procedure for healers and visionaries in every culture. The Aborigines used it to find their way through the desert on hundred-mile "walkabouts." Moses used it to find his people's promised land, a land he would reach only in his Imagination. Martin Luther King Jr. dreamed of a different promised land, though he too would die before his destination in physical reality. Einstein described general relativity after a leap of his Imagination, and American rocket scientists roamed the lunar surface in their Imaginations long before "one small step for a man, one giant leap for mankind."

This same kind of Imagination has helped you achieve any goal you've ever seen in your mind's eye, from passing a test in school to finding someone to love. The Imaginative process involves full application of the human brain's incredible capacity to observe and learn, endless deep practice negotiating this physical reality, and riding through the realm of the nonphysical, using Wordlessness and Oneness as vehicles. This was the process my friends and I tapped into as we cruised across the Karoo, seeing, hearing, smelling, feeling thousands of plants and animals that aren't there. Yet.

IMAGINATION AT PLAY

I've never felt quite as physically cold and emotionally warm as I do in Phillipolis. Few of the buildings have any heat, and the chilly Karoo air cuts through all clothing like an ice pick. Our posse clumps together in Kate's house, trying to share body heat, as her daughter Maya toddles around barefoot, oblivious to the cold. (Maya was born to a Setswana teenager, one of Africa's "throwaway babies," before becoming the light of Kate's life. "Mummy is pink," she explains, "and I am dark pink.")

Kate, ever the educator, tells us that the local people have to feed their families on about 250 rand a month—approximately $3.60. She gives us that amount and sends us to the village store, challenging us to buy enough to keep a family of four fed and healthy for thirty days. This makes us truly appreciate the meal we share with Kate's friend Ouma Nan, one of the village matriarchs. Our knees touch as we cram into her tiny house, sharing stew and fried dough from a pot in the center of the room. With Kate translating, Ouma Nan tells us that for most of her life, if we white people had been caught socializing with her, everyone in the house would have been arrested. She speaks with great eloquence and sorrow, but no bitterness at all, about the horrors of apartheid and the destruction of her people's ancient way of life.

We spend the rest of the day on a walking tour of the village, visiting the preschool, joining Kate as she teaches young people and adults. We show the children of Phillipolis how a Flip camera works, and let them film each other. We walk a labyrinth in the town square. As the day wears on, the retinue of children following us grows to include pretty much everyone in the village younger than fifteen. I love hearing them speak the local language, which seems to have as many different "clicks" as we have consonants.

That night, back at Kate's house, we let our Imaginations go nuts. The rule of the evening is that everyone has to Imagine as many different ideas as possible for "restoring Eden" in the Karoo. The ideas don't have to be good, just interesting. With a huge poster and a lot of Post-it notes, we start outlining ideas. We picture raising money to replant the Karoo. We see the breeding herds of springbok getting bigger. We decide we'll hire local kids to care for the herds, paying them by letting Americans "buy" springbok for a dollar a pop and having the local herders Flip-film and email weekly updates on each little herd to the American "investors." Once we start thinking about Flip films, we quickly Imagine preserving the Khoisan culture and unifying the village by having young people make documentaries about the village elders, so there will be a record of the old ways and the hardships of apartheid.

The later it gets, the more Imaginary situations we create. We'll remodel some of Phillipolis's charming old farmhouses as inns for ecotourism. We'll reintroduce captive white lions into the wilderness. The academics among us will write journal articles about the Londolozi model of ecosystem-friendly economic development. Boyd and I will both write books for popular audiences. Our rock concert organizer will raise funds with concerts. The drama therapist will bring in college students to teach the children and reenact ancient dances. We'll heal the wilderness, eliminate poverty, manage AIDS, bring in the whole world to help! Kate's living room is roughly the same temperature as a meat refrigerator, but our Imaginations get so overheated that by midnight we are literally pronking around the room.

Eventually our teeth begin chattering too violently to permit speech, so it's time to pack it in for the night. I crawl into a bed that Kate tells me was brought from Londolozi—the very bed Mandela used when he stayed there. In the ten seconds before I fall asleep, I ponder the Imagination of a man who created one of the greatest peaceful revolutions in human history from his tiny prison cell. However audacious our Imagination session was, Mandela had us beat.

The next morning we meet for breakfast, feeling a little shy about the wild ideas we created in the wee hours. But as we sip our tea, something odd happens: our cell phones begin to ring. All of them. We haven't been able to use them before this; a satellite must be passing directly overhead, allowing calls to go through. Whatever enables them, the calls all have one theme: people wanted to help us.

I hear from a famous, wealthy American celebrity who wants to contribute to development in Africa. The business consultant from Dubai gets a call saying that a Middle Eastern conservation group is interested in some sort of collaboration. The social work professors receive a thumbs-up on article ideas they recently submitted, and their sketchy plans to write up the Londolozi model of development are warmly encouraged the by journal editors on the phone. Kate's mother, Mo (also a teacher), answers her cell, chats briefly, and hangs up looking dazed: one of the most famous educators in South Africa just called to say he's retiring and wants to devote the next few years of his life to "whatever you're doing."

I'm not making this up.

This is what I learn on that trip to the Karoo: No matter where you are, no matter how small or pathetic you may feel, freeing your wayfinder's Imagination by embarking on an adventure turns you into some kind of crazy-strong electromagnet. Take out all the stops, drop into Wordless Oneness, laugh and play and love and dream beyond all reason, and miraculous things begin happening. Doors open. Paths appear. Team members you've never met find their way through time, space, and every other barrier to help you. You simply wait, Imagining, as the islands rise out of the sea to greet you. It's not necessary that you believe this. Imagining it is enough.

HOW NOT TO IMAGINE

The process of envisioning an outcome occurs to anyone with a brain, but many people misuse this technology of magic, rendering it ineffective. Religions insist that having faith in their model of reality, their authority structures, gives the faithful the power to work miracles. New Age dabblers insist that if they can just focus their mind on a huge house and a career as a movie star, they'll "manifest" what they want. These methods try to force reality to cooperate with the small imagination of our personalities. It doesn't work. A wayfinder's Imagination doesn't dominate reality. It feels into Oneness, falls in love with "what wants to happen," and gives itself to the vision created by that love.

The difference is very clear to me because I once spent months continuously trying to force my imagination into physical reality. Between Adam's prenatal diagnosis of Down syndrome and his birth, I read stories of miraculous healings from the scriptures of various religions and hoarded tales of strong-willed people who had gotten their way by using mind over matter. I spent weeks trying to *will* Adam to be "normal." It was an exhausting, jaw-grinding, white-knuckle effort, and all along I had the sick feeling it wouldn't work.

By contrast, in the few moments when I relaxed my attachment to what my personality wanted, my wayfinding Imagination went to an entirely different place—a future where Adam's Down syndrome would be the doorway to unconditional love, joy, and mystery. At such times I felt kind, unseen conscious presences caring for me with indescribable tenderness. They weren't giving me what my personality imagined I wanted. They were helping me want what my mender's Imagination was giving me.

This experience led me to conclude that the unconscious part of my psyche was tapped into a wider Imagination than my conscious mind. The part of my brain that processes eleven million data points per second, and is also tapped in to the Oneness of all space and time, was very pleased about the way Adam turned out. To "manifest" material outcomes with Imagination, I had to surrender the view of my small self to my larger Self, which had very different goals and motivations.

Here's an exercise that can help you feel the difference between mere imagination and a wayfinder's Imagination, using the relatively simple situation of your physical home. By now it should go without saying that all these exercises should be prefaced by dropping into Wordlessness and connecting with a sense of Oneness.

Imagination Liberation: Feel What Wants to Happen

1. Go to the least pleasant place in your house, apartment, yurt, lean-to, or whatever.

2. Sit down in the space, and get as comfortable as you can.

3. Without words, feel the dissonance in the space, the jarring items that cause it to be less than perfect for you.

4. Let yourself feel what the space wants to be—not what you want it to be (you'll get stuck in the same patterns that have kept the space as it is) but what *it* seems to want.

5. Close your eyes, and with your Imagination, closely observe the room as it wants to be. Notice where it wants a slash of color, more openness, a cozier texture, a flower.

6. Reach into Oneness and feel yourself connect with items that "want" to be in your space. Call them until you feel a sense of tugging; then let go. As in the exercises related to "calling" animals, this *total release* is the mechanism that activates your connection through the Everywhen.

7. Return to normal life, but remain aware: the items for your space will be trying to reach you. You may see them in stores, or they may come some other way—as a gift, a piece of driftwood on the beach, a donation from a neighbor who's moving.

8. When they come, receive them with gratitude and put them where they want to be, in the room that wants them to be there.

THE MEDIUM OF IMAGINATION

Doing this is an art, not loosey-goosey finger painting but the disciplined skill that made Michelangelo comment, "If people knew how hard I work, they wouldn't be surprised by what I can do." The wayfinder works with Imagination the way an artist works with paint or clay or marble. He feels what the medium can do by becoming it, letting it guide him with the constraints of its inner nature even as he guides it to become what he envisions. One of the great new arts of our time is the use of computers. If Wordlessness is like logging on to a metaphysical Internet, and Oneness is like sending and receiving messages on the Web, Imagination is the way menders write programs, create graphics, design and build websites in the realm of pure thought, pure energy.

I usually avoid computers, but once, for a period of several months, I felt driven to learn how websites are made. Because my chosen industry, writing and publishing, was being completely disrupted by new technologies, my Imagination (to my conscious mind's great surprise) came up with an idea for an Internet-based business. The whole enterprise would rely on computer technology, and perhaps for that reason, I suddenly became fascinated with learning to build a website.

It was very strange; during the months that I learned the basics of writing code, I morphed into a prototypical computer nerd. I slept little, stopped exercising, and spent hundreds of hours peering at chunky instruction manuals, tapping in the code they taught me, then running the programs I'd written to see if they worked. (They did—after approximately ten thousand failures apiece.) My hair grew shaggier. I developed acne. When my rimless glasses broke, I glued the lenses to a reshaped paper clip and kept programming. When the paper clip broke—this is true—I took clear packing tape and stuck my glasses lenses directly to my face. I simply could not tear myself away from the computer long enough to go to an optometrist.

To master wayfinder magic, you have to have this kind of passion for the medium of Imagination. You have to be willing to spend hours in Wordless Oneness, feeling the medium of reality as it encounters your consciousness. You need to explore what might (let's just Imagine this) be a subjective sense of the "quantum foam" that is the basic medium of all matter. Menders in every culture spend thousands of hours learning in this way before they become competent Imaginers. The way to "program" the thought realm isn't as simple as stamping our tiny princess feet and demanding that reality conform to our wishes, but with commited deep practice you can feel yourself gaining traction.

Here are two more exercises you can use to practice Imagining your own future. Remember to stay relaxed and Wordless, as connected to the One world as you can be.

Imagination Liberation: Visit an Uncharted Island in Your Own Life

1. Sit in a quiet place when you won't be interrupted for five to ten minutes.

2. Think of a place in your life where you feel a sense of lack, dissatisfaction, or uncertainty. Close your eyes and picture it.

3. By noticing what you don't like about this part of your present reality, clearly Imagine a different reality where you'd be more satisfied. Notice and describe this situation in great detail. Where there are fuzzy areas, give the situation permission to happen as it wants to happen, to violate your expectations, even do something you might not like. Fill in the entire scene, including full sensory detail. Hear, smell, taste, touch, and see the new situation.

4. You are now sitting at your destination. Just because it exists only in your Imagination doesn't make it unreal—every real thing humans have created existed first in Imagination. Appreciate and enjoy your new, improved life situation. Feel and express gratitude for it.

5. Open your eyes and go back to living as usual. Let go of your Imagined life and keep trying to make things turn out the way your personality thinks they should. But trust that your Imagination is working with the situation you've envisioned, the best possible outcome for you and everyone else who may be involved.

6. Remain alert; the changes you have Imagined are already trying to occur. You'll have opportunities to either allow them in or push them away. Allowing them in may be more frightening than you think. Stay on the canoe and keep sailing (by staying in Wordlessness and Oneness), and the island will come to you.

HOW TO SPOT SUCCESS

You'll know you're beginning to work competently with Imagination when three things happen:

1. Within you, the nervous scurry of conscious thought will cease. Your emotional attachment to achieving certain outcomes will disappear. Instead you'll feel a deep, calm sureness that your

ultimate goal has already been reached, your true desire satisfied, even if you can't physically see it yet. You'll be completely content with whatever is happening, knowing that it is the perfect set of conditions for the best future you can Imagine. The tiny boat of the present moment will obviously contain everything you need; you'll feel certain that the island is sailing toward you.

2. Around you, signs of guidance will begin to appear, the way the beam of light appeared on Nainoa's shoulder. Synchronicities, chance meetings, and information will give you whatever you need to make the Imagined thing materially real. People, animals, and things will find their way to you, even fight their way through barriers, to offer their help. Many of these meetings will be so improbable that to call them "chance" seems ridiculous. Yet none of this will surprise you at all; your Imagination will take it for granted, because its huge, omnipresent Self is programming, testing, and running the program that underlies all the events.

3. The situations you Imagine will occur in physical reality. Don't take my word for it. Believe it when you see it.

AWAKENING FROM THE DREAM OF FORM

If you spend a great deal of time Imagining reality from within Wordless Oneness, you may begin to see the world quite differently. You'll begin to realize that the way you once interpreted reality is in fact just another use of imagination. Because all observation is screened through perception, what we see as reality is always colored by our thoughts, and neuroscientists now realize that the brain is always shaping waking perception just as it shapes our night dreams. In fact, David Eagleman, a neuroscientist at the Baylor College of Medicine, writes that "the difference between being awake and being asleep is merely that the data coming in from the eyes *anchors* the perception . . . waking perception is something like dreaming with a little more commitment to what's in front of you."

Many ancient wayfinder traditions compare the proper use of Imagination not to falling asleep and dreaming, but to *awakening* from a dream.

Perhaps you've had the experience of waking from a nightmare and having to think for several minutes before you're really sure the dream wasn't real. Maybe you've had the opposite experience after something tragic happened to you: for a few seconds, as you woke up in the morning, you forgot that your loved one had the terrible illness, that the World Trade Center really did collapse in those few mind-numbing seconds. Then, horribly, you remembered, and the awful sorrow, fear, or rage returned. The doomed little being you saw as your real self got up to struggle through another long day's journey into night.

A wayfinder might ask how you're sure that this terrible reality isn't another nightmare—how you can be sure you aren't about to awaken again, into a reality altogether different and much more in harmony with your true nature. This is how people who have near-death experiences describe what it's like as they "die." I'm fascinated by these accounts, because I once experienced something similar. While undergoing surgery, I became alert and was able to look around the room, watching doctors operate on my body, though my physical eyes were closed. After a few seconds a brilliant white light appeared just above me. It felt conscious, completely familiar, and indescribably loving.

Recounting this experience in words is like trying to describe Niagara Falls by pointing at a hamster's dripping water dispenser. It was like awakening from a nightmare times a million million. I felt the same momentary disorientation, followed by the dawning memory of what felt much more real than the "dream" of my ordinary life, followed by relief so enormous it seemed to fill the universe.

Child development specialists say that babies love to play peekaboo because they haven't yet learned "object permanence." When Mommy's face disappears behind a blanket, they think she no longer exists (so the theory goes), and when she pops back in, the baby is amazed: Where the heck did *you* come from, Mommy? I like to toy with a different interpretation, based on my white light experience. Perhaps babies don't yet understand anything *but* object permanence. They're tuned in to Oneness, so the appearance of separation is unfathomable to them. When Mommy pops in ("Peekaboo!") they laugh with amazement that they briefly believed she was gone and relief that the universe is still functioning as it should.

When we fall in love, we are told, the region of the brain responsible for our sense of being separate from another "fails," allowing us the delicious sensation of connection with our loved one. But I think the brain's usual state of thinking we're separate is the illusion, the state that fails to perceive reality. Falling in love is a small awakening, and the further we follow our Imagination, the more we fall in love with all things. At some point we begin to realize that the way we've been seeing reality is only one limited, arbitrary, and comparatively impoverished view.

IMAGINING THE MENDER'S UNIVERSE

My near-death experience comes in handy when my friend Jayne is diagnosed with terminal cancer, during the writing of this book. Jayne's son Joey, who has Down syndrome, has been my son's best friend since both boys were knee-high. After the horrible diagnosis, Karen and I promise Jayne we'll help mother Joey and his sister after she's gone. The situation is all the more awful because these kids watched their beloved stepfather die, also from cancer, several years earlier.

The day before her death, Jayne finds the strength to joke with me about the fact that she has only one thing left on her To Do list. Her children, on the other hand, must go on living. There's nothing to say in the face of such loss; we just do a lot of hugging. The kids seem to be holding up very well, considering. Neither of them sheds more than a few tears as everyone bustles around arranging the funeral.

At the service I make sure Adam sits next to Joey, because I remember how the boys helped each other cope at the services for Joey's stepfather. Adam sat with his arm around his friend, squeezing his shoulder at the times when Joey quietly began to weep. This time Joey seems fine, almost detached. Then the funeral begins, and a friend of Jayne's stands up and begins to play the flute.

Suddenly Joey doubles up in his chair with a cry like a wounded animal. I've never heard such pure pain in my life. As he begins to sob I practically shove Adam to the floor so I can grab Joey. Maybe his heart and brain "entrain" mine, because as I hold him I feel an oceanic grief, far deeper than my own sorrow at losing my friend. I've never cried so hard in public myself, and yet I feel a strange lack of resistance to the sadness. It reminds me of the time in Africa when I tried to commune with the dying impala. Joey's grief is enormous, excruciating, unbearable, and completely clean.

After ninety seconds—the amount of time it takes the body to process a wave of intense, unrestricted emotion—Joey relaxes in my arms, panting as if he's run a race. I hold him as tightly as ever, but I can feel peace flowing through him now. Someone tells a story about Jayne, and Joey loudly corrects her, a good-natured, happy heckler. Then another spasm of grief grips him, and we cry again. It goes on like that through the whole service. It's like helping a woman give birth.

Adam has taken the seat next to me, and I sit between these two little men wondering, as I often do, if their consciousness is different from mine. Apes whose DNA is almost identical to humans live in a different mental universe—what might an entire extra chromosome do to the perceptions of people with Down syndrome? I remember my friend and editor Betsy Rapoport telling me about her conversation with an author who had autism. Betsy was discussing ultraviolet light, explaining that bees see things humans can't. "A bee could see streaks of color in this flower," she'd said, pointing to a plain white daisy. The author responded, "You mean you can't see the patterns in that flower?"

Sitting between Adam and Joey, I muse about the way they seem to be able to see in the dark, like cats. Does Down syndrome allow them to see infrared, below the visible light spectrum? Scientists tell us that 99.999 percent of the light in the universe is invisible to us. Can Adam and Joey see a different slice of that particular pie? Much more important, why is it that those affected by Down syndrome are capable of such extraordinary love? Does Down syndrome take from them the illusion of separation, that bit of frightened imagination that sends the rest of us reeling into darkness?

After the funeral, friends from Special Olympics bring in food for a meal, but Adam is exhausted and asks to go home. As we get in the car, he says, "Mom, I didn't cry."

"I know, honey," I say. "But it would be all right if you did. Even strong men cry at very sad times, and this is a very very sad time."

Adam thinks about this in silence for a minute or two. Then he says, "It's easier since the light came and opened my heart."

He speaks quite clearly, but I think I've misheard him. "What?" I ask. "Did you say a light came and opened your heart?"

"Yes," Adam says. "I was sitting on my bed in my room, and it came, and it touched my heart, and my heart opened. And ever since then, things aren't so hard."

We stop at a red light, and I stare at him. "When was this?"

"May tenth," he says. It's now February.

"You mean last year?"

"No. A long time ago. I was in middle school."

The signal turns green, and I drive silently for a while. "I'm really glad you told me that, Adam," I say finally. "Because I saw a light like that once too. And you're right—after it touches your heart, nothing is ever as hard again." At that moment I intensely regret that the tired old cliché "see the light" exists to trivialize something so utterly glorious. "I don't talk about it very often—I'm not sure most people understand," I tell Adam. "I'm really glad you do."

I glance over to see one of the biggest smiles Adam has ever smiled, which, believe you me, is saying something. We resume our usual companionable silence. Then, as I pull the car into our garage, I think of something that might give him comfort.

"You know, Adam, when I was with the light, it told me that it's always with us, even though we can't see it." I know he'll understand how the light can tell people things; it just does. But Adam's response takes me completely by surprise.

"Oh, I can see it," he says calmly.

My jaw drops.

"You can?"

"Sure," he says, sounding a little surprised that I can't.

"All the time?"

"Yes."

"Well . . . ," I have to think for a second. "So, *where* do you see it? Is it inside your chest, or your head, or next to you, or up by the ceiling, or what?"

Adam shakes his head slightly, smiling the patient, compassionate smile of a seasoned wayfinder talking to a dimwitted Cub Scout.

"Mom," he says kindly, "it's *everywhere.*"

And I Imagine it is.

FINDING THE ISLAND

Since our night of wild Imagination in Phillipolis, each person who was present has been creating physical versions of the things we Imagined. As is typical of magical things, the physical reality has unfolded slowly, appearing on the horizons of our lives like islands coming to meet us as we sit in the sacred canoe, the Wordless Oneness of the present moment.

Among other small victories, donors have contributed plenty of money to support Kate as she continues to work in Phillipolis. The political and financial arrangements necessary to restore the springbok migration have inched forward. Friendship and trust between the Restoring Eden crew and the people of Phillipolis have deepened. The master coach from Dubai has become an expert in healing trauma. Various film and writing projects—including the book you're reading right now—have gone from Imaginary to physical. (Boyd's book will be published shortly after mine.)

In short, all of us who went on that trip have kept sailing along by Imagination, rowing and tacking the sails and trusting the winds carrying us to undiscovered islands. It takes time. It takes thought. It takes effort. And it is completely magical. As we walk the pavement of our separate cities all over the world, still and always together in the Everywhen, our feet feel the rustling of the feet of the springbok.

Let your imagination pronk.

Nigel Dennis

CHAPTER NINE

PROBLEMS? WHAT PROBLEMS?
(USING IMAGINATION TO MEND YOUR LIFE)

The Vartys and I are having lunch on their deck overlooking the Msava River when the elephants in a breeding herd that's been browsing near the house all morning begin acting strangely, dashing around, trumpeting like Manhattan traffic. We humans move to the deck's railing to watch the activity in the undergrowth just below us. One cluster of wrinkled gray backs seems especially agitated—and extremely vocal. For about five minutes they scream like teenage girls at a Justin Bieber concert. Then the noise stops. Seconds later, four females edge slowly from the brush into a clearing right in front of us. They move in a tight cloverleaf formation, shuffling sideways. The Vartys, who've seen a lot of elephants from their deck, say they'd never seen them act this way.

"Wait," says Shan Varty, Boyd and Bronwyn's mother, pointing to one of the four females. "Look at that one—she's got blood on her trunk."

"And down her back leg," says Bronwyn, Boyd's older sister. "She's just given birth!"

As if on cue, the four female elephants draw slightly apart. Their inside legs, which form the center of the cloverleaf, are acting as pillars, supporting a tiny, wobbly thing that looks like a wet lavender pig with a limp sock on its face. The baby elephant is so new he can't stand without the support from his mother and aunties. They gently prop him up even as they move aside so we can see him. I mean, *they move aside so we can see him.* We will later discuss this at length without being able to think of any other reason for their behavior. We watch in silent awe as the proud new mom caresses her baby with her trunk. Finally Boyd breaks the silence.

"That," he says thoughtfully, "is a fresh elephant."

Later, sipping our postprandial tea, we debate whether the animals at Londolozi are aware that "their" humans are dewy-eyed conservationists, whether they're reciprocating when they do unheard-of things like showing off their brand-new babies to a pack of humans.

The fresh elephant.

"They *must* be responding to us," I say.

"It seems that way sometimes," says Boyd cautiously, "but we could be imagining it."

"Of course we're imagining it!" I exclaim, drunk on jet lag and baby elephant love. "That's why it happens!" I take a sip of tea and try to regain my rationality. "On the other hand, we should be able to test it. See if it's *just* imagination, or a physical phenomenon."

Bronwyn nods. "Well, why don't we 'call' an animal?" she says. "Something really unusual, so there's less chance it'll be a coincidence if we actually see it."

"I think we should call a unicorn," I say. This suggestion is immediately discarded on the grounds that calling unicorns famously requires the participation of virgins.

"Hmm," says Shan. "How about a nice fat python?"

"Not rare enough," says her husband, Dave.

"I have it!" Bronwyn exclaims. "Wild dogs!"

A general round of applause. African wild dogs are among the most endangered and least observed of the continent's large mammals. They're a separate species from domestic dogs, with a distinctive calico coat, large round ears, and long, lean, runway-model legs. Their hunting involves elaborate group cooperation; I've seen professional football teams that aren't half so organized. Wild dogs are extraordinarily, intelligently elusive, and human encroachment has devastated their numbers. They're rarely seen anywhere.

"No one's spotted a wild dog at Londolozi for at least ten years," says Bronwyn.

"Wild dogs it is, then!" I say. "Let's call 'em in."

Dave laughs. "Well, while you're at it, could you make it rain? The whole place is parched, and there's not a drop in the forecast."

He's joking, as are the rest of us. Even I haven't totally taken leave of my senses. It is in the spirit of Imaginative play, not fervid belief, that we all drop into Wordlessness, focus on Oneness, and do our best to "call" wild dogs and rain.

Then we go animal-watching. For three days we arise at 4:30 to be out tracking before sunrise. For three nights we stay up to see the savannah's night shift emerge under the brilliant stars (the skies remain cloudless). We go to bed around midnight and get up a few hours later to start out again. We see all sorts of animals and have numerous close encounters with virtually every sort of African beast—except wild dogs. Oh well, I think. I never really expected it to work.

By my final evening at Londolozi, we're all haggard and bleary. Sleeping very little and roaming the bush twenty hours a day hasn't been kind to our bodies.

"So," says Boyd as we bid each other good-night, "see you at 4:30 tomorrow morning?" His voice comes out like thick molasses. He looks like someone from a gritty documentary about crystal-meth addiction. For a moment, I drop wild-dog-seeking mode and go into Mom mode, worried about my friend's health. Then it hits me: we haven't been in Oneness at all during the past few days. Oneness is love, and we haven't been treating ourselves lovingly. We've been driving our bodies to exhaustion.

"No," I say. "Tomorrow we're sleeping in."

The others tried to protest, but they're much too weak. Part of me clings to a last internal protest: "Wait! I only have one more chance to see wild dogs." But I can feel the struggle, the weary dissonance, that thought creates in my body. When I return to what "wants to happen," I realize that the only compassionate option is to let our bodies sleep. So we do, for a long time.

I awaken at about ten the next morning, every cell of my body grateful for the long snooze. I feel healthy again. I also feel Oneness, like a strong, clear radio signal that has been thin and staticky for days. I pack my bags, hug the Vartys goodbye, and accept a ride in a Land Rover to Londolozi's airstrip. As I fasten my seatbelt on the small plane back to Johannesburg, the pilot says, "Please buckle in. We need to take off immediately to stay in front of the weather." That's when I notice towering anvil clouds rumbling in. As the plane takes off, it begins to rain. And a few miles away, for the first time in over a decade, trackers spot a pack of wild dogs running through Londolozi.

SOLVING PROBLEMS WITH YOUR IMAGINATION

This, along with the other "calling the wild" examples in this book, is an instance of using Imagination to influence events in the physical world. But this exercise wasn't a loose way of hankering for something and having reality serve it up immediately. My friends and I used all our skill in the physical world, as well as evaluating and correcting our use and misuse of the technologies of magic.

When menders use mind and body to help create the things we've Imagined, our technologies of magic intersect with our rationalist approach to life. We call this problem solving. Rationalism sees it as a purely logical process. New Age types often believe they can solve problems magically, but they don't use Wordlessness or Oneness. Instead of instantly "manifesting" the Rolex watches and Armani gowns they hold in their mind's eye, these people often end up drinking a lot.

The most gifted problem solvers in all cultures—the great scientists, engineers, and business people of our society, as well as ancient wayfinders—use Imagination to problem-solve in specific ways that are unusual for other people but very similar from wayfinder to wayfinder. They don't just use Imagination to get through stumbling blocks they encounter; they actually look for problems specifically to spark their Imagination (the way my friends and I decided to look for wild dogs). Skilled menders relish what most of us call "problems," recognizing them as the foundation of all good ideas, the source of all inspiration. This chapter is meant to help you use Imagination as they do.

USING PROBLEMS TO FREE YOUR IMAGINATION, AND IMAGINATION TO SOLVE YOUR PROBLEMS

Solving problems, not with ordinary imagination, but with the deep, magical Imagination of the creative artist, mystic, scientist, healer, and visionary, has four steps:

1. Ground yourself deeply in Wordlessness and Oneness. Failure to do this is why most attempts to "manifest" a desired outcome don't succeed.

2. Determine whether a problem exists at all in the physical realm, if it is purely imaginary, or if it has both imaginary and physical components.

3. Solve imaginary problems with Imagination. Ignore physical "solutions" that don't address the issue in its real sphere of existence (the imaginary realm) and so cannot be effective.

4. Clean up the physical aspects of the problem, if there are any.

As you read through this chapter you can practice these four steps on one of your own problems. Right now, think of a difficulty you're facing— preferably a repetitive, maddening problem you've been trying to solve for some time. Write it here:

_____

_____

Now open your Imagination, hold all beliefs lightly, and follow the instructions below.

Step One: Drop into Wordlessness and Oneness

Use any technique from part I and 2 of this book, or any other method of entering Wordlessness and Oneness, whatever works for you. As you drop into Wordlessness you may have trouble holding your problem clearly in mind. This is not a coincidence.

Step Two: Determine Whether Your Problem
Is Imaginary, Physical, or Both

Pretend you have a friendly animal with you. (If you happen to be sitting with an actual dog, cat, sheep, or herd of elephants, so much the better.) Consider the problem you wrote on the lines above. Here's the test: Can you explain your problem to an animal in such a way that the animal shares your belief that you have a problem?

If not, the problem is purely imaginary.

Wait! Before you start sending me enraged emails, hear me out. I didn't say your problem isn't *real*. It's real, all right. That was the major point of the previous chapter. Your broken heart, your fifty extra pounds, your credit card debt, the stalker who keeps texting you love notes with all those weird references to *The Sound of Music*—in short, all your problems are as real as death and taxes. But unless you can actually show them, right now, to a being who can't talk, they aren't physically real for you at this moment, in the physical spot where you're sitting. They exist for you only as stories in your imagination.

Many problems do have physical components an animal would recognize. When we're in pain, like Ned Rogers (see chapter 6), animals often know and seem concerned, as Kasey the monkey did. If your weird stalker came into the room, a dog, cat, or elephant (I'm not sure about sheep) would immediately sense an unstable creature and would become suitably alarmed. But if you're worrying about future catastrophe, nursing a grievance, or wallowing in self-pity, good luck communicating your problem to your basset hound, or even a talking parrot. They simply lack the imagination for such "problems."

Remember, the difference between ordinary imagination, which creates almost all our supposed problems, and Imagination, which is Wordless and therefore can't sustain painful stories, can be tested by seeing whether the thought you're thinking hurts or heals. Anything that causes no physical pain and can't be explained to a bunny rabbit is the product of negative imagination. It is real, but only in your head. Let go of what's in your head, and the "problem" will cease to exist.

Many of my clients get *furious* at me for saying their problems are imaginary. So let me be the first to acknowledge that I suffer immensely from this kind of dilemma. Here are some imaginary issues that, at one time or another, dominated my entire inner life: feeling totally alone in the universe; hating everything about my body; bewailing the fact that various people I loved no longer loved me; believing God despised me; worrying that I had some deadly disease; grieving my son's disability; fearing planes would fall from the sky carrying me or my loved ones; having way too much to do; realizing that I have seen everything that is done under the sun, and behold, all is vanity and a striving after wind. Okay, I cribbed that last line from Ecclesiastes, but believe me, honey: been there, done that.

Now in each and every case I've just mentioned, I truly thought my problems existed in objective reality, not just my imagination. I was wrong. The distressing things that caused all my pain—the problems— were purely and solely in the realm of thought. Here's a comparison between the *situations,* which were physically real, and the *problems,* which were products of my imagination:

SITUATION (WHAT HAPPENED)	PROBLEMS (WHAT HURT)
Through early adulthood, I was extremely emotionally stunted and didn't experience any strong positive emotional connections.	"I am totally alone in the universe."
My body never looked the way my culture said it should, and for many years it was crippled by chronic pain.	"My body is a horrible, loathsome monster."
Many people I dearly love no longer have active relationships with me.	"I've lost the ones I love."
Through my first thirty years, I was told frequently and vehemently that God was a narcissistic, judgmental humanoid male who would never, ever forgive me if I left my religion of origin (which I left).	"God hates me."
I had many physical symptoms and limitations that, for years, no one understood.	"I'm dying of some ghastly affliction."
My son has an extra chromosome in every cell; he's mentally and physically challenged.	"My son will have a blighted life; I've failed as a mother."
Planes sometimes crash; my loved ones and I sometimes fly in planes.	"We/I/they will die in fiery horror!"
There are many tasks necessary to keep my life running the way I like it.	"I have too much to do!"
Most human activity seems totally pointless to me, and we're all going to die.	"All is vanity and striving after wind."

You might want to write down the situational basis of your problem, the one I asked you to write down on page 156. Here's some space:

SITUATION (WHAT HAPPENED)	PROBLEMS (WHAT HURT)

If you feel stymied at this point, I should admit that this is a bit of a trick question. As we began this exercise, I asked you to drop into Wordlessness and access Oneness. If you are firmly rooted in these states of being, you might not have been able to fill in the blanks above. From the Wordless perception in which we are all One, most problems simply don't exist. Extra credit if you couldn't think of a single real problem that's bothering you right now. The rest of us yokels will continue to Step 3 of our problem-solving process.

Step Three: Solving Imaginary Problems in the Realm of Imagination

My partner, Karen, is a social work professor at Arizona State University's College of Public Programs. One day another professor, proofreading a grant application, found a typo in Karen's curriculum vita. It said she worked for the "College of Pubic Programs." Although "Pubic Programs" sounds much more exciting than "Public Programs" (the waxing seminars alone must be thrilling!) it wasn't strictly accurate.

Given this problem, what would you do? Probably just what Karen did: laugh, blush, and head for the computer to correct the error. You wouldn't print out a slew of résumés and then run around trying to change each one with White-Out and a pen, or call grant administrators to say, "You see where it says I work in the College of *Pubic* Programs? That's a typo. It should say '*Public* Programs.' Could you just pencil in an 'l' there? My bad."

Imagination is the way we write code on the energetic Internet, formulating new ideas, actions, and objects. *Most of us are working with flawed Imagination programs that churn out the same "misprints" over and over, believing something that doesn't lead to effective behavior or happiness.* But instead of finding the misprint in our own thoughts and correcting them there, we continue to try to fix the same damn error in dozens of identically "problematic" physical situations. Metaphorically speaking, we don't change the computer code, but instead try to alter every paper copy by hand once it's printed. This is such a pivotal error in our cultural mind-set that it's worth a few more examples.

Erica was a beautiful, sweet-natured acquaintance of mine who married a wealthy older man and had three strapping sons. Then Erica's husband left her for a younger beautiful, sweet-natured woman. Erica needed money and companionship, so she began looking for another rich husband. She was quite open about this as her problem-solving strategy. She eventually married an elderly man who was rich as Satan and almost as much fun to live with. "Part of me will be relieved when he dies," Erica told me frankly. "Living with him is not an easy job." Husband #2 finally expired, leaving Erica a small fortune. But five years later her funds ran low. "I'm working on the problem," she assured me the last time I saw her. "Do you know any rich older men?"

Alan's problem was that he performed brilliantly for his employers but never got the credit or remuneration he deserved. He had changed jobs half a dozen times by his fortieth birthday, adding many zeroes to the bottom line of each company he served but always losing out when it came time for bonuses and promotions. "I still haven't found the right company," he told me. "How come everyone in corporate America is a total ass?"

Cindy was a writer with a fertile creative mind. Not only did she write beautiful poetry and essays, but she also had genius ideas for marketing them online. She shared all her ideas with other writers and publishers, hoping they'd help her get her career off the ground. Each time the other parties stole her ideas, building the websites and marketing initiatives Cindy had created, giving her neither career assistance nor money.

Greg is handsome, funny, smart, successful, and straight, just the sort of man you'd expect to be thronged by women. Yet while his friends married and had families, Greg never even had a long-term girlfriend. He rarely dated, and when friends lined him up with eligible women, he invariably found them appalling. "Every single woman I've ever gone out with has done something unforgivable on the very first date," he told me. "Why do I have such unbelievably bad luck?"

Two words: Pubic Programs.

All these people had created mental computer code with misprints in it, errors that printed out the same way in one physical scenario after another.

All of them spent enormous time and energy trying to solve their problems of the imagination by changing their physical situations, printing out the same error from the computer, then trying to correct it on paper. If you keep running into the same problem, it's because you have a misprint in your imagination, your mental model of reality. Find and correct the erroneous code, and the physical problem will disappear. In the process you'll free your mind from the limited imagination that caused the problem, allowing it to Imagine the healing visions of the mender.

SPOTTING THE IMAGINARY TYPOS BEHIND PHYSICAL PROBLEMS

Like Karen, whose eagle-eyed colleague found the typo on her résumé, you have a helpful proofreader continuously pointing out misprints in the code you write with your imagination. Your own subconscious mind, the alert, subtle, nonverbal self, is specifically designed to spot typos, get your attention, and motivate you to change the problem at the level of your thinking, the only place you can create the needed repairs. The signal your proofreader uses to point out bad code is a neon-vivid highlighting device that basically says "In This Area, Your Life Totally Sucks."

My life coaches and I always start a session by asking the client, "What's the area of least satisfaction in your life right now?" (I do have a few rather daring coaches who start by shouting out the pithier phrase, "So, what sucks?") For some people, the area of least satisfaction can be a tar pit of dread, rage, and despair. For those who have fewer typos in their imagination, "least satisfaction" means things that are slightly less thrilling than other aspects of their joyful lives. The four examples just mentioned fall in the midrange of suckiness. Erica was worried about running out of money, Alan felt underrewarded at work, Cindy was sick of people stealing her ideas, and Greg couldn't find a romantic partner.

Before sending these people out to make laborious changes in the physical world, a good coach would find the mental misprint that was spewing out the same flawed situations over and over again. The way to do this is to let suffering point out the errors in the code of imagination, showing that you've overridden your wayfinder's Imagination with a feeble imposter. Let's do this for you, right now, using your practice problem. Write your answers to the following questions in the spaces provided.

1. When you think about your problem, what do you feel physically?

_____

_____

2. Where in your body is the physical sensation related to the problem?

_____

_____

3. How would you describe this sensation? Is it a burning, tightening, choking, numbing, tickling? How big is it? What color is it? What shape?

_____

_____

4. Describe the emotion related to this sensation. If you had to put it into one of the four categories "mad," "sad," "glad," or "scared," where would it go? (It might fit in more than one category.)

_____

_____

5. Allow the sensation to fill your awareness without any resistance; let it run riot. Now find a thought that's associated with this sensation. If you pay attention, you'll "hear" the thought internally. Several thoughts may come up: pick the one that's associated with the most miserable sensation. Write the most horrifying, disconsolate, or enraging thought that accompanies your awful sensation.

_____

_____

Congratulations! You've just isolated a typo in the computer code of your imagination. Your imagination is so powerful—even when it's not a wayfinder's magical Imagination—that every physical situation you create without fixing this misprint will create the same damn error, the same Pubic Programs, with absolute fidelity. It's useless to try to solve your problem in the world of form without fixing the error in the formless realm first. That's why the seemingly "inactive" magic of Wordlessness and Oneness absolutely must precede trying to create something magically wonderful in the physical world.

It's easier to see this in other people's lives than in our own, so consider Erica, Alan, Cindy, and Greg. After going through the exercise above, they identified the following typos in their minds. Erica's most miserable thought was "My only value is my sexual desirability." For Alan, it was "I'll never get the respect I deserve." Cindy's error code said "I'm creative, but I can't do business." And Greg's mental misprint was "I can't trust anyone."

All these people—and you and I—wrote the erroneous patches of code in our mental computer programs because of painful experiences. All of our parents made mistakes, and all of us suffered various traumas and losses. But I'm not even going to talk about those situations here, because *the experiences that create misprints in our energetic code are interesting but not important, and not all that useful.* What's important and useful is changing the code.

CORRECTING THE CODE OF YOUR IMAGINATION

To fix the programming errors that create your problems, replace the thoughts behind the Areas of Suckiness with a Wordless observation of the world. This taps you in to Oneness, which eliminates most problems from your experience so completely and immediately it's a bit anticlimactic. (For me, one of the most delicious things about working with people who spend a lot of time practicing the technologies of magic is that there's virtually no drama or wasted effort as we solve problems or examine mistakes, just a shared enjoyment of the process.)

To show you how this works, recall the imaginary problems I mentioned a few pages ago, the ones that caused so much *Sturm und Drang* in my own life. You've already seen how my mental code made problems out of the various situations I described. Well, here's how I see the very same situations from the perspective of Wordlessness and Oneness.

SITUATION (SAME AS BEFORE)	AS I SEE IT FROM WORDLESS ONENESS
Through early adulthood, I was extremely emotionally stunted and didn't experience any strong positive emotional connections.	All my life I have been surrounded by love. In fact I am made of love, as is every other thing. Aloneness is impossible, illusory.
My body never looked the way my culture said it should, and it has experienced lots of pain.	I am temporarily inhabiting an amazing animal that is willing to suffer so I can learn.
Many people I dearly love no longer have active relationships with me.	For a moment, minuscule aspects of love can drift apart in the sea of love; it's like a dance.
Through my first thirty years, I was told frequently and vehemently that God was a narcissistic, judgmental humanoid male who would never, ever forgive me for leaving my religion (which I left).	What?
I had many physical symptoms and limitations that, for years, no one understood.	Physical existence has taught me things through pain that enhance my capacity for joy.
My son has an extra chromosome in every cell; he's mentally and physically challenged.	I live with a spiritual master. If you disagree, I respectfully do not care.
Planes sometimes crash; my loved ones and I sometimes fly in planes.	Oh look, a plane.
There are many tasks necessary to keep my life running the way I like it.	Here I am. What shall I do?
Most human activity looks totally pointless to me, and we're all going to die.	What a strange, delicious game we're playing!

Of course, I don't see things this way all the time, only when I'd rather not suffer. And I'm not saying my perception of Oneness is absolute truth. It's just a pain-free way to Imagine reality, a healing stand-in for the mind-set from which various situations looked like painful problems. When I choose to Imagine that my perception of Oneness is true, I'm kinder, happier, healthier, more productive, and better at everything, from making my bed to making a living.

How would you perceive your problem if you Imagined, just for experimental purposes, that Oneness is an accurate description of reality? Rewrite your own problematic situation, and then capture it as it appears when you Imagine the world this way.

SITUATION (WHAT'S HAPPENING)	SEEN FROM WORDLESS ONENESS

When Erica, Alan, Cindy, and Greg dropped into Wordlessness and connected with Oneness, their problems all but vanished. Erica had a breakthrough when she began Imagining herself through the eyes of her Siamese cat. To the cat, Erica wasn't a pathetic aging sex object; she was a powerful, resourceful human with almost infinite options for thriving. As Erica became more convinced that this Imagined view of herself may be true, she realized that her keen eye for investment could lead to a career in finance. She also made excellent personal investment strategies and rebuilt her fortune without needing another miserable, exploitive marriage.

Alan went Wordless through the paths of play, focusing on moments when his love for doing work as a game overwhelmed his dark thoughts about evil management. By focusing his attention on his abilities, he earned respect from the person who set the tone for all his social interactions: himself. He began Imagining that he was really the cool-beans dude his Wordless self saw him to be. His behavior became more confident and relaxed, and coworkers and bosses started treating him much, much better.

Cindy, the writer, went into a mode of silent observation and realized that she was very intuitive. She could feel the transmission of emotional energy between herself and the people she hoped would help her establish a career. Once she began watching alertly, instead of rerunning her self-denigrating stories, she saw that her energy was so tentative other people didn't even realize she wanted to work with them. She was broadcasting weakness, and they sent back slight disappointment that Cindy seemed unavailable for collaboration. She began Imagining that her work was in high demand, reached out with more enthusiastic energy, and was soon hired to write a blog for a smart, literate website.

Greg realized that he'd been vigorously avoiding Oneness his whole dating life. The mental code "I can't trust anybody," written during an awful childhood, sent out a powerful fear signal that felt to Greg's acquaintances—especially women—like a massive force field of rejection. Greg had to spend considerable time in Wordlessness, Imagining a new, safe universe, before he felt safe connecting with a philodendron, let alone a woman. He practiced letting himself feel Oneness with plants, then animals, re-Imagining them as loving and accepting. It turned out they'd been that way all along. Greg adopted a pound mutt, and a few years later fell happily in love with a female Team member he met at the dog park.

These felicitous results weren't one-offs, solutions to just one problematic situation. Happy solutions began appearing throughout these people's lives as they replaced their mental programs by Imagining a reality filled with peace and connection. "Pubic Programs" changed to "Public Programs" in hundreds of situations once they'd corrected the errant strip of code that caused the problems. Other situations that might have developed into dreadful problems disappeared quickly, or never happened at all.

Lest you think this is because the problems weren't really serious, remember there are people who live in extraordinarily problematic situations while remaining continuously tapped in to Wordlessness and Oneness, and they seem to Imagine that these situations are problem-free. I've already mentioned Aung San Suu Kyi and Imaculée Ilibagiza, who learned to live this way despite the murder of their loved ones and constant threats to their lives. The Dalai Lama wrote *The Art of Happiness* after seeing his country sacked and occupied, his people massacred, his culture deliberately destroyed, and virtually every other component of his expected life taken from him. The spiritual teacher Byron Katie likes to say, "When I walk into a group of people, I know they all love me. I just don't expect them to realize it yet." This joyful grounding in Oneness means there is literally no way to hurt her feelings. Is she Imagining things? Of course she is—things that heal. And it's working for her.

All of these people act in the physical world to change less than optimal situations. They go to the doctor when they're sick, heat up soup when it's cold, encourage and champion those who suffer, lead the occasional massive social movement based on peace and justice. The Wordless, Oneness-based Imagination isn't inert or paralyzed. It solves all sorts of problems in the physical realm—that's one of its favorite games. Which takes us to Step 4.

Step Four: Cleaning Up the Physical Elements of Problems

When my friend Jayne was dying, her dog Sam seemed very much aware of her distress. At times when she felt fear, sadness, or physical pain, Sam would try, often with maddening persistence, to get through the tubes and bars of her at-home hospital bed and physically touch her. He'd lay his head on her lap or try to lie next to her, offering her comfort. The irony is that Sam also had cancer. Not having a human imagination, however, he didn't experience this as a problem. For him, the only problem was "Jayne's uncomfortable." And that part of the situation really was a problem that could be solved, or at least ameliorated, with good hard physical and mental work. Sam could lick Jayne's hand, and we humans, with our wonderful legacy of inventions, could give her intravenous fluids, antibiotics, and morphine.

This simplification of problem solving into present, physical action is beautifully addressed in the opening chapters of *Eat, Pray, Love,* which find Elizabeth Gilbert kneeling on her bathroom floor, sobbing, as she's been doing for many nights. She has what most people would see as a very big problem: she's entrenched in a life and marriage that look perfect— a husband, a house, plans for a baby—but she wants out. She's scoured her mind and heart endlessly, looking for solutions, but come up empty. Finally, in desperation, she begins to pray.

> The prayer narrowed itself down to [a] simple entreaty—*Please tell me what to do*—repeated again and again. I don't know how many times I begged. I only know that I begged like someone who was pleading for her life. . . .
>
> Then I heard a voice. . . . How can I describe the warmth of affection in that voice, as it gave me the answer that would forever seal my faith in the divine?
>
> The voice said: *Go back to bed, Liz.*
>
> I exhaled.
>
> It was so immediately clear that this was the only thing to do. I would not have accepted any other answer. I would not have trusted a great booming voice that said either: *You Must Divorce Your Husband!* Or *You Must Not Divorce Your Husband!* Because that's not true wisdom. True wisdom gives the only possible answer at any given moment.

This is what dear old Sam was offering Jayne, something any animal would completely understand. This is the combined power of the first three technologies of magic—Wordlessness, Oneness, and Imagination—

solving an actual, physical problem. The rest of Gilbert's story follows her as she travels around the world, resolving her life situation and emotional pain by following the path of a true wayfinder. While she resolves mighty questions in her Imagination, she never encounters any actual problem that she can't solve with divinely simple physical measures like eating, praying, or loving. The title of her book sums up an entire problem-solving strategy that could work for a whole human life.

Consider your practice problem, the one you wrote in the blanks above. Is there any aspect of it that is creating a gap, right here and now, between the physical reality you want and the physical reality you're experiencing? Remember, this rules out abstractions like "I need more money": unless you are at this moment trying to purchase something you want, that problem is imaginary. Real, present, physical problems are simple. A horse would understand the solutions. A cat or anteater would totally get them. If you're cold, go someplace warmer, put on an extra sweater, get a blanket. If you're lonely, ask someone for a hug, or read the writing of someone who found the way out of loneliness. If you're in pain, relax—and use whatever physical mechanisms you can, the way Jayne is using morphine.

In short, go back to bed, dear.

Once you've done all you can to make yourself physically comfortable in the present moment, and you're so grounded in Oneness and Wordlessness that you have no emotional discontent, you may turn your Imagination to things like building a fortune, eradicating social injustice, or saving the world. In fact that's what you *will* do as you express your true nature—the wayfinding Imagination will go much further than your comparatively tiny mind could dream.

But the problem solving you do with a free Imagination will lose the panicky air of necessity and take on the much more powerful energy of play. I like to call it "puzzle cracking," because it begins with a perspective in which very few "problems" arise. The next chapter is all about using your Imagination to crack puzzles. But before we go there, I must admit that a free Imagination, combined with mental and physical work, all targeted at the same "problem," often creates miracles. I don't know how; I've just seen so many inexplicable things happen this way that I'd be lying if I didn't mention them. If you start Imagining from the peaceful void of Wordless Oneness, you're going to see changes in the physical world that match what's happening in your Imagination.

CLEANING UP PHYSICAL PROBLEMS SOLELY BY ALIGNING WITH THE WAYFINDER'S IMAGINATION

Let's start with something that was considered hooey in my childhood, but is now widely accepted by medical science: our imagination affects our physical bodies. The way we think can resculpt the tissues of our brains and change our physical health dramatically, though no one's sure exactly how. We know that we can worry ourselves sick, causing hormonal havoc through stress. We can also Imagine ourselves well, to a degree researchers are just beginning to understand.

For example, in one recent experiment 65 percent of patients with irritable bowel syndrome who took a placebo saw improvement in their symptoms, compared to 35 percent who were taking nothing. This happened *even though the doctors told them all along that they were taking a placebo.* When they ran out of pills they knew were just sugar, these patients' symptoms recurred as if they had stopped taking real medication. Several of them finally went to health food stores, bought some damn pill or other that contained nutritional supplements rather than medication, and started taking those. Then, sure enough, their symptoms improved. Just the act of taking pills helped them Imagine their physical tissues back to health.

In another experiment, elderly men were asked to imagine they'd gone back in time. They lived in a facility decorated with items from the first half of the twentieth century, heard radio programs from the same era, and were not allowed to use or discuss anything that happened after 1950. At the end of the study, the test subjects appeared to have aged in reverse: they had stronger immune function, better sensory perception, more grip strength, and get this—their fingers had lengthened!

Unfortunately that study was done in the 1990s, and I am now living in a concrete bunker decorated with 1980s paraphernalia, refusing to talk about anything that happened after the Reagan administration, so I can't write about it any more. Also my massive shoulder pads and large hair are making it difficult to type. My point is that even before we set out to invent an object or a process in the physical realm, the code we write with Imagination begins seeping from purely imaginary reality and creating new realities in our flesh-and-blood bodies.

PHYSICAL PRINTOUTS FROM
CORRECTED IMAGINARY CODE

Not only our bodies, but our relationships, careers, and other "problematic" situations often change spontaneously as we re-Imagine the world. We behave differently, in subtle and not so subtle ways, as we become more and more used to using the first three technologies of magic. Without any problem solving other than Imagination, perhaps through the Energy Internet, our lives begin to fix themselves. Here are some things that happened to my own "problems" when I switched from imagining the world mechanistically to Imagining it as menders do.

SITUATION (WHAT HAPPENED)	SPONTANEOUS PHYSICAL CHANGES AFTER RE-IMAGINING THE WORLD
Through early adulthood, I was extremely emotionally stunted and didn't experience any strong positive emotional connections.	My life is absolutely flooded with people I adore, who give every indication of adoring me back.
My body never looked the way my culture said it should, and it experienced lots of pain.	I came to enjoy living in my body. Chronic issues like excess weight and pain disappeared.
Many people I dearly love no longer have active relationships with me.	I feel love and joy when I think about these people and my relationships with them.
Through my first thirty years, I was told frequently and vehemently that God was a narcissistic, judgmental humanoid male who would never, ever forgive me for leaving my religion of origin (which I left).	I experience an almost continuous sense of being infinitely loved by a benevolent higher power.
I had many physical symptoms and limitations that, for years, no one understood.	Though I was diagnosed with several incurable diseases, all my symptoms are in remission.
My son has an extra chromosome in every cell; he's mentally and physically challenged.	Adam feels and brings me infinite joy; a book I wrote about him launched my career.
Planes sometimes crash; my loved ones and I sometimes fly in planes.	I love flying.
There are many tasks necessary to keep my life running the way I like it.	Mysteriously, if I do only what I want, everything gets done.
Most human activity seems totally pointless to me, and we're all going to die.	I love playing the human game and have no fear of death.

You might want to experiment with your own life by picturing situations from a wayfinder's Imagination and watching how things play out for you. Based on what I've observed in my own life, in hundreds of other coaches, and in thousands of clients, I suspect that as you use the third technology of magic, every "problem," from your chronic heartburn to your epic heartbreak, will begin to shift, soften, and change in the direction that makes you happier.

If you keep this up for any length of time, things are going to start getting strange, the way they did at Londolozi when my friends and I finally got our Imaginations aligned with Wordlessness and Oneness. There's no way our physical behavior caused rain and wild dogs to appear simultaneously. It could have been a coincidence, but it would've been a whopping one. It's one thing to recognize that your body and mind respond to Imagination. It's another to see distant parts of physical reality apparently doing the same thing.

WHEN THINGS GET WEIRD

As your everyday imagination turns into the wayfinder's Imagination, you'll start to feel like the sorcerer's apprentice: pretty much everything you Imagine will begin appearing in your physical reality. Unlike the apprentice in the cautionary tale, however, you won't abuse your power, because anything acquisitive or grasping comes from ordinary imagination, not Imagination, and so has very little power. Only love does real magic. As long as the Vartys and I were trying to force-manifest wild dogs and rain, nothing happened. It was only after we felt our way back to compassion that the things we Imagined appeared.

I thought the animal calling experiment had failed for me because I didn't see the wild dogs the day they arrived at Londolozi. But on the day I return, months later, I learn the animals have done something more improbable than anything we Imagined. That particular pack of wild dogs stopped their usual nomadic wandering to establish a den and breed, something they do only rarely.

"Please, can we drive out to see the den?" I beg my friends. I know we won't actually see the animals; wild dogs are known for being so furtive that almost no one ever gets a good look at them. I just want to examine their tracks, which to me can be almost as interesting as seeing the beasts themselves. So Boyd and Bronwyn, ever obliging, drive me to the abandoned termite mound where the wild dogs have holed up.

Almost immediately after we park the Land Rover, two slender calico creatures emerge from the den and stand there smiling doggy smiles, as if in welcome. Then, one after another, five little puppies spill out of the termite mound and begin playing just a few feet from us. The adults lie down to watch, content and relaxed. Once again the animals of Londolozi seem to be doing something inexplicable, trusting us near the most precious thing in the universe: their babies. I sit there stunned with gratitude, wondering once more if this could possibly be real. If not—if I'm dreaming it all up in my head—I can only say that I never again want to leave the realm of Imagination.

Imagine that.

Bigstock Photo

CHAPTER TEN

LET YOUR IMAGINATION
CRACK YOUR PUZZLES

There aren't any keys at Londolozi—they tend to get lost and become litter—but every time I visit, the guest cottages have fancier locks. At least on the outside. Inside, the doors have always had simple sliding bolts, but the exteriors boast constantly upgraded wrought-iron gizmos that have to be unscrewed, unhooked, yanked up or down while being pulled sideways, and Lord knows what-all.

This constant upgrading mystifies me until one afternoon, when I return to my cottage to find an enormous male baboon standing at the door, examining the fancy-schmancy lock. The expression on his face reminds me of one of my old professors, who used to focus so intensely on logical problems that his eyes looked like they'd burn through paper. The baboon doesn't even flinch when he sees me, just yawns in a way that says, "It's not that I acknowledge your existence, it's just that I could easily puncture your skull with my incisors." This brings back even more memories of my professor, so I sit down on a rock to reminisce. I hope the baboon won't figure out how to deal with the lock before I figure out how to deal with him.

Eventually a ranger comes by, carrying a slingshot expressly used to chuck small pebbles at invasive primates, and the baboon reluctantly climbs a tree. As I open the lock, I can feel his laser eyes scrutinizing my every move. He's lost that battle, but the unsolved puzzle is eating at him, and I have a hunch he'll eventually solve it.

The baboons of Londolozi don't need to get into the guest cottages, but oh, how they love to try! If they do manage to break in—usually when a guest fastens the mechanism incorrectly after leaving the room—the baboons go on a wild rumpus, raiding minibars, drinking hand lotion, opening suitcases and stealing the contents. They put panties on their heads and lipstick on their knuckles. They nap and crap on the fine linens. They trash the place like rock stars, requiring a potent, ecofriendly "baboon soap" for cleanup. Hence the arms race: humans change locks, baboons puzzle out how to open the new mechanisms, and repeat.

These animals are almost our equals at solving puzzles once we've invented them, and their near-obsessive love of puzzle cracking is obvious. But you never see them smelting iron deadbolts, building guest cottages, or making their own damn lotion. Humans learned to do all these things with the very same puzzle-cracking compulsion that drives baboons. But we have a huge advantage: language. It allows us to take quantum leaps in puzzle cracking, where other apes pretty much plod along.

It's ironic that the same abstract verbal thinking that makes us such fertile problem *generators* also makes us world champion problem *solvers*. Most people use their imagination far more often to problem-create than to problem-solve. But once we reach the place of the wayfinder's Imagination— the amused, intense, fascinated mind that sees everything as a possibility, and nothing as a real tragedy—there are no limits to what we can invent. We can find our way through anything the wild world throws at us.

In the last chapter I defined "problems" as either imaginary thought demons or simple things you can change for the better right here and now; in this chapter I use the word "puzzle" to mean the difficult situations about which many wayfinders worry: how to make a living, stay healthy, find true love, be accepted by others, feed the hungry, eliminate cellulite, avoid joining a cult, clean up the Texas-size mess of plastic in the Pacific Ocean, save the world.

THE THREE STEPS TO CRACKING ANY PUZZLE

You need only three things to solve any puzzle with Imagination: the playful curiosity that comes from a basically problem-free worldview, a definite purpose for solving that particular puzzle, and the self-operating creativity of your wondrous, computer-like human brain. The conscious part of this process requires that you deliberately set your Imagination to find its way through the puzzle; in other words, you metaphorically write code on the Energy Internet to create a puzzle-solving program. Once you do this, your mind—and perhaps something larger, the One Mind—runs its wayfinding software and spits out solutions. You set this up, but you don't actually *do* it, any more than you do the math for a computer spreadsheet. This kind of puzzle cracking is delicious and powerful magic, and there are infinite ways to use it. I'll just offer a few basics here, to get you started on a process you were born to use and enjoy.

Again, as you read through the following instructions, you may want to practice on a puzzle from your own life. In the following space, write down a "problem" you're trying to solve. This is the puzzle you'll work with throughout this chapter. Let's call it Puzzle X.

PUZZLE X ("PROBLEM" I'VE BEEN TRYING TO SOLVE)

_____

_____

Step One: Get into the Wayfinder's Problem-Free Mind-set
You know how to do this: just drop into Wordlessness and access Oneness. Some people think this will take away their motivation to fix their lives, because conventional wisdom says that the more urgent and horrible our circumstances, the better we are at coming up with solutions. However, research on creativity consistently shows that people are much, much better at coming up with creative solutions when they're unconcerned about the outcome, when they're basically playing, as menders must.

For example, when subjects are offered money to solve a problem that requires thinking outside the box, they arrive at solutions much more slowly than when they're just tinkering, without any positive or negative incentives. Dire necessity narrows and limits the brain's ability to connect ideas and arrive at fresh solutions. So does any form of rigidity, dull repetition, or judgment. Wordless Oneness is by far the optimal condition for brilliant puzzle cracking. If you feel a problem is *very serious,* that you *must* find the solution, get over it. Your wayfinding Imagination runs on fun, not stress.

Step Two: Define Your Ultimate Purpose for Cracking a Given Puzzle
Most people try to crack whatever puzzles life brings them, without ever stopping to ask if the solutions will serve their true nature. From the day you were born, the people around you took it for granted that you'd work hard to overcome certain obstacles simply because it was cultural custom. You were probably expected to go to school, get a job, and raise a family. Along the way you'd have to solve countless puzzles, from first-grade

spelling tests to cutthroat corporate politics. Billions of people devote their lives to solving such puzzles. Surprisingly few ever ask themselves why.

Reclaiming your true nature begins with knowing the purpose for *all* your puzzle solving. In fact, because social structures are becoming so fluid, failing to define your purpose these days leaves you wandering aimlessly from problem to problem, feeling lost and confused, wondering why no one is showing up to tell you the next step. Without the rigid structures of past societies, wayfinders not only can, but must, head toward some consistent purpose. Otherwise we'll get utterly lost in the chaos of this wild new world.

Think of something you're planning to do tomorrow. Then answer the question, "What is my purpose in doing this thing?" If the answer isn't clear right away, sit with it for a minute. Are you doing it to have fun, to please your mother, to keep your hair from sticking straight up like Albert Einstein's? Once you've got an answer, ask yourself, "What is the purpose I serve by achieving *that* purpose?" You can think of this as a "higher purpose." And there's probably an even higher purpose you'll serve by achieving that. Ultimately everything you do is connected to a series of higher and higher purposes. Keep asking "What is my purpose for doing *that*?" until you arrive at something that yields no higher purpose, but is a desirable end in itself. For example, here's how the exercise went with one of my clients, a guy named Alonzo:

Q: What are you going to do tomorrow?
A: Attend a professional conference.

Q: What's your purpose for attending the conference?
A: To find good people to hire for my company.

Q: What's your purpose for hiring good people?
A: To increase productivity.

Q: What's your purpose for increasing productivity?
A: To help my company survive and grow.

Q: What's your purpose for helping your company survive and grow?
A: To make sure I have a good job for the rest of my working life.

Q: What's your purpose for having a good job?
A: So I can have enough money to be financially secure.

Q: What's your purpose for being financially secure?
A: To live a long comfortable life and support my loved ones.

Q: What's your purpose in living a long comfortable life?
A: Just . . . to live a long comfortable life.

Q: What's your purpose in supporting your loved ones?
A: Well, so they can live long comfortable lives.

When you find yourself bumping repeatedly into a purpose that is an end in itself, its own excuse for being, you've arrived at what I call your "ultimate purpose." Alonzo's ultimate purpose is "having a long comfortable life." Clarifying that will help him choose which of infinite possible puzzles to crack. There's no use even taking on a challenge that has no possibility of fulfilling his highest purpose. And there may be other options that lead much more directly to his ultimate purpose than whatever he's planning to do.

I'm amazed that so few people have ever considered even the first iteration of this exercise. "What is my purpose in taking my kids to school (or attending my neighbor's wedding, or going to work, or mowing my lawn)?" they ask, looking at me as though I've just asked to fondle their eyebrows. "Well, because I have to." They're unconsciously serving the purpose of fulfilling societal expectations. Once I can get them to articulate that, they can start identifying the higher purposes beyond their immediate expectations. Usually they end up describing the same ultimate purpose as Alonzo's, something like "I want to live as long as possible, provide for my family, and be comfortable."

This is a beautiful articulation of the ultimate purpose locked into the evolutionary programming of every living creature: algae, tapeworms, even politicians. Countless humans have put every ounce of their puzzle-cracking skill into living long and comfortably. As a result, today a record number of humans are living long, well-fed, comparatively luxurious lives. Yet many of us spend our time and money taking more antidepressants to boost the effectiveness of our current antidepressants. We have what every living being is programmed to want—enough food and shelter to survive and reproduce—but it doesn't fulfill all the needs of our true nature.

Many of my clients express devastating disappointment after climbing a pyramid of achievement toward material success and finding that, as one woman put it, "When you get there, there's no 'there' there." Surviving to procreate in comfort is our evolutionary mandate, but it doesn't bring our hearts and souls back home. To do that we need a wayfinder's Imagination.

BEYOND THE PURPOSE OF LONG LIFE AND PROCREATION

Perhaps, like me, you've had the good fortune to be suicidally depressed at some point in your life. Wanting to die throws a curveball into the evolutionary ultimate-purpose game. If you have no desire to live and can't imagine bringing innocent children into a world of wretched despair, what purpose is left?

One bitterly cold night when I was seventeen, I sat in Harvard's Lamont Library (which I called "Lament"), considering this question. The study carrels at Lament are covered with graffiti from generations of students, which no one removes on the grounds that it's actually pretty interesting. (This is one of the many things I loved about Harvard.) That night, after much glum contemplation, I wrote on a small blank space between other students' comments, "My ultimate purpose is not to live. It is to experience joy, if joy is possible."

That moment permanently altered the course of my life. I wouldn't feel really joyful for a few more years, but I had unknowingly set my wayfinding Imagination to crack just one huge puzzle: how to be happy. Articulating that ultimate purpose influenced everything I've done since. It made me a risk-taker, an expectation-ignorer, a person with an agenda that made no sense to most people. I studied a weird blend of subjects, which my freshman advisor said would take me nowhere, simply because they interested me. I switched my major to Chinese, got a Ph.D. but didn't try for an academic career, kept my Down's baby, and ignored all professional practices unless they felt intrinsically joyful. I still act this way. It may be insane, but it's purposeful. What many friends and advisors have told me is a totally random series of choices has actually been the most direct path I could find toward the ultimate purpose of experiencing joy.

Though I've never abandoned the statement I carved into that Lament Library carrel, I've amended it a bit. As I found that joy always brought a sense of being One with all things, my ultimate purpose changed from feeling joy myself to maximizing joy for all beings—you know, "Each man's joy is joy to me" and all that. This is how I find my way through the world. It's my purpose for everything I do, including writing these words.

Think about your ultimate purpose, the reason beyond the reason beyond the reason you want to solve the life puzzle you've identified. Write your ultimate purpose here:

_____

_____

Now commit to solving only the individual puzzles that take you toward this ultimate purpose.

This can get a bit confusing, because each puzzle you solve may be a step toward multiple purposes. Think of your ultimate purpose as the peak of a pyramid of puzzles, like the ones pictured below. Each small arrow shape represents a life puzzle, and each solution leads to a higher-level puzzle. As you can see, many puzzle pyramids overlap, at least for a time.

For instance, finding a compatible mate who's a good earner would move you up a step on the money, joy, and romance pyramids all at once. But suppose you fall in love with an unemployed spendthrift? In that case, you have to decide which purpose to serve: If you choose to marry your penniless beloved, you've left the "money" purpose to follow "romance."

If you break up solely because of the financial issue, you've left "romance" to move toward "money."

I'm focusing on these three pyramids because modern culture tends to conflate them. Your parents, television ads, movies, and friends might implicitly or explicitly tell you that money, romance, and joy are just one pyramid, bottom to top; that getting a perfect lover and lots of cash are the very puzzles you must solve to reach happiness. But I've coached hundreds and hundreds of people who keep doing jobs they hate (thus climbing the money pyramid while leaving the joy pyramid) or cling to relationships that make them utterly miserable (thus choosing the purpose of romance over the purpose of joy) or both. I've never seen this make anyone enduringly happy. On the other hand, every single time I've seen someone choose the purpose of joy-for-all-beings over these more typical purposes, wayfinding miracles have ensued.

Step Three: Crank Up Your Magical Metaphor-Making Mind
This brings us to the second stage of Imaginative puzzle cracking: reaching into the Everywhen for solutions that help you achieve your higher purpose when finding your way through a difficult life puzzle. Problem solving is much less magical when we're fixated on the material objective of a long comfortable life. When we set our puzzle-cracking intentions to the purpose of joy-for-all-beings, something—maybe the miraculous human subconscious mind, maybe Something more miraculous still—can offer up solutions so brilliant they knock us down, so simple they make us smack our foreheads, so beautiful they bring tears to our eyes.

All these solutions include an intensely magic word: the word "like." Humans, with our highly developed language skills, have a unique ability to think in metaphors. Language itself is one huge metaphor; we accept that a word *is* the thing it represents. This isn't true, but the ability to Imagine it's true allows us to connect information, actions, and objects in unprecedented ways. The key to understanding all the astonishing puzzle solutions created by the human Imagination, every human insight or innovation for navigating the wild world, boils down to the little concept *This is like that.*

My friend the baboon is very nearly as smart as I am, yet when he sees a log floating on a river he wants to cross, he thinks, "Log on river." A human may look at the same log and think, "That log is moving like a horse," or "That river is like a road." Bing! The concept of boating is born, the puzzle of river crossing solved, by the magical concept "This is like that," which baboons, apparently, rarely use.

In every ancient wisdom tradition, wayfinders are taught to see metaphors in everything and to use metaphor to solve the puzzles that face humanity—especially the puzzles in the pyramid of joy-for-all-beings. I've listened to Native American medicine men tell long metaphorical stories that made my bones shiver, as though my body were recognizing the symbols my mind could barely follow: *This story is like the journey of my soul.* Asian mystics said enlightenment was *like* the moon reflected in a thousand teacups, *like* an uncarved wooden block, *like* a cloudless sky. Jesus, the world's all-time most popular wayfinder, was a veritable geyser of metaphors: "The kingdom of heaven is *like* a treasure," he says in the New Testament, but also "*like* a net," "*like* a mustard seed," "*like* a pearl," "*like* yeast." I'm sure if Jesus were a modern American, He could tell us how the kingdom of heaven is like a Laundromat, an Olympic bobsled team, a double order of fries and a Coke. The guy was a metaphor machine.

Metaphor is also the method by which our scientific and economic wayfinders have cracked the puzzles that gave us modern technology. James Watt realized that the valve on his teakettle was *like* a piston in an engine, and both could be moved by steam. Ta-da! The Industrial Revolution was born. Darwin recognized that species diversify *like* a tree branching. Einstein noticed the *likeness* between his own body riding away from a churchtower clock on a train, and a photon of light moving away from the same clock. In commerce, as the business writer David Murray writes, "creative thinkers are metaphorical thinkers. Period." As for the arts, they're Metaphor Central; every painting, poem, dance, or song is a metaphor for something.

Remember, ours is the only society in history to divide the roles of mystic, healer, scientist, and artist. Other cultures see all these skills as occupational functions of the wayfinder's Imagination. The secret to mastering creativity in any field is knowing how to *work with metaphor without getting caught in language*—a delicate tightrope walk, because language is so intimately married to metaphoric thought. For me, it helps a lot to know how the brain uses metaphor to solve puzzles, hopping back and forth between verbal and nonverbal programming.

UNDER THE HOOD OF IMAGINATION:
HOW THE BRAIN CRACKS PUZZLES

Generally speaking, the left side of the brain uses language to *analyze*—literally, to cut things up. Much of what you learned in school was knowledge chopped into manageable chunks, then fed bit by bit into your brain through words and numbers. This installed a lot of neuron pathways in your brain's left hemisphere, physical links that, according to neurologists, are relatively short and straight.

Your right hemisphere is devoted less to analysis than to *synthesis,* the process of combining, blending, or connecting different things. It's constantly asking itself, "What is this *like?*" Some of the neurons in your right hemisphere are longer than those in the left, and they physically wander around inside your head, as if feeling for each other. When two previously unconnected neurons meet, you may understand something in a way you've never understood it before. That's the moment you may exclaim, "Aha! *This is like that!*"

Using the "This is like that" key, you can program your wayfinder's brain to find your way through almost any puzzle you encounter in your life, including how to achieve your ultimate purpose. Remember the problem you wrote down earlier, the one we're calling Puzzle X? To crack it, you just have to think of some other thing—we'll call it "Thing Y"—that is *like* Puzzle X. Focusing on Thing Y will help you solve Puzzle X and achieve your purpose. The instructions below will walk you through this process a few different ways.

SOME CONCRETE WAYS TO RUN
YOUR PUZZLE-CRACKING PROGRAM

There are many games that help you write and run the puzzle-cracking program of your Imagination. Each of these methods boils down to the following four steps:

1. Use conscious, verbal thought to define the puzzle you want to crack.

2. Establish your purpose for cracking it.

3. Drop into Wordlessness and accessing Oneness, which revs up your nonverbal right hemisphere.

4. Power your Imagination with play and rest, like an alternating electric current.

If you take all these steps, eventually the solution—or at least an idea that will help lead to a solution—will pop out of your Wordless right hemisphere and become a conscious, verbal thought. This isn't *thinking* as you were taught to do as you prepared for your SATs. It's your true nature's amazing method of finding its way through the material world, working to create something that occurs first only in your Imagination.

METAPHOR GAME #1: MINING YOUR METAPHOR-MAKING MIND

Think of your Puzzle X, and go into a state of relaxed peace. (Doing both at once requires the discipline of a wayfinder, since your verbal mind may be tempted to see the puzzle as a problem, which will derail your puzzle-cracking hardware.) For purposes of demonstration, let's say your Puzzle X is one of my clients' favorites, "How can I make a living doing something I love?" After stating your question, drop into Wordlessness and accessing Oneness for thirty seconds or so. This will automatically expand your intention to include the ultimate purpose of joy-for all-beings (which lets your magical metaphor-making mind function optimally).

Now you're going to generate several metaphors related to Puzzle X. Do this by noticing how your puzzle is *like* any object you happen to see around you right now. To show you how this works, I'll do it right now. I'll notice objects near me, then let my brain suggest how each object may be *like* the process of making money doing something enjoyable.

RANDOM ITEM	SOMETHING ABOUT THIS ITEM THAT CATCHES MY ATTENTION	HOW THIS ITEM MAY BE LIKE EARNING MONEY JOYFULLY
Baseball hat	A baseball hat protects a player's eyes from sunlight.	I work more happily if I block distractions the way a hat blocks sunlight. I could put up a timespace "shield" to keep myself from being interrupted.
Photograph	Photos used to be slow to develop and hard to retouch. Now digital photographs develop instantly, and almost anyone can learn to do simple retouching on a computer.	Maybe I can use new methods to do something quickly that used to take lots of time. Then I can offer people something they value without putting in massive time and effort.
Dog	Dogs do everything for fun, and people support them lavishly for this very reason.	If I maximize my fun levels until I feel the buoyancy and happiness dogs do, maybe people will pay me just to hang out and bark.
Coffee mug	My favorite mug is one my daughter painted for me. I drink my coffee from it every single morning.	If I can offer people something personal, something designed just for them, they'll go out of their way to own or use it.
Hourglass	An hourglass tells time in an elegantly simple way, while clocks and digital watches are complicated and high-tech.	Maybe there's a simple, elegant, low-tech way to do something I've been doing in complicated ways.

I know these ideas work, because I've implemented every one of them. I hired a wonderful assistant to screen distracting calls (my walking baseball cap). I videotaped lectures for training coaches so that when I teach, I can actually converse with the trainees instead of just lecturing (using high-tech replication of a time-consuming physical process). Whenever I find something that makes me as bouncy and cheerful as a dog, I get paid to tell people about it. I design personal interventions for clients (the way my daughter painted a mug for me) so they'll be highly motivated. And I often teach complex skills like Oneness by having clients interact with very low-tech props like spoons.

Now it's your turn. With your Puzzle X in mind, randomly pick five physical objects you see around you. Without pushing or worrying about quality, let your mind spin metaphors comparing each object with your puzzle. *The metaphors don't have to be "good."* Trying to make them "good" will totally crash your Imagination software. The *less* structured and disciplined you are at this stage of puzzle cracking, the better your solutions will ultimately be. Once you've filled out the form below, you may find random metaphors begin popping into consciousness without your even intending to create them. At that point you're using the third technology of magic at its optimal level.

RANDOM ITEM IN MY IMMEDIATE VICINITY	SOMETHING ABOUT THIS ITEM THAT CATCHES MY ATTENTION	HOW THIS ITEM MAY BE LIKE THE PUZZLE I WANT TO SOLVE

METAPHOR GAME #2: EXTEND METAPHORS TO GET ADVANCED SOLUTIONS

After reading an article I'd written, my daughter once commented, "Gee, Mom, it must be great making a living extending metaphors." She got that right. Every dilemma I've ever helped a client solve, everything I've ever done to improve my own life, every way I've ever found through anything difficult, was an extended metaphor. My first self-help book, *Finding Your Own North Star,* extended the metaphor of "your right life as the North Star" for hundreds of pages, discussing internal "compasses" that guide us, rough "ground" we have to cover, "clouded" beliefs that may block our view of the stars, yada yada yada. The idea of a wayfinder charting a course across open water is yet another extension of this single metaphor. It almost feels like a cheap trick, but the fact is, I've actually managed much of my own life by extending this metaphor beyond all reason, and readers also seemed to find it helpful.

Some puzzle-cracking metaphors work better than others. Most are sort of lame, a few are pretty good, and some illuminate blazing mental light bulbs the moment they occur to you. Keep coming up with metaphors for Puzzle X, and you'll eventually get a light bulb moment. If one of the metaphors you wrote in the blanks above seems to work, extend it. For example, perhaps your elderly mother-in-law is like a gargoyle because she's horrifying and grotesque and seems to be permanently attached to your house. Well, what puzzles can you crack with a gargoyle? In medieval times, people thought they drove away evil spirits. Maybe you can sic your nasty mother-in-law on telephone salesmen, Jehovah's Witnesses, and other people you'd like to drive away.

As you start paying attention, you'll see more and more objects, situations, and stories as metaphors sent to help you crack the many puzzles in your life. Maybe keeping your house clean is like watching television because there's so much crap you don't want to see. Well, you can bar selected channels from your TV; maybe you can bar certain categories of stuff from your house in the same way: nothing that doesn't either fill a need or enrich your life is allowed in *at all*. Or perhaps raising children is like painting your house because it takes forever and you keep making mistakes. Painting-related metaphors could help you prevent spills and clean up messes in your parenting. Maybe your career is like skiing because you have to throw yourself forward (which feels dangerous) to stay safe.

Try generating lots of metaphors like this, then extending them on and on, mercilessly. Again, don't worry whether or not they're "good." I can't emphasize this enough: *The wayfinder's puzzle-cracking Imagination isn't the conscious mind at work, but the subconscious mind at play.* Be silly. Be easy. Let your Imagination do this for you.

METAPHOR GAME #3: THROW IN THE KITCHEN SINK

If you're not used to churning out metaphors, the following game can put you in the zone. You can't force a good extended metaphor to pop into consciousness, but you can increase the rate of metaphor generation in your Imagination by feeding lots of random information into your brain. The more stuff you have knocking around in there, the more grist for your wayfinding Imagination. So after you articulate your puzzle, distract your-self by focusing on several totally unrelated subjects in quick succession—everything, including the kitchen sink. The more *dissimilar* these subjects are, the more likely your metaphor-making mind will come up with a use-ful answer.

I've seen people use this technique to come up with some amazing solutions to life puzzles. One was an audience member at a speech I gave about creating your right life. When George was a soldier in Iraq, he often had to ride in a serviceable but uncomfortable vehicle that made his legs cramp up and his back hurt. He handled it like a good soldier, but during his whole tour of duty he never got used to it.

When George came home from the war he couldn't get a job. He applied for all kinds of work, but no luck. One day, thoroughly dis-couraged, he stopped job hunting to hang out with his wife as she ran several errands—to the car wash, the fabric store, the post office. That afternoon George's right hemisphere put all these data points together. The car wash, with its whooshing machinery, reminded him of travel-ing in a military transport. At the fabric store, he realized he could make his least favorite vehicles more comfortable by sewing a flexible fabric seat that would give soldiers more physical support. At the post office it occurred to him to make and send some of these new seat attachments to his buddies who were still in Iraq. George spent a few days designing a strong nylon sling with metal clamp attachments, which he sent to an army friend overseas.

Long story short: George's innovation eventually came to the attention of military leaders, and now George has a contract with the U.S. military to design comfort-enhancing modifications for military vehicles. He runs his own company out of his garage, employs several other people who couldn't find decent jobs in a brutal economy, loves his work, and makes a lot of money.

Amanda's marriage ended when she was in her early sixties, leav-ing her with little money and work experience. She thought she might become a special education teacher because she'd once devised all sorts of creative ways to help her son, who has autism, learn to read. But going back to school for a teaching degree was slow, and Amanda felt too senior—not to mention too broke—to put in that kind of time. One day she was surfing the Internet looking at degree programs, thinking she might take a distance-learning course. After she had examined a dozen different websites, her metaphor-making mind clobbered her with a giant "DUH!" She created an online learning center through a website, teaching mothers of kids with disabilities how to help their children learn reading and math.

The writer Amy Sutherland loved her husband very much, but wasn't so fond of his habits—for example, the way he left dirty laundry on the floor and grunted monosyllabic responses to conversational questions. Then Sutherland wrote an article about something she'd always found interesting: how trainers work with exotic animals. She watched trainers work with dozens of creatures in all sorts of situations. Eventually she realized she could use a lot of these techniques—for example, rewarding tiny behaviors in the direction of whatever you want, and giving absolutely no response to unwanted behaviors—on her husband. Not only did she improve her relationship, but the *New York Times* article she wrote about animal/husband training was so popular it became a best-selling book, *What Shamu Taught Me about Life, Love, and Marriage.*

Your turn. Think of Problem X, then read, watch, do, call, or otherwise connect with at least five sources of information that have nothing to do with one another. Let your metaphor-making mind stew. And if that's not enough, try the next helpful hint.

METAPHOR GAME #4: REV THE EUREKA ENGINE BY SPEEDING UP YOUR RIGHT HEMISPHERE

Every strategy for dropping into Wordlessness and Oneness will rev up your brain's creative capacities. All the technologies of magic engage your right hemisphere and turn up the rate of unconscious puzzle-cracking comparisons. They also incline you toward pure sense perception and physical wandering, and away from "normal" thinking. This is why so many geniuses have reputations for being absent-minded. In these people, the part of the mind that's "absent" is logical thought; the mind that synthesizes new ideas is very present indeed.

"Let the most absent-minded of men be plunged in his deepest reveries," wrote Herman Melville, "stand that man on his legs, set his feet a-going, and he will infallibly lead you to water." By the same token, wandering around in nature, particularly observing something that moves continuously, like water, plunges our brains into deepest reverie. If you've stated your puzzle and purpose, thrown in the kitchen sink, and still aren't coming up with solutions, *move*. Walk, run, drive, swim, skate, ride a horse. If you can't get out of bed, watch a fountain, a flame, goldfish in a bowl, the sway of leaves in the breeze outside your window. Get lost in observation and kinesthetic rhythm, which put your analytical faculties in a mild daze and crank up the engine in your magical metaphormaking mind.

This process is famous for making solutions pop into consciousness fully formed, a phenomenon psychologists call the "Eureka effect." Supposedly the Greek mathematician Archimedes experienced it while taking a bath to relax after a hard day of pondering how to calculate the mass of an irregular object. As he lowered himself into the water, the story goes, the solution hit Archimedes like a wet sponge: "Wait! A body immersed in water displaces water equal to its mass!" He jumped up and ran around Athens buck naked, shouting "Eureka!," which is Greek for "I found it!," no doubt making his fellow Athenians wonder if he'd rediscovered a significant body part when he took off his clothes.

Anyway, when the Eureka effect hits, you *know* you've got the right solution, because your right hemisphere has formed metaphorical comparisons and worked out a lot of kinks *without your even knowing it was happening*. Archimedes, Melville, and other creative masters knew instinctively how to make this puzzle-cracking magic do its work. But in many cultures wayfinders are trained to do it very consciously. They deliberately send their consciousness into subconscious territory, finding their way through puzzles that defy analytical understanding.

The following exercise is a conglomeration of guided journeys or visualizations that crop up in the mender training of many cultures. Joseph Campbell described the hero's saga as the "hero with a thousand faces"; you can think of this story as the journey of the wayfinder with a thousand faces. It's one of the most powerful ways to run your puzzle-cracking right-brain program. As you read it, notice that the territory it describes is a metaphor for the brain itself, with its civilized, organized components (like the left hemisphere), and its dark, fertile wildness (the right hemisphere).

METAPHOR GAME #5:
STRIDE IN YOUR SEVEN-LEAGUE BOOTS
TO YOUR MEDICINE PLACE

Get comfortable and relax. If you like, you can record the following instructions or download the free audio version from marthabeck.com. Then listen to the recording with your eyes closed, letting your Imagination have full control of what you "see" mentally. The most important instruction to follow as you do this exercise is *not to think up anything*. Don't decide what "should" be there, or try to invent impressive images. *Just watch what happens*. If nothing happens, that's fine too.

Imagine you're sitting in your favorite room inside your house—a fully enclosed room, not a patio or open deck. As you sit peacefully in this room, something odd happens: one of the walls develops a doorway-size translucent patch, and the matter inside the doorway dissolves. Through the opening you can see a city, though not a city you know. Look down at your feet. A pair of boots has appeared next to them. These are what European folklore calls "seven-league boots." Each step you take in them covers seven leagues, or twenty-one miles. Put on the boots.

You feel powerfully drawn toward the opening in the wall. You walk through it and begin striding very rapidly through the city, seven leagues for each step. Almost immediately, you leave the straight-line structures of the city and find yourself in countryside, passing villages and farms. Soon you reach a zone that's even wilder; the only signs you see of human habitation are small groups gathered around campfires. Leaving even this marginally civilized zone behind, you reach a deep wilderness, one few humans have ever seen.

Let this wilderness be whatever it wants. You may expect a pine forest and find yourself in a jungle, or aim for mountains and end up in a desert—it's all good. Wherever you are, this wilderness is beyond ancient. It's primordial. The farther you go, the deeper and wilder it feels. If you began your journey in daylight, you notice the sun setting. If you set out at night, it gets darker still. Now you're walking by moonlight, but that's fine, because you can see in the dark like a panther. Something at the very center of the wilderness is calling to you; you feel this as an intensely sweet yearning in your heart.

Now you feel you're drawing near the deepest, wildest, oldest place of all. Take off your seven-league boots—they'll reappear whenever you need them—and walk slowly through the last few yards that surround this sacred, ancient area. This is your "medicine place." It could be a cave, a clearing in the trees, a pool, a mountaintop. As you reach it, you feel intense joy, because this place is the origin of a wonderful magic that exists especially for you. Take a moment to look around. See things your truest self has been keeping here: objects, people, memories. Don't think up things. Just look around. If you don't see anything interesting, that's fine.

Sit down in your medicine place and draw in a deep breath of its pure, pure air. Smell the trees, earth, flowers, or water. As you exhale, become even more relaxed. You're home. Drink in the peace, beauty, and utter safety of this place. You feel surrounded by an enormously loving energy. With each breath, the sense of being known and unconditionally accepted grows stronger.

Now look up and see that another being has entered your medicine place. It might be an animal, a person, a mythical figure, an angel, or anything else—don't think it up, just see it. Whatever form it takes, this is a totally wise and loving being, who has only your highest good in mind. The being's eyes light up with joy when the two of you recognize one another. Call the being your guide.

Your guide comes and sits beside you. With or without speaking, he or she asks if there is anything troubling you. Tell your guide about a problem you're facing. Describe it only briefly; your guide knows the details. When you're finished relating your problem, stop and wait for a minute. Your guide is going into the magical realm—even deeper than your medicine place—to find you a solution. Wait patiently, breathing the sweet air and soaking in the feeling of absolute peace.

(Leave a minute of silence here if you're making a recording.)

Now turn to see that your guide is holding a box—maybe a large, ornate one, maybe just a tiny carved box you can hide in your hands. Don't think it up, just see it. There's no urgency here in this completely safe and peaceful place, but you're curious. Open the box. See what's inside it.

The object inside the box is a symbol of the solution to your problem. It may be an obvious symbol, one that instantly shows you how to fix the situation, or it may make no sense to you at the moment. Either way is fine. Your only job is to take it back to your "ordinary" life and keep it near you until you understand its purpose.

The seven-league boots reappear and you put them on. Say goodbye to your guide, but remember that the two of you can meet any time, so this isn't really a parting. Now walk out of your medicine place, seven leagues at a step. Go back through the wilderness, past the campfires, the villages, and farms, and into the city. See your home and walk into it, straight through the walls, back into your favorite room. Sit down in the same place you started. Take off your seven-league boots. They disappear. So does the opening in the wall.

Now contemplate the object you brought back from your medicine place. Keep it near you and let it give you ideas every time you think about the problem you discussed with your guide. Ask yourself, "How is this object like the puzzle I'm trying to crack?" Create an extended metaphor—or several—until the "likeness" of your sacred object to your puzzle begins to reveal itself. Toss in the kitchen sink. Rev up the Eureka effect. If your answer hasn't yet come into consciousness, don't worry. It will.

IT'S NOT ABOUT THE PUZZLE

The physicist Richard Feynman was in his twenties when he agreed to work with scientists in Los Alamos to develop weapons that could defeat Hitler. Because the project was top secret, the place and personnel were isolated, and in Feynman's words, "There wasn't anything to *do* there." So he started picking locks. At one point he discovered that three of his colleagues had used the lock combination 27-18-28, after the base of natural logarithms, which is 2.7182. (Like we all didn't see *that* one coming.) He left a series of notes in the other scientists' lockers as a joke. This caused an uproar, as his colleagues became convinced there was a spy on the premises. It took Feynman a while to persuade them the intruder was just his big, bored brain looking for a puzzle to crack.

In the end, you see, the ultimate purpose of every puzzle-cracking escapade isn't so much *having* the solution as *finding* the solution, sending our Imagination on that baffling trip beyond what we already know, finding its tumultuous, watery way toward an unseen destination, feeling the thrill of discovery and invention.

This is what my friend the baboon was seeking as he tinkered with the lock on my guest cottage. All animals love puzzle cracking insofar as they can manage it. But we humans have changed the face of Earth with our extended metaphors and creative solutions. Much of what we've done has reflected our fear-based, self-centered imagination, and to that extent we are a destructive species. But those who reclaim the true nature of the mender's Imagination, grounded in presence and shaped by compassion, can find their way in a wild new world. Perhaps they can even renew, re-wild, and restore the world itself.

He can crack more with his jaws,
but you can crack more with your imagination.

CHAPTER ELEVEN

WHEN EVERYTHING GOES RIGHT BECAUSE EVERYTHING GOES WRONG

My friend Donna is a truly beautiful person. Tall and delicate, with gentle eyes and a deeply compassionate personality, Donna continuously gives to everyone and everything around her. When we met, while walking our dogs, she reminded me of a saint in a stained-glass window, quietly shining blessings from a presence that seemed detached and rather sad. She also had that Team vibe, and the more I learned about her, the more details of her life proved to fit the wayfinder's archetype. There was the enormous sensitivity, the history of early loss, the overwhelming desire to ease suffering, the deep connection with animals. Donna also possessed the skepticism of a scientist, so when I broached the subject of a human Team mustering to repair the world, she, . . . well, let's just say she tried not to judge me.

Naturally once I get to know Donna, I want to get her to Londolozi. I've come to see the place as a kind of Team belly button, a physical location where a divine umbilicus sucks in direct hits of soul nutrients, psychological oxygen, antibodies to cure the ills that assail humanity in our time. Didn't Mandela's time at Londolozi help him enhance the inner peace that would save his country from potential chaos? Hasn't a whole model of restoring Eden grown from the Londolozi example? Aren't the local people thriving by husbanding nature rather than having to destroy it to survive? There are many extraordinary healing places on earth, but there's a reason this particular place is named "protector of all living things." I was certain the world-weariness I always sensed in Donna could be healed by a visit. All menders need mending.

Donna and I have dinner shortly before I'm scheduled to take a group of clients to Londolozi on a week-long retreat. That very day a health crisis has forced one of the clients to cancel her trip. I decide this is Fate: that client's spot was meant to be Donna's. To my absolute delight, Donna agrees. Just a few weeks later I'm clambering into a Land Rover to share her very first game drive. My anticipation level is off the charts. For me, the joy of observing an awakening wayfinder is so intoxicating it makes Ecstasy look like aspirin.

For ten minutes or so we drive through the grassland without seeing any animals, though Donna comments that she felt strangely happy—lighter somehow, and clearer. Then a giraffe lopes out of the trees. It's nothing every American hasn't seen a million times on TV, in movies, at theme parks and zoos—except that the difference between meeting a giraffe in the wild and watching one in any other context is like the difference between making love and reading a pamphlet on sexually transmitted diseases. When Donna sees that huge, graceful creature, the air around her actually seems to light up, like fireworks igniting. She laughs. I thought I'd heard Donna laugh before, but I haven't. This is her real laugh, a laugh like a church bell, pure distilled joy.

As the game drive continues, Londolozi begins acting like an amped-up petting zoo. I've never seen so many spectacular animals in such a short time. They seem drawn to Donna's laughter like American children running to greet the local ice cream truck, but with less body fat and purer intentions. We are greeted by three different leopards, one of whom gazes into Donna's eyes as if recognizing his own long-lost mother. We round a corner to find a bull elephant shaking his ears and trumpeting, but he doesn't appear aggressive so much as welcoming. I'm beside myself with happiness to be beside so much happiness. Thanks to Donna's courageous decision to embark on a big adventure, my devious plot to change her life is working perfectly.

Then it all goes to straight to hell.

The following morning the rest of the retreat participants arrive, and we all separate into two groups for the morning's activities. Boyd and I coach half the participants in one Land Rover while the rest go on safari with a ranger. Donna, who's gone with the ranger, is now fully engaged in rediscovering her inner child, so she decides to climb a tree. A really big one. Having signed all the release forms acknowledging that she alone chose this adventure, she practically runs up the tree, then descends with equal nimbleness. But on her final step to the ground, she lands on something unstable and falls backward onto her right arm. When the whole group reconvenes later that afternoon, she says she's "sprained" her wrist. "I only hurt my ego," she assures us, laughing that beautiful new laugh.

What I don't know is that though Donna looks like a fragile flower, she's actually a Spartan warrior. The freak fall has broken both bones in her right forearm, in a nerve-rich area near her wrist. The pain must be indescribable, but Donna's initial reaction is merely to wrap an Ace bandage around the break and apologize for distracting the group. On the third day of the retreat, when we noticed that Donna looks pale and isn't eating, Boyd and I get really concerned.

So, on the camp doctor's recommendation, Donna spends her third day in Africa jostling over dirt roads, being driven to the nearest hospital six hours away. The skilled physicians (South Africa is famous for the high quality of its doctors) put on a plaster cast but say the break is so tricky it will have to be set surgically by a hand specialist back in the USA. At least pain medication allows Donna to regain her appetite, and she enjoys a meal in a small town—a meal that unfortunately doesn't meet Londolozi's strict standards of sanitation. When she returns she is already showing symptoms of a virus unfamiliar to her system. She's now jetlagged, badly wounded, feverish, undernourished, and exhausted—but with all that, she seems to be increasingly open and present, not less so.

I, on the other hand, am devastated. In a feeble attempt to improve the situation, I get Donna a first-class ticket home on an airline where she'll enjoy a full, flat bed with real pillows, a down comforter, and constant care from the flight attendants. When Karen puts through an emergency call from the States, I assume she wanted to confirm Donna's reservation. But no. She's calling to tell us that Iceland has blown up—or at least a long-dormant Icelandic volcano has—filling the European air with ash and grounding all flights for an indefinite period. We manage to squeeze Donna into a cattle-car seat on a much less luxurious airline, where she can sit up for the whole trip and make multiple stops, the better to experience her pain, fatigue, and dehydration.

As the great philosopher Roseanne Roseannadana used to say on *Saturday Night Live,* "It's always something. If it's not one thing, it's another." I mean, really. Iceland? Really? I've taken dozens of people to Londolozi, and none of them has ever had a major problem, except for this one woman who is so precious to me and seemed so vulnerable. For her, everything seems to go wrong, wrong, wrong.

Or maybe not.

As Donna and I have discussed her great misadventures, she's repeatedly insisted that the physical pain, sleep deprivation, and overall discombobulation of her Londolozi experience were exactly what she needed to radically change her life. Her normal skepticism, which fell away in that first bright surge of laughter when she saw the giraffe, never had the chance to reinstate itself—she was in too much physical pain. The psychological work of the retreat sank deeply into a psyche too busy handling fatigue and illness to sustain its defenses. The path of torment drove Donna deep into Wordlessness—so deep she couldn't brace herself against Oneness. When the other participants described her as lovable, when animals mirrored the untamable beauty of her true nature, Donna simply wasn't strong enough to deflect the truth.

Perhaps this is why Donna is one of those rare adults I've seen change suddenly, dramatically, and permanently in midlife. The adventurous, tree-climbing kid with the musical laugh never made it back into hiding. Before she'd even started healing her body, Donna had committed to mending everyone and everything else more actively than ever before. She became a brilliantly intuitive, intelligent, gentle coach, and in the process found a community of like-minded souls who adore her. She has gone from being a quiet storm of love and generosity to a full-on monsoon. Even now I don't think Donna believes in my concept of the Team. But she is so, *so* on it.

ADVENTURE, MISADVENTURE, AND IMAGINATION

Adventure, which almost by definition involves misadventure, is one of the most powerful ways to free the wayfinder's Imagination, to create new visions of our own future and the future of everything else on earth. Imagine our whole species as one enormous brain, each person a single neuron. Every time you make a new connection with something you've never seen before, the entire brain (humanity as a whole) gains an insight or a creative idea. Who knows, maybe you're the only possible link between someone or something that desperately needs mending and the forces that are desperately trying to mend it. Maybe your own life, career, or health can only find the most satisfying zone when you connect the things that want to connect through you. Maybe your going on an adventure, with its host of unpredictable misadventures, is the only way to activate the link.

Let's define "adventure" as anything you do to actively invite into your life a problem or puzzle you could just as easily avoid. Willingly encountering unfamiliar situations, you maximize the experiences that, though often inconvenient and uncomfortable, trigger huge leaps of Imagination. When you go adventuring, you become a walking version of the long, wandering right-hemisphere neurons that help create inspired ideas. Examine any great advance in the arts, sciences, or structures of society, and you'll find it was born in the Imagination of a human neuron, a person who went adventuring through unknown territory and ideas.

For example, if you like the paintings of the French Impressionists, be glad they adventurously studied art from places like Asia that helped them Imagine a whole new way of painting. If you enjoyed the amazing stage production of *The Lion King,* you were watching Julie Taymor's adventures in Indonesia, where she learned shadow-puppetry techniques. If you're into jazz or rock and roll, be grateful to the slaves who blended their ancient African harmonies and drum rhythms with Western melody lines into a new kind of music, transforming their truly horrendous adventures into joy or consolation. If you're an American and revere our ideology of freedom and egalitarianism, you owe a lot to the Europeans and original Americans, the Indians, who ventured in one another's worlds; the Indian structure of government, based on a combination of individualism and representational leaders, was a seminal inspiration for the political system the United States now enjoys.

Here's a specific example I love: Remember Squanto, the friendly Indian who, as my first-grade teacher taught me, was instrumental in helping English colonists survive in the New World? Mrs. Nelson described for us six-year-olds how Squanto taught the Pilgrims to increase crop yields by fertilizing each corn seed they planted with a small dead fish. But Mrs. Nelson didn't mention where Squanto learned this technique: France. Squanto's real name was Tisquantum, and he was captured by an English explorer in 1614 to be sold as a slave in Spain. He made his way to France and then England before finally getting home, only to find that virtually everyone in his village had died of European diseases. The American Pilgrims didn't survive because God sent them a "noble savage." They survived, for better or worse, because of a multilingual international adventurer who combined his people's traditional wisdom with things he learned on a trip he never wanted to take.

THE AGE OF ARMCHAIR ADVENTURES

In the past it took decades or even centuries for the ideas of one adventurer's adventure to affect millions of other humans. (Charles Darwin's 1836 adventures on the HMS *Beagle,* for example, led to discoveries that still haven't made it to certain parts of my home state.) But around the end of the twentieth century, the global brain hit a tipping point in its capacity to learn quickly from even a single individual. Today, just by clicking around YouTube, anyone with access to the Internet can see wonders that once would have required enormously difficult, time-consuming adventures, both to acquire the information and to communicate it.

It's wonderful to go on armchair adventures made possible by our new, magical technologies. When you have a few minutes to spare—maybe right now!—here's an adventure you can experience with just a few minutes and an Internet connection.

AN ARMCHAIR ADVENTURE FOR TYPICAL TEAM TYPES

Want to see the incredible body art of the Omo people, who live in an isolated region of the Ethiopian Rift Valley? (Trust me, if you love beauty, fashion, or just plain amazement, the answer is yes.) Well, here they are: www.youtube.com/watch?v=1sYPBRy8ljQ.

Ever wondered what it would be like to participate in one of those ancient ceremonies where wayfinders used sound and rhythm to facilitate Wordlessness, Oneness, and Imagination? Stick in a pair of earphones and go to this link: www.youtube.com/watch?v=0Xkbj8 MDZXo&feature=related.

Here's a glance at one of the few remaining uncontacted tribes on earth, in video taken from an airplane as it circled over the Amazon rainforest, using a camera that could zoom in on the tribe from a kilometer away: www.youtube.com/watch?v=sLErPqqCC54.

Ever heard of the "hundredth monkey" phenomenon? Supposedly, one adult female in a troop of Japanese macaques learned to wash potatoes and rice by tossing them into the sea, where the food would float and the sand would fall away. She taught others in her troop, and when about a hundred of them learned the trick, it mysteriously began turning up in other troops of monkeys on other islands. No one knows how the practice was communicated (at least, no one who doesn't understand Wordlessness and Oneness). Click on this link, and you can watch the original troop, on location in Japan. You'll also hear them communicating in sounds that some scientists think are approaching the level of verbal language: www.youtube .com/watch?v=gz8FlSKJ2JE&feature=fvwrel.

And, just for variety, why not watch an elephant seal befriending— actually, more like falling in love with—a human Team member on a cold beach in Georgia (not the state, the country)? http://www .liveleak.com/view?i=4e2_1271613335.

Don't stop here—the suggestions that come up on YouTube as you watch these videos can keep you adventuring as long as you want. The stranger the sights you see, the deeper, wilder, and more resourceful your Imagination will grow.

When my father was born, in 1910, no single individual could hope to see all the sights in the videos listed in the box above. Even the most intrepid adventurer in the Age of Exploration (approximately the fifteenth century to the seventeenth) would have been lucky to see any of them. Seeing two would have been astonishing beyond words. And even if someone had that kind of grit and luck, he couldn't have shared his experiences except through arduous drawing, handwriting, or storytelling, with the relatively few people he'd meet in his lifetime. Our present ability to have adventures is mind-blowing; our ability to share them even more so. The huge brain that is the human species has never learned even a fraction as fast as it is learning right now.

This accelerated capacity to access and share adventure is dramatically changing the way humans live all over the world. As I write this, protesters in Egypt's Tahrir Square are bringing down a thirty-year dictatorship, largely by trading information over cell phones and laptops. Twitter—*Twitter,* for heaven's sake—has become a tool that can unseat tyrants. Various despots across the world will fight similar uprisings, using military force and suppression of information, but even if they succeed in the short term, they can't hold out for long against the rise of new technologies. Too much knowledge is traveling too quickly through too many human-to-human synapses. Totalitarianism, which depends largely on control of information and forbidding free assembly, is dissolving in the transparency created by the freedom to have enlightening, mind-expanding adventures.

All of this gives me hope that the Team of world menders still has time to devise new ways of thriving as individuals, as a species, and as the residents of a delicately balanced global ecology. No one can anticipate the changes that can be made by even a single humble person in the wild new world. The more you personally free and feed your wayfinder's Imagination by going on adventures, the better everyone's chances.

THE HERO'S CALL TO ADVENTURE

The anthropologist Joseph Campbell constructed a model of the "hero's journey," compiled from hundreds of traditional adventure tales told by wayfinders all over the globe. The hero's story begins with the protagonist happily going about a normal life. Then, out of nowhere, he or she receives a "call to adventure." Interestingly the next step isn't acceptance, but "the refusal of the call." As anthropologist Sheila Seifert says, "The protagonist chooses not to move forward in life because he or she chooses to not give up his position, power, ideals, goals, or responsibilities; the refusal is often based on his/her fear of the unknown and comfort in the familiar. Usually secondary characters support the protagonist's refusal." Donna initially refused to accompany me to Africa—not because she wasn't interested (she was), but because it was just *so much* more convenient and inexpensive to stay home. No sensible person leaps at the first wild-ass opportunity to go do God-knows-what.

Fortunately for storytellers, in the classic hero's tale the refusal of the call is followed by an event Campbell called "supernatural aid." Some mysterious being, object, or coincidence enters the hero's life, and it's Goodbye, comfort zone, Hello, adventure. In Donna's heroic adventure, the "supernatural aid" was the vacancy that opened up just in time for her to join our safari group. When I told her about it, I could almost feel a subtle energy pulling her. "I just knew that I had to do it," she told me later. "I wasn't sure why, but something in me just said 'Go!'"

If I'd known Donna was going to have a freakishly difficult time in Africa, I'd have told her not to come with me. But she was on a wayfinding adventure, and that means going into the next classic stage, the "road of trials," in which, Campbell says, "the hero is tested and found vulnerable, but the outcome reveals a part of her that she did not know existed." Today, despite all the pain and bad luck she endured in Africa—or perhaps because of them—Donna claims that the trip gave her exactly the experiences she needed.

Not all heroic stories involve travel to exotic places. Brad answered the call to adventure the first time he went to an AA meeting and admitted he was an alcoholic. Susan, a psychologist who is also a dancer, refused and then accepted an invitation to give a creative arts seminar to a group of geeky computer engineers, little knowing that she was embarking on an entirely new career as a business consultant. Anne set out on a huge adventure when she decided to write her first novel. Zach lived for years with a secret: though his parents thought he was majoring in accounting, he'd actually switched his focus to marine biology, adventuring through the part of human knowledge that sparked his enthusiasm. By the time his parents found out, their negative reaction was just one more challenge on his "road of trials."

Right now, take a moment to look back on your own life for times you answered the hero's call to adventure. These were moments when you behaved anomalously, perhaps even breaking the implicit rules of your social group or your belief system, to choose an uncertain and inconvenient path of action. Perhaps you had no idea why you made the choice. You may remember feeling strangely pushed or pulled as you set off, or someone may have showed up to encourage you, or a whole parade of events might have coincided to get you moving in the new direction. Some of your adventures may have involved traveling geographically, but you also may have sailed off into unprecedented thoughts, behaviors, or relationships.

If these calls to action were true heroic catalysts, they weren't followed by effortless, enjoyable success. Many of my clients get confused by this. "If I was 'supposed' to [go back to school, marry the handsome stranger, breed supermassive ferrets, or create a new flavor of cheese]," they ask me, "why did everything go wrong?" The answer is that an adventure on which nothing goes wrong is just a vacation, and wayfinders aren't designed for mere vacations. The best way to stretch ordinary imagination into a mender's Imagination is to travel the road of trials.

THE FRUITS OF THE DIFFICULT ROAD

If it's true that this is the time for the Team to mend the world, this book may have found you in the throes of an adventure. Or you may be actively resisting an irrational inclination to do something wild and soulful and totally unnecessary, something your family and friends think is ridiculous, something that just won't stop calling. As Mary Oliver says, "When you feel the mist on your mouth and sense ahead the embattlement, the long falls plunging and steaming—then row, row for your life toward it."

Whether you feel called to start a career, raise a child, tutor prisoners, or sit in your pajamas thinking through a philosophical problem, doing so may well put you through a living hell. On the other hand, according to hero stories from countless cultures, here, in Seifert's words, are some of the rewards you'll earn for traveling the road of trials:

> The protagonist becomes self-assured and often receives physical gifts and emotional rewards. Since personal limitations are broken, the protagonist can see the big picture [and] . . . understands how the ultimate goal can be accomplished and the mission completed. . . .
>
> [By the end of the adventure] the protagonist has the ability, power, or wisdom without limitations to relax in whatever world (physical, mental, emotional, or spiritual) he finds himself. He is able to combine the workings of unenlightened (old) and enlightened (new) societies into one world.

In other words, those who have been through some form of the hero's adventure (whether as wayfinders or in some other archetype) are the only humans with sufficient Imagination to mend the world in which we now find ourselves. The very strangeness and difficulty that frighten or torture us on the hero's road of trials also enlarge our Imagination enough to absorb alien concepts, enabling us to create meaningful change. With an expanded Imagination, an adventuring mender can create a harmonious balance between old, unenlightened behavior and a new way of being that heals what we've broken. Wayfinders are born to be heroes. Whether or not that

promise is fulfilled depends on whether a born wayfinder heeds the initial
call to adventure—or at least the call that comes again after the initial refusal.

ADVENTURE AND THE BLENDING OF OPPOSITES

Did you know that you tend to be more sexually attracted to people whose
immune system is different from yours than to people who share your
immune profile? This factor, measured by a gland inside your nose that
picks up on other people's pheromones without your conscious knowledge, prevents accidental inbreeding (by making you uninterested in people
whose genotype is related to yours) and ensures that your babies will have
the broadest possible range of immunities. Analogously, the adventures that
create the broadest, most powerful, and most useful wayfinder's Imagination are those that bring together elements of wildly different worlds.

This is one reason I find Africa so fascinating; as a North American, I
come from the youngest, wealthiest, most mechanized continental culture
on earth, while Africa is financially the poorest and least developed continent, as well as being humanity's ancient home. Connecting these two
extremes leads to leaps of Imagination, whether the adventurer is an African encountering America, or an American encountering Africa. One of
my favorite pastimes is finding stories of African heroes whose Imagination was ignited by contact with the norms of the First World.

For example, in Kenya I met an amazing woman named Ingrid Munro.
A Swede who married a Canadian, she has spent most of her life in Nairobi. Ingrid's father was a physician who lived in Kenya for some time
before moving back to Sweden. While Ingrid was back in Nairobi on a visit,
she got a call from an African surgeon who said he was about to operate
on a little homeless street kid who'd been hit by a bus. The surgeon knew
Ingrid's father, and he asked her if she'd mind calling Sweden and helping her father talk him through an operation that could save the boy's leg.

Ingrid not only complied, she ended up adopting the boy. Then
she became interested in the beggar women who'd helped him survive
before she met him. She began brainstorming about ways these women
could work their way out of poverty using tiny bits of investment capi-
tal. That was many years ago. By the time I met her, Ingrid had helped
more than 300,000 beggars overcome destitution and become successful entrepreneurs. The organization she helped found, Jamii Bora, has

its own banks, insurance company, and city planning department. (If you want to hear Ingrid firsthand, go to http://video.google.com/videoplay?do cid=7351863330550836974#.)

Here come the African adventurers: Jamii Bora is run by those women who once lived on the streets of Nairobi, begging for pennies and helping children like Ingrid's son survive early childhood. When I asked some of them how they'd risen from poverty, these heroes told me that the small loans they received (about $50 apiece) had been helpful, but by far the most powerful ingredient in their success was the way Ingrid saw the world. "She would say us, 'You can do it. I see you succeeding,'" one woman told me, as others nodded their agreement. It was the Imagination of the mender, freeing the Imagination of the street beggars, that called them to further adventures. Their road of trials would not only bring them out of poverty, but spread through their mender's ways to hundreds of thousands of others.

Another hero is William Kamkwamba, whose adventures began in a tiny library in Malawi. Unable to afford the $80 fee to attend school, fourteen-year-old William borrowed an American fifth-grade textbook on electricity. Though he didn't speak English, he was fascinated by a photograph in the book that depicted an electricity-generating windmill. That photo sparked his Imagination, and William started puzzle-solving like there was no tomorrow. With the textbook as his guide, he spent two months creating his own windmill, using a broken bicycle, a tractor fan, and chunks of rubber cut from his own sandals—all of this while his entire village was starving its way through a famine. William's relatives and friends thought he'd lost his mind—until his rickety windmill produced enough power to run a radio, then a light bulb, the first electricity his village had ever seen.

Eventually word of William's achievement made its way into the local press, then the international news. You can see footage of him describing his windmill and seeing America for the first time at www.youtube.com/ watch?v=arD374MFk4w. He's since built more windmills, solar panels, and deep-water wells, and hopes to bring reliable electricity to his whole village. He commented in his book, *The Boy Who Harnessed the Wind,* that his invention process would have been immensely easier if he'd known about the Internet. Given what he was able to do with one textbook, it boggles the mind to think what he'll do now that his Imagination can roam scientific and engineering devices from all over the globe. Think about William the next time you Google.

And then there's Ishmael Beah, whose home country of Sierra Leone was devastated by civil war in the 1990s. Beah was captured by a military gang, given drugs, and brainwashed into becoming a "soldier"—basically a homicidal puppet—in his young teens. After a few years in hell, Ishmael was one of two child soldiers from his battalion to be rescued by an aid organization. He survived a harrowing "rehab" and was eventually chosen to represent Sierra Leone at a model UN conference for young people in New York City. There he met a professional storyteller (read "wayfinder"), Laura Simms, who spent hours listening and talking to him.

Ishmael returned to Sierra Leone only to be swept up in another wave of violence as the war continued. In his book *A Long Way Gone,* he describes how the images of his future that he'd gained from his adventures, and his conversations with Laura Simms, helped him Imagine escaping the country and finding his way back to America. He made it all the way to Laura, who eventually adopted him. She was able to open her life to Ishmael because his adventure and her Imagination opened his mind to the possibility of a new future. (Meet Ishmael at http://www.youtube.com/watch?v=5K4yhPSQEzo.)

This is the kind of thing that happens when a Third World wayfinder accepts a call to adventure and winds up intersecting with a First World experience that frees his or her Imagination. In a way, this kind of adventure is almost a cliché: the poor, backward African inspired by the wealth, magnificence, and optimism of "advanced civilization." But any wayfinder will tell you that when two unfamiliar worlds intersect, the exchange of Imagination always goes in both directions.

WHAT ADVENTURES IN AN ANCIENT WORLD CAN TEACH MENDERS FROM THE NEW WORLD

Donna and I, both educated Americans, found inspiration and a new way to Imagine humanity's future in Africa. Surrounded from birth by a culture that sees "progress" in the unbridled expansion of human cities and technologies, we'd never Imagined that humans can thrive by healing our own inner lives and the natural world around us.

Though nature has been crippled by human activity in Africa as everywhere else, the damage there is less extensive, precisely because "development" has been slow. Try to mend the woods of Manhattan, and you've got yourself a predicament. Restoring Switzerland to its pre-human-habitation state would be another one. Healing the bison migration in the American Great Plains would require the demolition of innumerable Walmarts, not to mention cities and towns. But Africa, our species' home, is still close enough to its primeval condition to help us Imagine restoring Eden. Just a few blocks from the densely populated ghettoes of Nairobi is a wilderness preserve where I visited humans whose lives are devoted to helping orphaned wild baby elephants. Londolozi and its neighboring "mended" ecosystems are bigger than Switzerland. And there are no Walmarts in the Karoo. The people, animals, and plants in these places can expand a First Worlder's Imagination as much as an adventure through Times Square can broaden the horizons of an African child.

And then there's Africa's magic.

Anyone with a trace of the mender archetype begins to light up walking through the ancient home of the first humans, staring into the same animal eyes our distant ancestors held sacred, climbing the same trees beloved of our great-grandparents' great-grandparents' great-grandparents. Maybe it's not just Africa; perhaps every wayfinder feels pulled toward a different place, an adventure custom-made for his or her individual life. It doesn't matter where the call to adventure takes us; it only matters that we go.

Whatever inconvenient, senseless thing is calling to you right now, go ahead and say no, as long as you can. The call will simply come again—repeatedly, insistently—until you say yes. Then buckle your seatbelt, because this will not be a comfy trip. Once you accept your heroic assignment, it will always be something; if it's not one thing, it will be another. Take a first-aid kit, some water-purifying tablets, an extra fund of cash squirreled away in your sock. Keep an eye on Iceland. Expect any and every form of complication and disaster, and also expect these very misadventures to stretch your Imagination around your real mission in life. Your hero's journey may break your heart, your bank, or your arm. But it will also mend your soul, your life, and your part of the wild new world.

FREEING IMAGINATION THROUGH ADVENTURE

All that's necessary for you to embark on an adventure is choosing to do something you've never done. Travel to new places. Learn new skills. Use new technologies. Seek constantly for learning and innovation rather than familiarity and comfort.

Wayfinding Adventure: Go Someplace You've Never Been

Answering the call to big adventures is a lot easier if you practice with small ones. Today, go to a place near your home where you've never been before. Get your coffee at a different restaurant, shop in an unfamiliar grocery store, take a walk through a neighborhood you've never noticed.

You'll probably feel slightly uncomfortable. Your brain will be forced to create new neuron pathways to familiarize itself with even a small innovation. Watch that feeling without fearing, resisting, or avoiding it. Learn to be comfortable with the discomfort that is inextricably linked to all adventures.

Wayfinding Adventure: Learn a New Skill

Most of us admire some skill we haven't mastered, or even attempted. Have you always wanted to make ceramic pots, or play the guitar, or dance the tango? Admiring a skill you haven't mastered is one form of the call to adventure. You've refused the call before; this week, say yes. Take a lesson, or buy some supplies and start messing around. Again, notice the frustration and bafflement that you'll feel, especially as you begin. Watch how everything goes wrong. Get used to it. Persist until you have at least a small success.

Wayfinding Adventure: Use Technology in a Way You Haven't Before

Today's world is dominated by adventurers who dare to venture not into unknown places, but into unknown technologies. If you're a technophobe who's never used the Web, design another armchair adventure via You-Tube, like the one I described earlier. If you're a computer scientist who builds motherboards by hand but hates going outside, learn to make a fire with two sticks and muscle power. If you're a girly girl who hates cars, learn to change your own oil; if you're a manly man who loves cars, learn to knit a sweater. We are the tool-using animals, and the more tools you can use, the better your brain will navigate our wild new world.

Wayfinding Adventure: Plan a Big Event

Looking far enough into the future to find a free week on your calendar, plan to go somewhere you've always wanted to go. To maximize your fun, organize the trip around some purpose that mends the world: volunteer for disaster cleanup, volunteer with Habitat for Humanity, plant trees in a deforested area.

If you can afford it, take your adventure to some foreign region. If you're not in the money, think about adventuring into the wilderness. Eat a lot of trail mix and perhaps edible greens you can find in the area (Google it). Wherever your adventure leads you, take along some Team friends and enough Post-it notes to make crazed plans for saving the world.

Wayfinding Adventure: Celebrate Your Road of Trials
Whatever's going on in your life right now, you have problems, slow-downs, complications, and frustrations (call me psychic). Instead of resisting and resenting these difficulties, reframe them as a road of trials. See yourself as the hero in a story being told around a thousand campfires— the tale of Michelle and the Faulty Plumbing, or Doug's Great Combat with the Supervisor from Hell. Go on a quest. Tell the story. You'll find that the more annoying or even devastating an adventure is to live, the better wayfinding tale it makes.

CALL OF THE WILD NEW WORLD

The irony of the hero's adventure is that after going through terrible things in terrible places, experiencing nightmarish wounds and trials, the hero doesn't want to go back. He's learned things that make him a new, deeper, happier person, and as Seifert says, "sometimes he prefers to live in the enlightenment [rather] than return to a 'home' that might not accept the ultimate gift."

As I wait with Donna for the small plane that will take her away from Londolozi, I see the familiar sadness back in her eyes. Her broken arm, in a temporary cast, looks awful, the hand swollen and bruised black. She's weak from lack of sleep and the intestinal trouble she contracted during her medical jaunt. She was thin upon arrival; now she's beginning to look skeletal. I feel a wave of horror that I talked her into this trip where everything has gone so wrong. No wonder she looks miserable.

When the plane arrives, I go to give Donna a hug and one more apology. She looks at me with stricken eyes.

"I can't leave," she says, beginning to cry. "I don't want to go back. I have to be here. I belong in Africa." Instead of begging her pardon for dragging her into misadventure, I find myself assuring her that she'll return soon. Like every classic hero, she's deeply in love with the place that conspired to crack the shell of her usual quiet emotional isolation. After going through more hell than anyone I've ever dragged to Londolozi, she feels she's found heaven on earth. And this, I promise, is how you will feel about your own hellish adventures. Eventually.

At this writing, Donna is planning another Africa adventure with her husband, Joel. But much more important, she's learned through experience that she never left Londolozi. Having continued her adventure through the psychological upheaval of learning a mender's magic, she can enter Oneness at any time. There, in the Everywhen, all her adventures are still happening. The giraffe still bursts from behind the tree, the elephant gazes into her eyes, the tree breaks her arm and the shell around her heart, African friends still gently tend her wounds, the earth thunders and erupts, the rivers and clouds offer their liquid solace.

No hero's journey ever ends, and your next adventure is already happening. The moment you accept the call to adventure, the road of trials begins finding its way from your unconscious awareness into your consciousness, freeing and expanding your Imagination, helping you become the healing you hope to create. To quote Mary Oliver again, all your heroic adventures will "break your heart, by which I mean only that it break open and never close again to the rest of the world."

PART IV

THE FOURTH TECHNOLOGY OF MAGIC

WORDLESSNESS

ONENESS

IMAGINATION

FORMING

CHAPTER TWELVE

FORMING—NOT FORCING—
WHATEVER YOU WANT

"One lousy cheetah!" I fume. "Is that really so much skin off your nose?"

No answer. The sky remains impassively blue, the breeze across the savannah calm and fresh. I've been trying to "call" a cheetah for at least ten days, and this is my last safari drive before heading back to the States.

It's not that I particularly need to see a cheetah. "Calling" one is just my ongoing experiment with the technologies of magic. In science, an experimental result must be replicable to be considered valid; in other words, you have to be able to create the same end through the same means, or you can't say you're actually causing what you think you're causing. So no matter how many times "calling" worked, I'm always trying to replicate the results one more time.

Today I'm out with my friend Sal (Rowan's mother) and some other Team friends who've gathered at a wilderness preserve called Phinda to celebrate Sal's birthday. We've spent the previous day and night in joyful festivity, and most of the guests are back in their rooms, sleeping off well-earned hangovers. Only a few of us dragged ourselves out of bed at 4:30 to go safari-ing, but this is my last chance at a cheetah, so I held back on the party fluids and headed out bright and early. Now it's eight o'clock on a gorgeous morning. The dawn-loving animals are almost certainly bedded down, snoozing, invisible.

"It's really strange," says Sal, sitting next to me. "I've been here about seventy times, and I've seen cheetahs on every single trip except this one."

Our Zulu guide winces. Trackers hate it when they can't find the animals their guests have asked to see. "There aren't even any tracks," he says apologetically. "Not on the entire preserve. They've gone to some other hunting ground for now."

I sigh and let it go. Either there really isn't an Energy Internet we can program with our minds, or I didn't write the code correctly this time. I once would have favored the first explanation, but after so many, many experiments, I'm leaning toward the second.

Four years have passed since the Day of the Rhinoceros, when I had my epiphany about a global Team of menders joining up to save the world. Four years of reading, interviewing, traveling, thinking, inquiring. As I've begun to see the commonalities in ancient technologies of magic, I've implemented each one. Though I'm intensely curious at an intellectual level, my real objective has always been to find and heal my own true nature, to experience more inner peace, love, and joy. Though I'm far from an expert practitioner, it's definitely been working. What I never expected was the radical change this process would catalyze in my outward life.

Shortly after Rhinoceros Day, two coaches I'd trained sat me down and said that though they had no idea why, they felt compelled to help me set up a business that would allow me to focus virtually all my time on the Team. (Prior to that, I'd thought of myself as a writer, not an entrepreneur, and had been coaching through a company I didn't own.) It didn't seem to be a coincidence that the two coaches who freed me to do Team work full time were named Meadow and Brooke—or as I call them, Field and Stream. Their generosity and genius helped launch me into more career adventures than I'd ever had before. Along the way colleagues, experts, clients, and other helpful people kept showing up just when I needed them. Many echoed Field and Stream's comments that they couldn't understand their own overwhelming urge to help.

The "synchronicities" in my experience became downright ridiculous. If I felt intrigued by a public figure, I'd end up meeting the person within days. When I ogled an iPad but decided it would be silly to buy one, a client I hadn't spoken to for months sent me one without explanation. When I injured one of my eyes and begged the Powers That Be to fix it, my ophthalmologist not only repaired the damage but suggested laser surgery; thirty seconds of surgery later, after a lifetime of near blindness, I suddenly had better than perfect vision. It's not that I "deserved" these things; it is just that everything I focused on with the first three technologies of magic seemed to trip over itself to get to me.

Everything, that is, except a cheetah.

Two weeks before this trip to Phinda for Sal's birthday party, my colleagues and I ran another of our Londolozi retreats. Everyone practiced the technologies of magic until the entire group could practically levitate. The evening after our clients left, Koelle, Boyd, and I drove into the bush to relax. Koelle went a little way off to meditate in a meadow. A few minutes later the biggest, brightest meteor flash any of us had ever seen, brighter than the setting sun, blazed in the western sky. For a moment it shone brilliant white, then turned emerald green before blinking out.

Koelle stood up and walked back to us. There were tears in her eyes. "I asked for that," she said quietly, "but I didn't expect my favorite color."

"Ri-ight," I said.

Boyd shook his head in disbelief, but admitted, "Hell of a coincidence."

"Do it again," I demanded. Replication, dammit, replication!

Koelle turned, walked away, and sat down on the ground again. Three seconds later another comet flashed through the sky, close to the path of the first.

"Well, that one wasn't green," I pointed out.

"Must be a meteor shower," said Boyd.

We stayed for an hour or so, eyes locked on the sky. *Nada*. We asked Koelle for more, but she shook her head. "I'm done," she said, unnecessarily, since both Boyd and I felt the same thing once we went Wordless. A third comet didn't *want* to happen, not in our wayfinding Imaginations. Of course it all could have been coincidence. But coincidences this improbable were happening so regularly that we were all losing our belief in the randomness of the universe.

So Koelle can apparently order up astronomical events like hamburgers, but the cheetah I was "calling" never showed up for me at Londolozi. My frustration about this turned to excitement as I headed for Phinda, because people kept telling me it was cheetah heaven. Cheetahs out the wazoo, Phinda veterans assured me. But now, after two days and three game drives, we haven't found even tracks. And I'm out of time. My experiment has failed.

As I accept this, my mind relaxes and I let myself just drink in the beauty of the day. We've driven to the summit of a hill, from which the savannah stretches away to the distant horizon. The chest-high grass ripples in the wind, nature's shining green fur coat. It's a miracle to me that the Zulu can track any animal, even an elephant, through this terrain. As I leave the world of language and feel Oneness click in, I become the grass, the plain, the distant clouds.

"Aha!" says our tracker. He begins speaking rapid Zulu to the ranger, who shouts "Hang on!" and mashes down the accelerator like the getaway driver in a bank robbery. As I clutch my seat, trying not to get thrown from the vehicle, I search the landscape for our target. I think I see it: a teeny tiny little white square above the grass, approximately four thousand miles away. It's the chest of a cheetah that has climbed a termite mound to survey the landscape.

I don't think I've ever traveled this fast in an open vehicle. After some fifteen minutes screaming along a dirt trail, we turn aside and drive through trackless high grass for another fifteen. I have no idea how the trackers know where to go, especially since the cheetah is almost certainly on the move and won't be anywhere near the termite mound where we originally saw him. Once we've reached the right general area, we begin trawling, driving aimlessly around. And then, at the very moment I completely despair, there he is, curled up in the grass under a cactus, almost invisible from even ten feet away.

"Okay," I said to my higher power, which I call Whatever (to avoid offending people with divergent belief systems, including atheism). "There's a cheetah, but I am not marking this on the 'miracle' score card. This is good old-fashioned human ingenuity. Ten days, two different groups of Team members, and a bunch of the best trackers on Earth. That's what this is." Still I feel proud of what human will and determination can do. There it is, the first wild cheetah I'd seen in years. I don't usually carry a camera in the bush—you can't really see animals when you're staring at a viewfinder—but at this moment I really wish I'd brought one. Even my cell phone would suffice to snap a quick photo, but I left it back at the camp.

That's when we hear the growl of another Land Rover, growing rapidly louder. It's rare for safari vehicles to go top speed, but today is shaping up more like a NASCAR event than a typical game drive. The second Land Rover barrels up to us and jams on the brakes. It holds only two people: the driver and Teammate Kelly Eide, a professional photographer. Kelly is wearing pajamas and looking around wildly.

"Where is it?" she asks. "Where's the cheetah?" When we point to it, Kelly whips out one of her large, impressive cameras and starts clicking away. The cheetah sighs and sits up obligingly, like a tired but polite celebrity posing with a fan.

Here is Kelly's story: After dancing the night away, she sacked out with every intention of sleeping until high noon. But around 8 a.m. her slumber was invaded by a troublesome thought: "I've got to get up. There's a cheetah I have to photograph." She pushed the thought away and went back to sleep, but the urge to go get pictures of this cheetah returned repeatedly, like the whine of a mosquito in her ear. After a while she got better at ignoring it. She was fading back into deep sleep when all hell broke loose on the roof of her lodge.

"It was a troop of monkeys," she tells me later. "And they acted like they were there for one reason: to wake me up." The monkeys bounced on the roof, pummeled the windows, hooted and screamed at the door in a most uncharacteristic way. Finally Kelly gave in. "I grabbed my camera and went looking for someone to drive me," she says. The ranger she found was another hungover party guest. He was none too happy about being seconded, with no warning, to help a guest in pajamas find an alleged cheetah at the wrong time of day, when there were known to be no cheetahs on the property. He was stunned when my guide radioed to say we'd found one.

Kelly hasn't been snapping photos for more than a minute before the cheetah runs out of patience, turns, and vanishes into impenetrably thick grass. The photographer and the cat rendezvous just long enough for me to get a picture to remember "my" cheetah and the small miracles helping conjure up a thousand things I think I'm doing with wit and effort alone.

THE FOURTH TECHNOLOGY OF MAGIC

The first three technologies of magic take place in the inner spaces of our perceptions, thoughts, feelings, and dreams. Using them reveals and heals our true nature: we see the truth of our lives in the stillness of the Wordless mind; we sense love and connection to others through Oneness; we prefigure our desires, solve our puzzles, and picture new solutions with Imagination. When all those technologies are used at once, it requires only a slight push to create, in three-dimensional reality, the conditions, objects, and events we've Imagined. That gentle push is the fourth technology of magic: the art of Forming.

Forming, as you may have cleverly discerned, gives physical *form* to things that previously existed only in thought. To return to the metaphor of computers, recall that we log on to the energetic Internet with Wordlessness, communicate by sending energetic messages through Oneness, and write code to create things "online" with Imagination. Forming is like printing out a page of a website you've created, or causing a machine to physically move around based on its computer programming. The object or action exists in three-dimensional space, not just as an arrangement of bits of energy. Once you transform something from virtual to physical, you can show it to people who don't use computers, don't have computers, have never seen a computer, don't believe computers exist. Mastering Forming means that you never need to make people believe in wayfinding skills; you just show them the results. And (as I learned from a cheetah, a troop of monkeys, and a sleepy photographer), should you stop believing in your own magic, the metaphysical realm may yank your chain a little, just to bring you back to reality.

HOW NOT TO FORM THINGS

Back when I was a good Mormon girl, a few church members told me that if I'd had enough faith, I could have "cured" Adam's Down syndrome before he was born. The general belief about performing miracles (not for all Mormons, but for a few) seemed to be that, if you belonged to the One True Church, kept all the rules, and really, really, *really* believed something, you can will it into existence. (Also, it helps if you thresh your own wheat.) Many other religious folk seem to think in similar ways. Enough rigid belief in a human system, enough absolute concentration on what you want to have happen, will create miracles.

Menders don't work that way.

Don't get me wrong—in every culture and tradition, people with mystical leanings try to will their desires into manifestation. Dark sorcerers, ego-driven shamans, and power-hungry priests of many religions have tried to conjure the things they want. Some use the technologies of magic competently enough to be quite powerful in a limited, localized way. But the things they Form tend to be grotesque little monsters, whirls of fear and manipulation that drag along for a while, then collapse and disintegrate like any other zombie.

Experienced wayfinders, by contrast, know that their magic isn't about fixating on the fantasies and fears of their personality, then forcing reality to supply their demands. Real Forming is a process of inviting universal Oneness to play with an individual human Imagination. This always begins not with intense, grasping focus, but with the nonattachment that comes with Wordlessness. Suffused with deep acceptance of the present moment, the wayfinder feels for what the One would love to create, then adds Imagined ideas born from his or her specific human experience. This marriage of the vast to the particular feels nothing like will. There is no need to make things happen, only a love so overwhelming we forget there was ever anything to need. Forming at full throttle is pure ease. It's the first three technologies of magic, plus a joyful, relaxed alternation of rest and play.

SWAPPING ELBOW GREASE FOR ENERGY

All of us have been taught to make things happen in the physical world. We know what it takes: setting goals, rolling up our sleeves, putting pleasure aside, and working, working, working, working, working. Then it helps if we work harder. Often we need others to help us work, so we must work to find them and work to motivate them with physical rewards (food, money, companionship, approval) and/or physical punishment (pink slips, prison, breakups, criticism). All of this is hard. It demands much time and effort from both the body and the calculating mind. As Genesis reminds us, "In the sweat of thy face shalt thou eat bread, till thou return unto the ground; for out of it wast thou taken: for dust thou art, and unto dust shalt thou return."

Well, yes, but . . . We now live in a world where a great deal of value is created with pure information rather than physical matter. Lots of people eat bread without their faces sweating at all. And that's not just a modern phenomenon. Later on in the Bible Jesus doesn't seem to break any more sweat restoring a blind man's sight than my ophthalmologist did with his laser-surgery machine. Forming, which uses mainly information and energy, allows us to do things that look miraculously powerful without much effort. It's one thing to say this, but it's better just to show the results. To do that, I often enlist the help of four-footed friends.

TWO WAYS TO HORSE AROUND

For several thousand years, in many cultures, generation after generation of people have spent countless hours working to tame and train horses. It isn't easy, because horses are tricky to work with; they're massive, strong, and easily panicked. The most typical cowboy method of creating a working relationship with a horse, based on millennia of handed-down custom, is some form of "breaking." Breaking a horse often involves weeks of coercion, using ropes, whips, chains, groups of men, and a lot of violent energy, which eventually convinces the animal that it has no choice but to do as humans command. Only after a horse is "broken," says conventional wisdom, can a human start forming a truly cooperative relationship with it.

Compare and contrast this method with the process Koelle and her mentors call "joining up" with a horse. Its objective is to create that cooperative relationship between human and animal using only presence, observation, body language, and energy. I've seen Koelle create this transformative magic with terrified, severely traumatized animals, horses who tried to bolt, buck, scream, and kick at any human who tried to "break" them and were therefore slated to be shot. She's connected with captured mustangs when they were still wild as the wind. Wild elephants and zebras respond to her very much as horses do, though out of respect for their way of being she's never tried to thoroughly tame one. Koelle has taught hundreds of people to join up with horses, including people like me, who had never been near a horse until the very first "whispering" lesson. In other words, anyone who chooses to learn this mender's method of communicating with animals can do it. It's a sufficiently advanced technology to look like magic, but that doesn't mean it's not science.

I partially described a join-up in chapter 4, but here's a description of the usual process, which is slightly different from the exercise I mentioned there:

1. A person walks into the circular pen where the horse is standing. Neither has met the other, and the horse has no training whatsoever.

2. From a short distance, the person encourages the horse to move around the pen for a little while (with a domestic-born horse, usually no more than two to five minutes).

3. If the person is calm and holds a clear Imagined intention, the horse soon begins signaling, with ears, lips, head position, and energy, that it feels safe with the person.

4. The person walks a short distance away, then stops.

5. The horse walks up until its nose is near the person's shoulder, stops, and waits for further instructions.

6. The horse follows the person everywhere, gently and quietly, with no ropes, whips, chains, or other forms of physical compulsion.

Koelle and I use this process and other ways of playing with horses (really, you can't call it working) to teach seminars. We call them "How to Make Things Happen," though Koelle feels this is false advertising. But it's easier to say, and more appealing to modern rationalists, than "How to Notice What Wants to Happen in the Everywhen, and Give It Permission and Space to Become Physical Reality."

The horse, you see, is a walking, breathing, living, loving metaphor for anything good you might want to create. More money, satisfying relationships, physical fitness, intellectual breakthroughs, emotional equanimity, healthy ecosystems, really good shoes—all these things respond to the same process and energy that harmonizes the energy of a human with that of an animal. Everything you need or want is waiting to "join up" with you.

So you're perfectly free to attack your life's work with gristle and grit, to break, control, force, and dominate everything and everyone you desire, the way many people still break horses. But if you're willing to practice Wordlessness, Oneness, and Imagination, and then take the final step by bringing in a rhythmic alternation of physical rest and play, you can become a true wayfinder and achieve far, far greater results with far, far less effort.

ACCIDENTAL FORMING
(HOW TO GET WHAT YOU DON'T WANT)

Every day, every hour, without even noticing it, you are conjuring things in your Imagination that have never existed before. You're using that amazing human ability to think abstractly, projecting your thoughts into the future and creating juxtapositions of things that have never interacted. But your Imagination may not be very free. If you haven't practiced puzzle cracking and adventuring, your *expectations* will get stuck in the often disappointing little region of what you already believe possible. Any negative pattern you Form repeatedly reflects the quality of your deep expectations. Even if you fill your head with ambitiously cheery thoughts, or chant positive affirmations until all your friends want to smack you, what you expect most deeply is what guides your behavior, which determines what you Form.

For example, Nancy believes that she will never make enough money to truly relax. Although she performs her job with desperate intensity and makes a very high salary, every time she gets a raise or a bonus she manages to incur expenses that keep her financial situation at exactly the point that matches her expectation of "not quite enough."

Gerard has a similar issue with time. He's always so busy he has little time for personal pleasure, family outings, or even sleep. Though he complains about this every day, his underlying, unarticulated expectation is "I am worthwhile only if I'm constantly *doing* something." He won't Form a more open schedule until he corrects this use of his Imagination.

Polly feels isolated, unable to find a romantic partner or even friends who really "get" her. Though she works very hard at connecting with people, her expectations were set during a childhood that combined her loneliness as the only child of a hard-working mother with high academic achievement that meant few of her classmates could keep up with her. Her expectations, not her deliberate thoughts, are dominating everything she Forms.

Another way of accidental Forming is to push against a negative pattern you've observed in others, trying to do exactly the opposite of your dysfunctional role models. This ends up being just as distressing as whatever it is you're trying to avoid, and often lands you right where you swore you'd never be.

For example, my client Bonnie grew up in a violent home. Vowing to break the cycle, she adopted an extremely soft, unassertive interpersonal style. Unfortunately this cringing energy is exactly what predators and abusers look for in their victims. Bonnie married an abusive man, and her sons grew up to batter their own wives.

Chuck was raised by parents who were obsessed with their wealth. He scorned their shallow materialism and became a proud starving artist. The problem is that no one thinks about money as much as rich people— except poor people. Constantly scrambling to pay for rent and food, Chuck obsesses about money every bit as much as his parents do.

My mother had fibromyalgia and was basically incapacitated by the time I was born. In an attempt to avoid the same fate, I became a hyper-exerciser, thereby developing fibromyalgia symptoms unusually early, when I was only eighteen.

Where are you Forming your life accidentally? Do you have horrible luck? Do people keep suing you? Are you always a bridesmaid, never a bride? Do you regularly wake up in strange hotel rooms wearing lederhosen, a three-day beard, and an unfamiliar sports bra? Such patterns are not thrust upon you by blind fate alone. You are Forming them yourself, using the fourth technology of magic unconsciously. Now it's time to master this process consciously, so that you can Form your life into the magnificent frolic it's supposed to be.

MASTERING FORMING

Most of the Forming process happens automatically as you employ the first three technologies of magic. Use all the skills this book has taught you so far to complete the following exercise. This is deep practice. To become a master Former, you'll need to repeat your efforts many times, always watching to see whether they're effective, and trying to increase your efficacy each time. You've been doing this in many of the exercises I suggested in previous chapters. For example, bending a spoon required some physical action, just not nearly as much as you'd need if you didn't use Wordlessness, Oneness, and Imagination before physically manipulating the spoon. True menders do everything this way, so that their ability to get things done becomes astonishing, while their lives become steadily less effortful.

Forming isn't a button you can push, the way you turn on your microwave. It's more like a golf swing. It looks easy and simple when you've never tried it, but as you play around with it, you find adjustments and subtleties that make all the difference between a solid *thwack* straight down the fairway and missing the ball entirely. Approach this exercise playfully, but with the intention to improve, as you would with any art or skill.

Step One: Think of a Little Something in Your Life
You Kinda Sorta Want to Form
Remember, this is only a practice session. Don't take on the twelve labors of Hercules quite yet. Trying to learn Forming by focusing on huge issues

you've been obsessing about for years is like trying to learn the rules of football by joining an NFL game in full swing. The key to Forming is a light touch, a total freedom from grasping energy. Until you've had quite a bit of practice, you won't be able to achieve that in areas where you're highly emotionally invested. That's why I suggest you practice on something you kinda sorta want, the way I kinda sorta wanted an iPad even though I really didn't need one. The thing you Form doesn't have to be an object; it could be an event, a relationship, a skill, an experience.

The best way to come up with suitable objectives for Forming is to rely on the various methods we've discussed for freeing your Imagination. If you have a problem, clean up the purely Imaginary parts in your mind, then use Forming to fix the physical aspects of the problem that remain. Finding a puzzle you'd like to crack is an excellent way to Imagine new solutions, which you can then Form. And if you're feeling bored or blank, a little adventure will give you new information, new metaphors, new insights that may transform everything in your world. Once something occurs to you, write it down in this space:

Something I kinda sorta want:

_____

_____

Step Two: Notice the Tension of Wanting and Not Yet Having

Most of us are very good at feeling impatient, frustrated, robbed, or neglected. We're *not* very good at observing these feelings with detachment. As you contemplate the thing you kinda sorta want, pay attention to the discomfort you experience from not having it. Since we're working with a molehill, not a mountain, this feeling won't be very upsetting. (If it is, exchange the thing you're trying to Form for something less emotionally volatile.) Before we've found the right zone of Forming, many of us get stuck in the negative emotion whenever we focus on anything we want and don't have, from frustration to rage, disappointment to despair, anxiety to desperation. This pattern will create more of the negative situation.

Alternatively, you may be pushing away your negative emotions about the thing you want, telling yourself it's no big deal, not worth ruffling the surface of your consciousness. That's true, of course; nothing is worth getting caught in mind-created pain. But *the objective here is to feel a full range of emotion without attaching to any Form.* Spiritual seekers often deny their desires, taking vows of poverty or celibacy, citing the biblical injunction that "money is the root of all evil" or the Buddha's position that desire creates suffering. But that's a misinterpretation of wayfinder wisdom. The Bible says that the *love of money* is the root of all evil, and the Buddha taught that *attachment* to desire creates suffering. The Bible suggests that "seeking first the kingdom of heaven" frees us to have every good thing our souls desire, "full measure, pressed down, shaken together, and flowing over." The Buddha gave up asceticism for a long, comfortable life of desire and fulfillment without attachment.

It's the emotional quality of gripping, clutching, and needing that bespeaks an underlying expectation of loss and deprivation, and causes us to create nightmares in the world of Form. Desire without grasping is joyful and playful. Hunger makes food more satisfying; it's forcing ourselves to deny our hunger that will eventually make us ravenous and insatiable. Without attachment we can receive the messages from the Energy Internet that tell us our needs will be met. With that as our expectation, our actions bring wonderful abundance into the world of Form.

If you find yourself getting attached to any outcome, Wordlessness and Oneness will come to your rescue every time. As you drop your mental stories and watch your own feelings, you'll notice that the gripping desperation of attachment is something you can release. This is what happened when I stopped chasing cheetahs and began enjoying myself at Phinda. Of course, it's more difficult to detach from things that mean a great deal to us; that's why we're practicing on little things. As you gain skill, you'll be able to want things very intensely, or abhor atrocities, or feel extreme signals to get the hell out of danger, without being graspingly attached to any of these emotions.

Step Three: Imagine Perfection . . . Calmly

Deep practice in Form involves doing with your body what you've already done with Imagination: aiming for a perfect outcome. You hold the Imagined perfection while you act, guiding your physical actions toward the Imagined outcome. The music student holds in her mind's ear the perfect trill on the piano; the tennis player Imagines a perfect serve; the poet feels for the string of words that will perfectly align his readers' felt experience with his own. Business people and politicians Imagine a perfect negotiation.

Parents with new babies Imagine keeping their temper and their sanity perfectly, despite sleep deprivation and boredom.

If, as you Imagine the perfect outcome for your situation, you find your jaw, chest, or various other body parts tightening, you're letting attachment creep into Imagination. Go Wordless, relax, and watch the perfect image until you feel only positive emotions: pleasure, delight, gratitude, satisfaction. No, the thing you're Imagining hasn't happened yet. Yes, you really can free yourself from all negativity about that fact. Otherwise you'll be chasing horses instead of getting them to come to you, roping and dragging and terrifying them until they break. That'll work, in a lame, exhausting way. But we don't want work. We want magic.

Step Four: Drop the Form of What You Want and Focus on Its Essence

Once you've established the emotional sensation of already having found your way through a problem perfectly, wipe the thought of the physical thing right out of your consciousness, but keep the emotion that arose from Imagining having it.

You may have experienced this when something wonderful happened in one area of your life (you got engaged, planned an exciting vacation, closed a business deal, escaped from prison) and then you pushed the thought of it aside to focus on some task that required your full attention, such as performing dental surgery or making a very fancy sandwich. While you were focused on the immediate task, you weren't thinking about the happy event, but the glow of it remained present, bathing the moment in a background blush of happiness or satisfaction. That's the energy of Forming.

Keep toggling back and forth between Imagining what you want in clear detail, and dropping the Image and returning your attention to the present while keeping the warm glow. Really lean on your Oneness skills, becoming totally present and aware of the moment. As you click in to the present while sustaining positive emotions, you're powerfully calling the situation you want from your Imagination into the world of Form. At that point your actions will be playful, enjoyable, parsimonious, and incredibly effective.

Step Five: Look for Any Evidence of a Response

Being in love with *both* the present moment and the future perfection you've Imagined makes you irresistibly magnetic. You may feel this inwardly. It's as though your joy at this never-before-Imagined scenario flows into the surrounding space, and the Oneness, never having experienced your perspective on the Imaginary thing, becomes intensely curious. You can sense this connection and heightened interest in the very air around you. You'll also see physical things responding to you. Birds and animals will come closer. People will smile more, ask you what you'd like, volunteer to cooperate with you. Your own body, your words and actions, will surprise you by being exactly what's needed and by happening almost without your conscious mental or physical effort.

Of course, on one level the objective is for the situation or object you've Imagined to enter your physical experience. But the real joy of this process is the playful join-up between you and everything around you. Because there is no thought in Wordlessness and no separation in Oneness, you become a pure observer of the delicious interaction between your mind and your external environment, watching Imaginary things take Form. You get to simply bask in the wonder and pleasure of feeling everything around you saying, "Yes!" to your heart's desires.

Step Six: Notice Anything You Kinda Sorta Want to Do

Sustaining the feeling of joyful interplay between the Imaginary and the physical is often enough to bring things galloping into your experience. But when Forming requires your physical participation, an impulse to act will rise up in you—such a pleasant or powerful impulse that it will actually be less enjoyable to hold still than to move. The action step will feel juicy, interesting, compelling. It may not be what you expect. Do it anyway.

Don't confuse a sense of anxiety or negative urgency with creative juiciness. Again, grasping will stop the magic of Forming, and you'll be left with plain old work. Wait until an impulse to act arises without any attachment. Sometimes it's easier to notice this when you're playing a part in someone else's Forming efforts. You may do flat-out heroic things for someone without knowing why. My friend Kelly had no intention of getting up after four hours of sleep to photograph a cheetah. But when she awoke with monkeys hammering on the roof, the impulse was so strong it sent her running through the camp in her jammies.

Speaking of sleep, here's another crucial thing to remember about the impulse to act: *the juiciest action step for you at any given moment may be to rest.* I can't emphasize this enough. Everything in nature ebbs and flows, and trying to flow without ebbing is a stressful, anxiety-based strategy. Wayfinding magic often needs you to literally fall asleep so it can proceed. The final step in joining up with a horse is to walk away from it. The final step in connecting with anything you're trying to bring from Imagination into Form is to let go, surrender, totally detach. Napping is one of the most powerful steps in many a Forming. If the impulse to rest or sleep arises, cancel everything and crash.

Because this isn't a high-stakes Forming, you may not feel a lot of juice in the impulse to act (or nap). Because this is something you just kinda sorta want to Form, you'll just kinda sorta want to do stuff about it. Still, doing that stuff will be very pleasant.

Something I kinda sorta want to do:

_____

_____

Step Seven: Sustain the Energetic State of Forming as You Do Whatever You Want

As you perform whatever action you just described, notice and gently side-step any temptation to start thinking verbally, steer back toward attachment, or "work the problem." Again, *this will immediately stop the magic of Forming.* The zone where magic occurs is so detached it may feel almost boring, but only by contrast with manic excitement. Keep paying close attention to physical results, repeating what succeeds (even a little) and correcting what doesn't. Soon you'll feel the smooth, flowing, delicious energy Lao Tzu called "doing without doing." The Force will accomplish everything for you, including the things it accomplishes through you.

PRACTICING FORMING UNTIL IT ACTUALLY STARTS HAPPENING

If the instructions above don't feel somewhat baffling to you, you're either an experienced wayfinder or you've misunderstood the instructions. Any verbal description, including the one above, can give you only a very rough approximation of the lived experience of Forming. This is another place where talking or reading about something is not the same as doing it.

For instance, the first time I tried a join-up with a horse, I'd read all the theory, memorized all the steps, watched one demonstration on TV and another one live, and had absolutely no idea what I was doing. The horse, as any part of the wild world always does, mirrored my confusion perfectly, stopping, starting, turning, wheeling, trying desperately to follow my contradictory signals. My body language was a mess, but the real issue was my energy: I was tense, hyperfocused, excited, a little needy. You've felt the same thing when an overly solicitous shopkeeper tried desperately to sell you clothes, or a classmate lobbied frantically to become popular. There's nothing evil about that energy. It just doesn't work. Or, to be more accurate, it works way too hard. What it doesn't do is play.

A few years after that first try, I found myself in a round pen with a horse, alone, for about fifteen minutes. Without anyone watching, without any fear, with nothing but happiness and curiosity to focus my attention, I found my way through my first solo join-up without a hitch. Did I jump up and down in triumph? No. That manic energy isn't on the Forming bandwidth. I'll never forget the playful joy of that moment, but I didn't need it then, and I don't need it now. You don't need something that *is;* you simply appreciate it.

Once you can sustain that sensation, simultaneously picturing something you kinda sorta want, feeling the pleasure of having it, and staying anchored happily in the present, you'll be pelted with pennies from heaven. Then you can move onto dollars from heaven, then friends from heaven, then elaborate flash-mob dances from heaven, cheetahs from heaven, and anything else heaven has on hand. You can find your way from anywhere to anything, especially in our wild new world.

THE UNEXPECTED JOIN-UPS
WITH THINGS YOU IMAGINED IN THE PAST

As you practice these steps over and over, expect something amazing: everything you've ever wanted (from the perspective of your true nature) will begin to join up with you. Achieve a wayfinder's level of calm and peace, and bada-bing, bada-boom, here comes all the stuff you wanted in childhood and adolescence, the job you fantasized about after you graduated, the lover you longed for when you were living alone, the physical reality of wild, silly dreams you made up to please your life coach. It's as if, having yanked hard on these things years ago, you created a momentum that keeps them coming long after you've forgotten you asked. In fact it's when you forget you asked that they finally arrive.

That's what eventually happens to me in regard to my request for one lousy cheetah. Less than two months after Sal's party at Phinda I find myself in Kenya, traveling with a group of philanthropists led by an intrepid, visionary Team member named J'Lein Liese. She's one of those people who shows up in a war-torn country as an unaccompanied tourist, promptly becomes a confidante of both the prime minister and the rebel leader of the opposition forces, and brokers peace over drinks the next afternoon. J'Lein's powers of Forming boggle my mind. I have no idea how she does it, but I always go along with her happily. Everyone does.

I've mentioned my cheetah fixation to J'Lein, so at one point she goes to "talk to someone," someone who has never met her but promptly becomes putty in her hands. Fifteen minutes later we're enjoying a strictly forbidden personal audience with a family of orphaned cheetahs who have been reared by loving zoologists in Nairobi.

Each species of animal has its own energy: horses are gentle and easily frightened, dogs are joyful and easily impressed, house cats are quirky and easily offended. But cheetahs . . . oh my. Cheetah energy is one of the most intensely sweet forms of affection I've ever felt. I kneel by one of them and pet his woolly fur, and he begins to groom my arm in return. Because cheetah's tongues are like industrial-grade sandpaper, it's physically excruciating; with every kiss, the cheetah seems to be removing significant layers of skin. But I'm so swept away by love I hardly noticed. For a long time afterward that arm will remain raw and sensitive, but instead of minding, I'm thrilled to have such a perfect reminder of how tender things are at the juncture between thought and three-dimensional reality, at the tipping point of creation, at the place where the wayfinder's bridge finally reaches all the way from Imagination into Form.

Kelly Eide

One lousy miraculous cheetah . . .

J'Lein Leise

. . . after another.

CHAPTER THIRTEEN

FORMING YOUR ART, MENDING YOURSELF

We hear him long before we see him. The sound is nothing like what you hear in the movies. It begins as a soft, high moan, like a human yawning, then grows steadily louder until it reaches 115 decibels—the volume of a jet engine or the amplifiers at the loudest outdoor rock concert—before dropping in pitch and fading to a series of resonant grunts. You can easily hear it a mile away, sometimes as far as five miles. If you're close to its source, the sound literally makes your organs quiver. It feels as if a lion can kill you just by roaring.

"Back up," Boyd whispers. I don't want to; I have the unshakable confidence that comes only from years of total inexperience. But I grudgingly follow Solly as he leads us in a wide circle to a *kopi,* one of the small peaks named for their resemblance to upside-down cups, that dot the savannah.

"Up, up, up," whispers Boyd from the back of the group. His usually laid-back voice seems unusually urgent. Another moan starts behind us, a Megadeath lead vocalist yawning casually right into the microphone. Five more decibels, and the vibrations would register in our ears not only as sound, but as pain. It seems to be physically pushing on my back. I climb faster.

"Here," whispers Solly when we reached a row of volcanic boulders halfway up the *kopi.* We sit down on the rocks, facing downward.

As if on cue, the lion steps out of the thick brush at the base of the hill. The rising sun turns him into five hundred pounds of glowing gold muscle and mane, a living illustration of the Gerard Manley Hopkins poem that begins "The world is charged with the grandeur of God. / It will flame out, like shining from shook foil." The lion lifts his head and draws in a huge breath, expanding his whole body like a massive bellows. Another moaning yawn emerges from between jaws that could crush a human head like a peanut. The sound grows louder . . . *and louder . . . and louder . . . and louder,* until I can feel my spleen beginning to disintegrate. I've never witnessed a more dazzling performance. It was so, so worth waking up at three in the morning to get front-row seats.

Of course, attending a lion concert requires slightly different tactics than camping out at a box office. To get these tickets, we've been tracking for hours, loping at a steady jog-trot through the bush. Solly has been leading, with Koelle and me in the middle, and Boyd bringing up the rear carrying a heavy rifle, though his bush skills mean there's virtually no chance he'll have to use it. To the Africans, the slight indentations in the soil, the disturbance of a grass blade I can't even see, might as well be neon signs telling them everywhere the lion has gone, everything it's done, practically every thought in its massive head.

I know just enough about tracking to be impressed. I started learning the day Solly beckoned me over to him, picked up a long stick, and drew a circle in the dirt. "What do you see?" he asked.

I stared at the ground inside the circle. There in the soft sand was an enormous paw print.

"Um, a lion track?" I answered. Solly nodded, and I inwardly congratulated myself. Nailed it! But Solly didn't move. He circled the same track with his stick again.

"What do you see?" he repeated.

I was confused. I'd gotten the Right Answer, hadn't I? Solly kept gazing impassively at the footprint. I tried again. "It's really big," I said. "It must have been, um, a male?'

Solly nodded again, almost imperceptibly. Then he held out one of his hands and twitched it slightly, eyes never leaving the footprint. I looked down again. This time, for some reason, I found it immensely interesting.

Later I'd realize that by using that tiny bit of body language, Solly had dropped me into Wordlessness. Instead of my Johnny-come-lately analytical neocortex, I was now looking at the lion's track with all the nonverbal sensory processes I'd inherited from millions of progenitors. Without thinking, I found myself holding out my own hand above the footprint, pretending I was the one with a giant forepaw. Then I noticed that the print was slightly smudged, as if it had corkscrewed about an eighth of an inch to the right. That movement was what Solly had shown me with his hand. I turned my own hand in the air and felt a slight torque go up my arm. Almost unconsciously, I balanced the action by turning my head to the left.

Something shifted inside me. I suddenly knew—not thought but *felt*— what the lion had probably done to make that print: he'd heard something behind him, to his left, and had stopped momentarily to glance back over his shoulder. I could feel the sharpness of his attention, his golden eyes searching the bush. He was looking for something: prey, an adversary, the other members of his pride? My own ears and eyes filled with every bird-song, cricket hop, and rustle of leaves, sifting a million tiny impressions for details that might be meaningful to a lion. When nothing presented itself, I turned my eyes forward to the next huge paw print, and then the next, and the next.

That was when I finally understood why Boyd and Solly could stare at dirt for hours at a time. They weren't just television-deprived or rolling on Quaaludes. They were *reading*. Every line of footprints was a story, written in first person by the animal who'd made it.

Once I entered the right brain state, the lion's tracks seemed to almost speak to me, like Sherlock Holmes talking to poor dim Dr. Watson. The imprints were deep and regular and right out in the open; probably he'd eaten recently and wasn't hunting. The paw pads were clear and sharp, not obscured by other footprints or softened by the breeze. The lion must have passed here very recently. In fact it suddenly occurred to me that he could be watching me. All my senses went on high alert. The footprint story became the most intensely meaningful mystery I'd ever read, the sort of clue trail that had kept me riveted to so many detective novels, so many episodes of *CSI* and *Law & Order,* but with the added spice of potentially saving my life. The story had me hooked. I wanted to follow those tracks all day.

Since then I've dragged dozens of other city-dwelling First Worlders into the bush for their first tracking lesson. I've seen the same reaction over and over: disinterest, followed by puzzlement, followed by fascination, followed by near-addiction. I'm inclined to agree with some anthropologists that reading tracks, an obvious evolutionary advantage, is knit right into our DNA. Footprints in the sand may be the ancestors of the alphabet, of analytical observation, of the scientific method itself. *What do you see? What do you see? What do you see?* That question has helped take humans in rockets all the way to the moon, through telescopes and satellites into other galaxies, through experiments into places where matter dissolves into pure energy. And it will help you track your right life through the wild new world of the twenty-first century. It will tell you what to do and create in the world of Form.

TRACKING YOUR WAY
THROUGH THE WILD NEW WORLD

When I was born, in the early 1960s, people in developed nations no longer needed to track. We'd enjoyed several centuries of cobblestones, railroads, and freeways. Industrialization paved over animal footprints, pushed back nature, allowed the human population to explode, and created unambiguous directions for millions of lives. In the America of my early years, men went to work every weekday, even though it directed most of their creativity toward imagining methods of suicide. Women, aside from occasional bouts of whelping, had basically the same life course options as furniture.

By the time I became a research assistant at Harvard Business School in the 1980s, things were changing. The simple fact that I was there showed that, but I learned much more about how the changes looked when I helped analyze a longitudinal study of 125 HBS graduates. The guys (they were all guys) who'd gotten great jobs right out of business school were struggling by the 1980s; they felt trapped and unfulfilled. The subjects who had seemed a little lost at first, who had wandered around and eventually created their own small companies, were thriving financially and psychologically.

"Wow," I thought as I read the data, "this is crazy!" The train-track career boys were actually less successful than those who were driving their lives more erratically and independently, like cars. With this in mind I began teaching career development, telling students they could "drive" their lives wherever they wanted. Maybe one day, I told them, they wouldn't even need roads! Maybe they could steer their careers like all-terrain vehicles!

I was wrong. Not because social forms were about to stiffen up again, but because even in my zaniest moments I never dreamed how fluid and unstable social and economic structures would become during my own lifetime. The term "wayfinder," remember, refers to people who can track their position and find what they need not just on land, but on open water. An all-terrain vehicle isn't a good metaphor for modern life, because everything is morphing in a huge, ongoing, liquid flood of change. Old-fashioned train-track careers, well-marked highways, the solid ground itself are being swept away.

According to a principle known as Moore's law, the capacity of digital devices doubles every eighteen months. (Many experts now think this is too conservative.) As I write this, the World Wide Web is about six thousand days old. By the time this book is published, the capacity of Web technology will be at least twice what it is now—as far removed from my current reality as my current reality is from the pre-Web world. To know what we should Form in this wild environment, we must radically release our expectations and pay a tracker's attention to all the signals that arise continuously from our environment and our own instincts.

Fortunately, we have at our disposal the technologies of magic developed by wayfinders when the world was truly wild, long before there were train tracks or freeways, let alone college degrees, entry-level marketing positions, corporate mergers, and all the other social structures we twentieth-century troglodytes thought were so solid. Today your best bet for creating a satisfying career and happy life is to toss out the rulebook and rely on the technologies of magic.

The rest of this book is about how to direct this process in physical time and space, but you've been learning how to do that since chapter 1. The procedure for reclaiming your true nature and finding your way in the wild new world is always the same: drop into Wordlessness, sense your environment and position through Oneness, Imagine what you want, and Form things—situations, objects, relationships, projects, activities—that express your unique perspective. There's a pleasingly brief word for this kind of radical creativity. It's called "art."

START WITH YOUR ART

Your art, as opposed to art in general, is any way your unique true nature expresses itself in the world of Form. You can track it by looking for moments in your life when you felt fascinated, lost in the act of creation. Whatever you Form in a truly authentic way will be compelling to more people than just you, because as the psychologist Carl Rogers wrote, "What is most personal is most general." Your essence is shared with the One Great Self, but your unique experience as an individual isn't quite like anything the One has seen before. In this wild new world, as never before in all human history, you can find others who love your art, who will support you for creating anything your true nature finds beautiful, informative, nourishing, or healing. There's no solid "road to success" in today's world, and no two career paths need look exactly the same. But the process of tracking your art can be shared, learned, and taught.

Consider, for example, the life and career of David Berceli. Gentle and intelligent, with a dazzlingly sweet smile, David grew up wanting to help and heal anyone he could. That desire, repeated in many situations, was a track, a sign that his true nature was that of a mender. David also loved religion. A mystical Catholic, he told me, "I got all the good things from church. I managed to miss all the negatives." He became a priest, and loved it. He was right on track.

Then David was assigned to work as a missionary in Lebanon, just as the country descended into war. He lived there for years, under constant threat of being blown to smithereens. Many of his friends and acquaintances were killed, and the rest lived in constant fear. So did David. The clear trail of joy, enthusiasm, and energy that led to his profession became vague. It disappeared entirely when he was most anxious. Nothing made him happy. But after a while he noticed a few faint "tracks" reappearing under very specific conditions. When a threat had passed, he'd sometimes let himself physically tremble. After that he'd feel calmer (a track!). When he didn't shake, he found no peace and no happiness; he'd lost the trail.

David became fascinated by the action of shaking. Doing research on animal physiology, he learned that all creatures tend to shiver after undergoing a trauma. Humans sometimes let themselves do this, but often we suppress our shaking, either to stay watchful or to prove that we're fine, dammit, just *fine*. By the time I met David, he'd written a Ph.D. dissertation on the healing powers of posttraumatic trembling. By following his own fascination through endless research and spending thousands of hours with trauma survivors, he had learned that people frozen in fear and pain could "unlock" their posttraumatic stress by letting themselves shake, even decades after a painful or frightening event.

David now travels all over the world, working with traumatized people in war-torn areas to repair the devastating effects of posttraumatic stress syndrome. Shaking is the Form of his personal genius, his art. David uses it to powerfully mend thousands of people who will never see a therapist, let alone a psychiatrist. In a few minutes or hours of guided shaking, David helps large groups attain a level of healing once thought to require years of counseling.

Now David lopes along the hot tracks of his best life the way Boyd tracks a lion. Despite a hectic schedule, constant travel, and immersion in some of the most anguished populations on earth, David radiates joy. He has the bizarrely powerful stillness, the "peace that passeth understanding," of someone who has eradicated all traces of fear from his own being.

"I won't leave this place," he told me when I met him, gesturing toward his own calm body. "Not even to catch an international flight or resist violence in other people." His physical body is the one bit of Earth where he can always find the tracks of his right life.

Can you imagine a high school guidance counselor steering young David Berceli toward this world-changing life's work? "Oh, yes," the counselor would have said, "you'll grow up to help huge numbers of traumatized people shake until they feel ever so much better." Or not. Fact is, no one before David had ever created such a career. But he is now in such hot demand that he's teaching apprentices and students all over the world.

THE WANDERING PATHS OF THE WAYFINDERS

Many modern wayfinders I know have similarly strange career paths. You've met several of them in this book. Lynn Trotta uses her understanding of "bird language" to help people connect with lost aspects of themselves. Her husband, Michael, is a Native American–trained "firetender" who has taught hundreds of troubled kids to heal their lives by tending campfires. Susan Hyatt, a tremendously talented coach, is also a green smoothie fanatic who helps her clients lose weight and reach optimum health. Dan Howard's life work is teaching people to rest "intentionally," achieving deeper relaxation through a few guided mental exercises than they've ever enjoyed before. All these people are genius artists, and I am not the only eager customer ready to pay for their respective arts.

As the change tsunami sweeps away jobs, companies, even industries, fewer and fewer of us are able to sustain our lives by sticking to old "concrete" career forms. To find security in an unstable world, you may have to track your own true nature to places no human has ever gone before. You may have to direct all the Forms of your life and career through this radical procedure. You can start the way I started studying lion tracks, by looking closely at a few very clear examples. The first track we'll examine is something I call "Your Ten Thousand Hours."

TRACKING YOUR TRUE NATURE, LESSON ONE: TEN THOUSAND HOURS

When technology reached a level that allowed scientists to observe the brain in action, a group of German researchers went into music schools to study the brain differences between students who had average talent and those who were true musical geniuses. As it turns out, there are none. Neuroscientists now believe that no one is born with more brain-based ability to perform a task than any other person. The single difference between ordinary musicians and geniuses was that the geniuses do a lot more deep practice, that is, Imagining some perfect Form, then trying to reproduce what they Imagined in physical reality. To be a world-class musical genius, a student has to deep-practice for about ten thousand hours.

This is as true in sports, computer programming, personal relationships, financial management, and any other complex skill as it is in music. Tiger Woods's dad taped a golf club to his tiny hands when he was an infant and made sure Tiger had put in ten thousand hours of deep practice in golf by the time he was shaving. Solly and Boyd were ten-thousand-hour animal-tracking veterans by late childhood. David Berceli has spent well over ten thousand hours reading people's posttraumatic tremors. Koelle began obsessively studying horse-whispering, all day every day, when she was fifteen. Dan Howard spends hours lying on his back on bare earth, feeling his way into deeper states of resting. When he rests deeply enough, he can somehow sense crystals in the ground; he dug up a few gorgeous jewels and gave them to me one day to demonstrate that deep-practicing rest is very different from just vegetating.

Wade Davis writes about a Polynesian named Mau who was chosen at birth to be a wayfinder and spent many of his infant hours in tidal pools, absorbing the rhythms of the sea. At age fourteen Mau "tied his testicles to the rigging of the vessel to more carefully sense the movement of the canoe through the water." While you picture the logistics of this procedure (whether you want to or not), let's think of something you care about that much, and I don't just mean the waitresses at Hooters. I mean anything you approach with interest that borders obsession. As many a tennis mom and piano teacher has found, you can push someone to practice, but not to deep-practice. That intensity has to come from within.

Ten thousand hours equates to about six hours a day for five years, or three hours a day for ten years, or an hour and a half a day for twenty years, or twelve hours a day for two and a half years. Is there anything that inter-ests you so much you've put in that amount of time deep-practicing it?

Almost everyone can answer that question yes. If you can't think of anything, you're not searching broadly enough. *Literally anything can be your art.* If you had narcissistic parents, you've spent at least ten thousand hours learning to understand narcissists. If you obsessively rearrange your clos-ets, it's likely you're an organization master. If you've put in ten thousand hours of reading, you're probably world-class at communicating in writ-ten language. When I taught college, I told my students they could submit their term papers as video recordings, since ten thousand hours of watch-ing TV had turned many of them into video geniuses. Nowadays I train coaches mostly by recruiting people who've already spent ten thousand hours trying to help others fix their lives. With just a light sanding and a coat of varnish, these geniuses are ready to rock their clients' worlds.

Use the spaces below to list anything you may have deep-practiced for ten thousand hours. Start with the obvious: breathing, finding delicious food, loving your children, grooming your pet tarantulas. Pay attention to specifics and patterns. Maybe you deep-practice singing along with the radio and always favoring country-music ballads. Perhaps you surf the Internet obsessively, persistently seeking YouTube videos of people falling down. If you collect anything, from stamps to meteorites to balls of lint, you've deep-practiced the skill of finding and getting valuable specimens. All of these activities are the Forms you've created from the Wordless place where wayfinders enter Oneness and Imagine the future. I've left you ten spaces, but don't feel bad if you have just a couple of world-class skills. There are only so many hours in a life.

THINGS I'VE DEEP-PRACTICED FOR TEN THOUSAND HOURS

1. _____

2. _____

3. _____

4. _____

5. _____

6. _____

7. _____

8. _____

9. _____

10. _____

Anything on this list counts as a clear, precise, "hot track" left by your true nature. It also constitutes part of your art, the way your true nature expresses itself in the world of Form. Now we're going to move off this topic for a moment to consider another set of tracks, left in a different substrate. Don't worry, this list will be waiting for you when we come back for it.

TRACKING YOUR TRUE NATURE, LESSON TWO: TO HELL AND BACK

A lot of people tell me, "I need to find my passion." They rarely realize that the word "passion" is from the Latin *pati*, "to suffer," or that passion originally meant "pain" (as in The Passion of the Christ). Knowing that, it becomes much easier to track your passions; even if you feel no interest in anything, odds are you have suffered. Wayfinders of all cultures know that healing the self from any kind of torment is the groundwork for healing others, for creating a positive change in the world of Form and thereby establishing your career, your life's work. Let's track your true nature along this path of passion. It's often the clearest trail.

Think of the worst thing you've ever survived. Describe it below. Then think of the next-worst thing. If you've had a long and/or eventful life, you may be able to list several ways you've been to hell: being jilted at the altar, having a miscarriage, developing tennis elbow, getting robbed at gunpoint, accidentally pressing "Send to All" on a very private email involving photographs of your special body parts. Pick your top five, in order of awfulness (the most awful is #1).

WAYS I WENT TO HELL

1. _____

2. _____

3. _____

4. _____

5. _____

    Though these experiences were dreadful, *because* they were dreadful, they are also precious. Pain gives our true nature an objective we can pursue with genuine passion. Whatever ways you've been to hell, you can make the experiences meaningful by leading others out of the same grim spots. The most motivating thought for a suffering wayfinder is "I can help other people who've been through this." This is a win-win-win-win idea. It helps heal the healer, transforms the tragedy itself into a gift of grace, blesses and repairs other beings, and radiates healing outward to the entire Great Self.

THE WOUNDED HEALER

If you're in a lot of pain at the moment, you may not feel particularly optimistic about misery taking you to your right life. Many people believe suffering makes them ineligible to create a powerful positive difference in the world. What they need, or so they think, is a perfect life and an advanced degree. Well, consider this story: After nursing a beloved father figure through his agonizing cancer death, my cousin Lydia was comforted by a woman who approached her at the funeral and said, "I know how you must be feeling. I mean, I've never known anyone who died, but I've had my legs waxed, and I bet this hurts just as much." I don't care what kind of degree this woman had; she is not going to be my chosen grief counselor. On the other hand, I have no idea what Maya Angelou's credentials are. I only care that she knows suffering and the end of suffering, and that her poetry helps me go from one to the other. The proof of the pudding is in the eating.

As future empathic healers, many wayfinders have lives front-loaded with the pain of a thousand leg waxings. Abuse, depression, illness, loss, addiction—these are standard issue for young menders. They have to be. Without deep suffering, menders can't possibly help the people who will later look into their eyes and ask, "Can I really be happy after living through this hell?" Count on it: whatever you're suffering is leading you toward your life's purpose. It's giving you depth, resonance, street cred. It's turning you into a healer—on one condition: you must not stop tracking. As Winston Churchill said, "If you're going through hell, keep going."

FINISHING THE ROUND TRIP

A lot of artists—filmmakers, writers, painters—specialize in showing how people land in hell. Their work plumbs the recesses of human depravity and despair, shows lives disintegrating into chaos, unsparingly depicts the madness of relationships and societies gone awry.

Big, fat, hairy deal.

I'll tell you this for free: anyone can go to hell. Most of us do so regularly; it's a very short commute from ordinary life. No one has to tell me that pain is ubiquitous and we're all going to die. I respect the talent of artists who dwell on this message, but they are worlds away from wayfinders, artists who Form creations that take their audience to hell *and back*. Bad artists ignore the darkness of human existence. Good artists often get stuck there. Great artists embrace the full catastrophe of our condition and find beyond it an even deeper truth of peace, healing, and redemption.

A Shakespeare professor once told me the Bard lost his mind, perhaps to senile dementia, after writing the great tragedies. That was the way this professor explained why Shakespeare's last plays, the romances, have happy endings, often involving spiritual, mystical, or magical events. I think this particular scholar was a good artist (totally cool with going to hell) feeling baffled and embarrassed by a great artist (who found the way back). "We shall not cease from exploration," wrote T. S. Eliot in *The Four Quartets,* "and the end of all our exploring will be to arrive where we started and know the place for the first time."

This is true of all wayfinders, not just playwrights and poets. Any art can teach human souls a way back from hell. David Berceli's guided shaking moves people right into a full experience of their worst repressed traumas, then carries them gently back to peace. During periods of darkness and doubt, Boyd uses his experience as a tracker to pick up the trail of his own life's mission, exactly as you're doing right now. Koelle helps horses (and people) get over phobias by gently and repeatedly exposing them to the very thing they fear most. My coaches zero in on the worst part of a client's experience, what we call the "area of least satisfaction," then usher them from that low point to confidence and clarity. All these people can help others back from hell because they've found their own way back from internal, infernal experiences.

TRACKING FORWARD

Every track runs hot and cold. Even as a beginner I had no trouble tracking a lion on a dusty path, but as soon as the ground turned rocky or the animal walked into thick scrub, I lost the trail. Great trackers can read tiny signs as if by magic, but even for them, trails go cold over some surfaces and in some conditions. The process then is always the same: return to the last clear track, form a theory about where the animal might have gone from there, and follow your hunch in that direction, trying to pick up footprints farther on. If nothing turns up, return to the hot track again, and start in another direction. Eventually, perhaps on the other side of the river, the rocks, or the fallen tree, you'll find another recognizable track.

There are times when the tracks of our true nature lead us clearly and unmistakably forward. Your next step to your right life may be absolutely apparent to you right now: you feel a compelling urge to marry your soul mate, study Norwegian, start your own bakery, or (my favorite) take a nap. If so, forward march! Follow the tracks, even if the next step seems scary and illogical and everyone thinks you're crazy. You'll never reach your goal except by following that hot trail.

On the other hand, you may feel completely baffled, directionless, uncertain of everything. *If so, it's because at some point you stopped following the tracks of your true nature.* Instead of trying to pick up the trail wherever you happen to be now, go back to the last hot track. Return to the last moment you were totally engrossed in your ten-thousand-hour activity, or the last time you took a step that brought you some measure of relief or happiness. The clearest tracks will meet both criteria: you created them when you applied your world-class skills to healing your own suffering.

In the space below, write down memories of times you got lost in deep-practicing something that relieved your pain or enhanced your joy. Maybe your passion for oil painting helped you go into a Wordless state where your depression couldn't follow, or you gardened your way out of anger, or cooking moved you into a hopeful energy where you nourished yourself and others emotionally as well as physically. Let your Imagination find any track, even a faint one

HOW MY TEN-THOUSAND-HOUR FASCINATION HELPED ME COME BACK FROM HELL

My love of [describe ten-thousand-hour activity] _____
helped me come back from [describe the worst thing you ever suffered] _____ the time I [recount an experience when you eased deep pain with deep fascination] _____

If you think through this memory, you'll realize you were using all four technologies of magic. Your ten-thousand-hour activity dropped you into Wordless fascination, connected you with a Oneness greater than yourself, helped you Imagine some beautiful action, object, or event, and then led you to make that something real in the world of Form. In that moment you were practicing a healing art, one slightly different from any other thing created by the One Great Self, ever. You are the world's master of this particular art.

TRACKING INTO YOUR FUTURE AS A MENDER

Try this: reframe the statement you wrote above as a role defini-tion. Say it out loud: "I help people who are dealing with [your hell] _____ by doing [your ten-thousand-hour art] _____. That's what I do." Of course, this isn't your only job, your only identity. *But it is probably a more stable, marketable role definition than anything based on professional or social models external to your true nature.*

This will become increasingly true as time passes and social change continues to accelerate. The technologies that underlie the huge transformations of our time are not only destroying old career tracks; they're creating new opportunities, mostly by putting people in touch with each other so directly and easily that clusters of interested people immediately Form around even the oddest-sounding art.

You can see how this played out in the lives of menders I've mentioned in this chapter. David makes his living doing the very thing he used to heal his own posttraumatic stress. Boyd's whole family has faced traumas, ranging from illness to loss of loved ones to airplane crashes, all of which drive them to create safe places and become "protectors of all living things" (the meaning of *Londolozi*), which became not only their passion but their livelihood. As a teenager Koelle sought the company of horses to heal wounds inflicted by predatory adults in her childhood. Brooke was robbed of her life savings and gained eighty pounds before learning how to create a profitable business and lose weight at the same time.

Here are some more examples of people who tracked their own fascination and suffering all the way to their life's purpose—some through familiar jobs, others new and strange ones. Kathleen's worst experience was developing panic disorder in her twenties. She learned to calm herself by having meaningful conversations with friends and is now a therapist. Anton was molested as a child and later used drugs to numb his pain; he found his way back to hope and love largely by surfing. (In rehab his "higher power" was the ocean.) He now teaches groups of recovering addicts to surf their way to recovery. Jeannie was bullied unmercifully in grade school, escaped into reading fantasy literature, and now writes stories she sells online to comfort and inspire other alienated kids. Clark grew up in a violent neighborhood and never felt safe until he rescued an abused pit bull, whom he trained to be his friend and protector. Now Clark helps run a program in which prisoners raise and train service dogs for people with disabilities.

If you are really born with the archetype of the mender, the idea of using your ten-thousand-hour art to help or heal something—other people, animals, plants, ecosystems—will give you the zinging sensation of a clear, fresh track. It will pull you forward, pique your curiosity and your enthusiasm, and tell you what to Form. Even if you're presently far from your right life, it will feel like relief and ease compared to any other path you might contemplate. And it will lead you straight into the part of the wild new world that is yearning for the gifts only you can bestow.

No matter what economic or social changes occur in the future, the mender's arts (one unique art for every mender) will always be in demand. Why? Because everything, especially humans, needs healing and values it above almost anything else you could offer. That's why even the homeless heroin addicts I've coached find money (around $200,000 a year) for street drugs. Mender skills are as potently comforting as drugs, but without negative side effects like dry mouth, weight gain, or a life of crime.

If the mender archetype doesn't appeal to you, that's fine. You can still use all the technologies of magic to reclaim your true nature and find happiness. This process will still help immeasurably with your career. But if you've lived the classic wayfinder life, you can and probably should make your living by creating your art. You may need a little help shaping a delivery system and finding the people to help; that phase of Forming is the subject of the next chapter. The real point is not that your wayfinding art can help you make money, though that's true. The exciting thing is that *in this wild new world, you can make a living doing nothing but your art.* That means getting up every morning and diving into your ten-thousand-hour passion. It means doing what most fascinates you until your former sorrows and weaknesses become your great joys and strengths. If you're a wayfinder, you've already been to hell. If you haven't been to heaven, it's time to start making your living by Forming your art.

PRACTICE FORMING YOUR ART

Here are a couple of additional exercises you can do before moving on to the next stage of Forming. Basically their purpose is to stimulate your Imagination, helping you come up with ideas for applying your fascinations to the problem of suffering as you've experienced it. They're fun to do with friends, especially friends who are on the Team.

Wayfinder Forming: Google Your Art
Fire up your computer, iPhone, brain implant, or whatever other device allows you to track in the wilderness we call the Internet. Using the "Ten Thousand Hours" list and the "Trips to Hell" list you made earlier, enter combinations of your skills and challenges into the Google search field.

For example, if you love to crochet and also have diabetes, you'd type "crocheting" and "diabetes" into Google. I just did, and by golly, it turns out there are sites devoted to "crocheting for a cure" for juvenile diabetes. If your skill is riding a bicycle and your personal hell was a bad divorce, you can Google "bicycle" and "divorce." I just found a site for divorced dads who do bicycle tours to bond with their kids, and a cycling group for "divorce recovery."

At the very least, this exercise can give you ideas about ways to use your art. It will almost certainly help you find a tribe of people who share your interests and can help you make a living. And it may just show you a "hot track," something your true nature immediately recognizes as your next step.

Wayfinder Forming: Take On the Big Stuff

A variation on the previous exercise is to Google your ten-thousand-hour skill and a social, even global issue that bothers you. For instance, if you're a fashionista who detests discrimination, you could search for "accessories" and "racism." Sure enough, there are folks selling accessories with antiracist messages, fashion designers working for social justice, and sites where any purchase of accessories sends a donation to foundations that promote racial understanding. Again, this could be a fire-starter or a way for you to connect using your own art.

Wayfinder Forming: Ten Ways Your Art Can Help
People Return from Hell

Using your computer, advice from friends, and any other stimulating idea catalyst, brainstorm at least ten different ways each of your ten-thousand-hour skills might be used to help people return from the hell you've experienced. The ideas can be completely impractical, ridiculous, even stupid. Just keep them coming. Somewhere in the process you'll find a hot track.

Wayfinder Forming: Tracking Your Way to Fearlessness

I returned home after our lion-tracking expedition in love with the sound of lions. I spent hours searching the Internet for the perfect roar, then installing it on my phone as a ring tone. It was hard to get close to the real sound, because sheer volume is such a crucial part of the effect. A techie friend managed to double the volume of my phone—not perfect, but better.

One night, around two in the morning, someone placed a wrong-number call to my cell phone. Before I realized what was happening I'd already leaped out of bed and hunkered in the bathroom behind the toilet, trembling. Only then did it occur to me that I'd deliberately subjected myself to one of the most terrifying noises in nature. An anthropologist I know believes saber-toothed cats hunted the original humans, and that our entire defensive brain is focused on avoiding encounters with lions. I was basically sleeping with the enemy. Yet when I'd been out tracking in a place where lions actually could have killed me, their roars were one of the most beautiful, musical sounds I'd ever heard.

The lesson I take from this is that when we're on the trail of something, all senses alert, attention soft and present, our bodies know we're at our safest. With the world getting stranger and more fluid every day, with a new wildness growing up all around us, tracking has once again become our safest haven and our path to security. Following the trail of your own passions—the passions of fascination and of suffering—is wayfinding at its most intense, zoned-in, and fearless. When you get unnerved by the wildness of the world as we know it, don't look for safety in institutions. It's no longer there. Instead look at your life; your history, your passions, the direction of your interests. Then ask yourself, over and over, what your ancestors asked each other on a million different trails.

What do you see?

What do you see?

What do you see?

Bigstock Photo

Hold on to your spleen.

CHAPTER FOURTEEN

HOW TO FORM A LIVING

"I think it's in trouble," I say.

"Nah," says Boyd. "Turtles hang out in the pool all the time."

"It's safer than the river," Bronwyn puts in, "and it's their home too, after all. They're welcome to take a dip with us. They just swim through."

I peer through the trees that lined the grassy banks of the pool, where I once coached a client while treading water (long story). For some reason the small shape in the water pulls at my attention. "It's not a very strong swimmer," I said. "For a turtle."

As we walk across the grass toward the pool, Bronwyn exclaims, "Oh, it's not a turtle, it's a tortoise!"

Tortoises, as you may know, are landlubbing turtles; they don't habitually swim. This one is churning her stubby legs mightily to keep her chunky little vault of a body on the surface. She's headed for the poolside, but I can see she'll never be able to climb out on her own. I reach into the water and pick her up. She's panting in exhaustion. I've never seen a tortoise pant. Didn't know they had it in them.

"Good grief, it's another leopard tortoise!" I say as Boyd gently takes the animal and sets her free in a patch of choice tortoise terrain. "That's the third one I've seen today. Are they in high season or something?" My friends shake their heads. They have no theory about why I'm running into different leopard tortoises every couple of hours. But I do.

You see, once you're using all four technologies of magic, something fascinating occurs: Oneness begins speaking to you, using any available messenger to get its point across through physical Form. Objects and events show up to reassure you, point out the best way forward, and nudge you away from problematic situations. On this trip to Londolozi, Oneness has apparently chosen to speak with me in Reptile.

Decades before, when I was physically sick, emotionally devastated, and generally incapable of any function I couldn't perform while curled into the fetal position, I chose tortoises as my animal mascots. Since then I've been collecting tortoise images—in jewelry, carvings, cool photographs—as reminders to keep plugging along slow and steady, to stick out my neck when I want to move forward, to maintain a resilient shell while keeping my insides soft. Since beginning to research the technologies of magic, I've occasionally wished I had a more exciting mascot, namely the leopard. Leopards or leopard-like animals (the mountain lion, the panther, the jaguar, even the humble housecat) are the mascots of menders all over the earth. So I was delighted when I learned that Londolozi, which is famous for its strangely human-friendly leopards, also boasts a critter called a leopard tortoise. This beautiful little animal looks like a turtle in an elegant cat-print body sock.

Because leopard tortoises immediately became my favorite symbol for my ownself, it feels quite poignant to rescue that compact, panting little body from the Londolozi swimming pool. I experience the joy you can get only by doing a good deed while burning virtually no calories. But even as I help the drowning animal, the Wordlessness at the back of my brain whispers that I'm on a two-way street. It seems that somehow, the leopard tortoises are also trying to help me.

This feels like an explanation for the barrage of leopard tortoises I've seen in a very short period. In all my prior visits to Africa, I glimpsed only a single specimen. This time they're everywhere: on the path from the Varty house to the camp; in the grass where we went tracking; beside the deck where we had lunch. One shows up in front of me as I walk back to my room after the incident at the swimming pool. Later, as I sit in my room trying to write, something on the other side of the glass door catches my eye. Sure enough, yet another leopard tortoise is marching back and forth across the cottage veranda, looking oddly purposeful, like a soldier on guard duty.

I stop typing and stare at this latest leopard tortoise until my eyes blur—approximately two-fifths of a second. Months of constant travel, public speaking, coaching, and writing deadlines have left me with the energy of a corpse, minus the high muscle tone of rigor mortis. Every cell of my body aches with fatigue, because while working frantically crossing many time zones every few days, I've forgotten how to sleep. I haven't managed anything more restful than a light doze for longer than I can remember (especially since my memory span has shrunk to twenty seconds). I slap myself in the face and stare at the leopard tortoise, telling myself to focus, focus, *focus*. Why are so many of these animals literally crossing my path? What's the message they seem bent on delivering? Are they telling me to keep on keeping on, no matter how tired I am? That seems right.

The tortoise stops for a moment, fixes one bright black eye right on me, then continues his march. Back and forth, back and forth, across the veranda, gaze locked on me. Finally, propelled by the same magnetism that drew me to the tortoise in the pool, I walk out to the veranda and pick him up. He's about the size of a flattened volleyball, beautifully dappled with gold, black, and brown. I hold him up at eye level, facing me, and he peers back at me from the confines of his shell.

"What are you trying to tell me?" I ask him. In my wooziness, I feel as if I'm conversing with Yoda, though the tortoise actually looks more like Don Rickles. That makes me comfortable. Who doesn't love Don Rickles? The tortoise pokes his nose out a little. I could swear he smiles at me.

"Okay," I say, "why don't you show me what I need to do?" I set the leopard tortoise back on the ground. His landing gear deploys immediately, and he practically sprints (in tortoise terms) to the shade of a small, low-lying plant a few feet away.

Where he falls asleep.

For fifteen hours.

That night I sleep too, deeply, with the tortoise curled up next to my door like the great spotted cat he isn't. In my dreams I walk through the savannah saturated with comfort, feeling the touch of my feet as if they are massaging my own shoulders, hearing the frogs, crickets, hyenas, and hippos as if their voices come from within my own buzzing body. I *am* the wilderness. The stones, plants, and animals are all continuous with my own nervous system. The tortoises are a part of myself reaching out to comfort me, as automatically as my hand might brush the hair out of my eyes.

I suspect this is how the life of a real mender always feels. Healing is a natural effect of the love experienced in Oneness, and Oneness can't help but respond to the energy of healing by offering more love. Helping another *is* helping yourself; whatever you give, you also receive. Some American Indian cultures refer to this gentle tornado of compassion as "mending the hoop of the people." The more you experience the world this way, the less interesting it becomes to sustain any other state of consciousness. Being a mender is a great way to live.

And these days it's also a great way to make a living.

WHY MENDING THE HOOP OF THE PEOPLE
IS A SOUND FINANCIAL STRATEGY

In March 2011, as you may recall, a massive earthquake occurred off the coast of Japan, creating a tidal wave that briefly turned earth to ocean as far as six miles inland. Hundreds of people used "magical" technologies—mostly video cameras in smart phones—to record their experience of the disaster. A week or so later I found myself watching one particular You-Tube video with particular fascination. It begins with sirens blaring and water lapping its way into the city of Sendai. Things start looking pretty serious, then truly dangerous, then utterly mind-blowing. For six full minutes the wave continues to rush in, carrying away boats, cars, and finally buildings, until it's two stories deep. The video is mesmerizingly nightmarish. Watch it (www.youtube.com/watch?v=2uJN3Z1ryck).

I was viewing and re-viewing this clip, trying to wrap my mind around the enormity of the disaster, when strangely, my computer opened another video. I don't know how this happened; I must have hit a key somewhere, but it seemed as if the scene popped up spontaneously on my monitor. It showed the surfer Mike Parsons catching what turned out to be a freak wave (www.youtube.com/watch?v=IsHzU0ynRZk&feature=related). As in the tsunami video, the wave starts out looking impressive, then becomes alarming, then jaw-dropping. At its apex it measures sixty-four feet, nearly the height of a seven-story building. When the wave crests and breaks, the amount of water crashing down on Parsons looks as if it too could smash a city, let alone one unarmored human standing on a plank. Yet after riding the wave to its finish, Parsons surfaces not only hale and hearty but whooping with joy. He's just lived every surfer's dream. The Big One came, and he was in exactly the right place, at exactly the right time, to catch it.

These two videos are the best illustration I can offer for what's happening to the global economy—including your personal financial situation—right now. The world is awash in what the Harvard Business School professor Clayton Christensen calls "disruptive innovation." Established ways of doing business are being battered, then uprooted and demolished, by powerful, fluid ways of using machines, buying, selling, and conducting human affairs. What we tend to call "solid" economic structures aren't any safer than the wooden or concrete buildings in Sendai when the tsunami hit. On the other hand, very small business entities that can "surf the change"—that is, adapt to a shifting environment rapidly and flexibly—are doing better and better, not only surviving but having a thrilling ride.

Consider the book you're reading. Books were once more precious than gold because they were laboriously handcrafted. Then, for a long time, they were literally "penned" only by the actual author, after which a printer would set them in movable type, make many copies, and sell them through retailers. Typewriters made the process slightly easier, but when I wrote my first book, it still took thousands and thousands of people— publishing personnel, paper makers, printer-repair mechanics, truck drivers, book sellers—to get the words from my brain to faraway readers. All those laborers still exist, but if I wanted to post a truly enormous blog, I could send this manuscript (the word means "written by hand") through virtual reality to literally billions of people, almost instantly, with very little effort or expense. In my field, as in many others, individuals can now do things cheaply and quickly that once required lots of workers doing lots of jobs.

Similar events are happening in virtually every industry, mostly because of technological innovation. During the twentieth century transportation technologies made it cheaper for manufacturers to hire labor in less developed nations than at home. Now near-instantaneous information transfer means companies and individuals in the United States can hire employees in India to do so-called knowledge work: accounting, legal paperwork, advertising, graphic design, scheduling, and more. Online retailers are diverting foot traffic from department stores. The music industry as it once existed collapsed when it became possible to email a song. Newspapers are closing all over the developed world as people choose to go online for information.

The economist Thomas Friedman won the Pulitzer Prize for observing that, because of technology, "the world is flat," meaning that nowadays making money is a game played not in huge pyramid-shaped organizations, but on a fairly level playing field. One isolated genius in Bangladesh or Siberia can log on to the schoolhouse computer and gain immediate access to as much information as a researcher at the Library of Congress. Everywhere individuals and small groups (surfers) are using this reality to do business in new ways, and they're outcompeting big organizations (concrete structures). If you have an old-fashioned job, the change tsunami is either sweeping through your industry already, or it's right offshore, ready to smash into your "safe" situation.

There are two ways to deal with this huge wave of change: you can either hunker down in an old-fashioned company that's probably a financial death trap, or you can go surfing. If you choose the first option, good luck to you, my friend. Even if your job survives in some form, the neighborhood is going to disappear. You'll find yourself working harder and harder for less and less money just so your company can continue to exist. It's much safer to climb on a surfboard, a small-scale, low-cost way to make money that gives you enormous delight while offering something to consumers they can't get anywhere else. And what would that be? Why, of course: your wayfinder art.

THE WHOLE NEW WAYFINDER'S MIND

Thomas Friedman's favorite business book (if we can trust the cover blurb) is Daniel Pink's *A Whole New Mind: Why Right-Brainers Will Rule the Future.* Pink sees the change tsunami in the developed world as part of a shift from information-shuffling to creativity. "We progressed from a society of farmers to a society of factory workers to a society of knowledge workers," Pink writes. "And now we're progressing yet again—to a society of creators and empathizers, of pattern recognizers and meaning makers."

In this new economy, where manual labor and knowledge work will be so mechanized they won't require much human input, the most profitable products and services won't be high tech but "high concept" and "high touch." Here's Pink's description of these terms. As you read it, bear in mind the wayfinder archetype we've been discussing throughout this entire book.

> High concept involves the ability to create artistic and emotional beauty, to detect patterns and opportunities, to craft a satisfying narrative, and to combine seemingly unrelated ideas into a novel invention. High touch involves the ability to empathize, to understand the subtleties of human interaction, to find joy in one's self and to elicit it in others, and to stretch beyond the quotidian, in pursuit of purpose and meaning.

In other words, the artistic, imaginative, unorthodox personality of a mender is the most profitable thing you can have in the wild new world. The economic transition isn't complete, but it's happening. The wave is rising, and I'm willing to bet that you were born to surf.

Pink describes six "senses" that will be particularly valuable in this wild new economic world. He doesn't mean things like sight or hearing, but "sense" as in capacity for perception, as in "sense of humor." To be a high earner requires a sense of design, story, symphony (the ability to coordinate disparate things into meaningful patterns), empathy, play, and meaning. As a wayfinder (if you're not one, no offense, but why are you still here?) these six senses are the sweet spot of your personality, the things that make you happiest. Your art almost certainly involves one or more of them. To thrive while fulfilling your highest purpose, you just have to offer your art to your tribe as a product or service.

YOU'RE A CONTENT CREATOR, NOT A DISTRIBUTOR (AND THAT'S A GOOD THING)

Using your ten-thousand-hour specialty to bring people back from hell is a precious gift to the world. Your capacity to delight, inspire, comfort, and heal is desperately needed by people who will be happy to pay for your art. But to make this exchange, you need a method of delivering your art in the world of Form. Since there are as many arts as there are individuals, there is no way I can identify all possible Forms your art may take. It may help to think of your art as Forming something in one of the categories below. Remember, whether something occupies time (like a performance), space (like a painting) or virtual reality (like Facebook), if it can be transferred from mind to mind, it has entered the world of Form.

FORMS YOUR ART MAY TAKE (The components of your business model)		
NEED FILLED (DEMAND)	OBJECTS (GOODS)	ACTIONS (SERVICES)
Education	books, movies, sound recordings, etc.	storytelling, teaching, public speaking, etc.
Human connection	clubs, organizations, group activities, aid work, etc.	coaching, counseling, organizing, fundraising, etc.

Beauty and aesthetics	paintings, sculptures, jewelry, architecture, design, etc.	music, dance, acting, standup, TV or radio shows, etc.
Tools for making a living	appliances, cars, electronics, websites, etc.	classes or personal instruction in trade, craft, or art, etc.
Daily needs	houses and other buildings, clothing, etc.	Pet care, child care, cooking, shopping, errands, etc.
Physical health and comfort	foods, beverages, medicine, soap, lotion, perfume, etc.	massage, acupuncture, surgery, personal training, etc.

Whether your art is researching pharmaceutical biochemistry, making stained-glass windows, or delivering vegan live-food cuisine to people too busy to graze on their own damn lawns, it probably fits at least loosely into one of these categories. Now this is very important: *notice that every single item in the chart has value in and of itself.* You couldn't say the same about the vast majority of twentieth-century jobs. Most jobs weren't about *creating,* they were about *distributing.* To run a newspaper, you needed far more paperboys (and girls) than you did journalists. The apparel industry required far more salespeople than clothing designers. It took a huge workforce to get movies and TV shows to a large audience, but there were only a few writers and actors creating the performance.

As the world gets flatter, it's the distributors' jobs that are disappearing. A news blog requires no paperboys. A clothing designer doesn't need stores or floorwalkers to sell clothes, just a computer, a camera, and a PayPal account. Forget the hundreds of technicians needed to make a movie or TV show; today any suburban mom can put a video of her darling twins online and see it go viral, all by her lonesome. (Check out this one—*tens of millions* of people have already watched it, and you won't regret seeing it yourself: www.youtube.com/watch?v=_JmA2ClUvUY.)

Focusing on your wayfinding arts makes you a *content creator,* and in the economy that's emerging right now, being a content creator is the best job security you can have. No computer knows how to get people back from hell; your art can't be mechanized. No one else combines your ten-thousand-hour skill with your particular passion; they can try to mimic it, but your personal energy is unlike anyone else's. Think of all the people who have tried to replicate the success of people like Oprah, J. K. Rowling, or Lady Gaga by imitating them. It just doesn't work, because you can't fake the deeply personal energy that makes a content creator fascinating.

Best of all, because of the magical distribution technologies, you can easily find your tribe—people who need your art—even if they're scattered all over the world. No, scratch that. You don't have to find the people who need your art. *They'll find you.* They're already looking for you. The only thing you have to do is show up in the places they're looking.

HELPING YOUR TRIBE FIND YOUR ART

In his bestselling book *Tribes,* the business author Seth Godin spells out the economic importance of people with common interests, how they'll shape the fluid, tsunami-struck world we now inhabit: "A tribe is a group of people connected to one another, connected to a leader, and connected to an idea. . . . Do you believe in what you do? Every day? It turns out that belief happens to be a brilliant strategy. . . . The most profitable path is also the most reliable, the easiest, and the most fun."

Tribes of customers are forming because people in today's economy want meaningful work, meaningful products, and meaningful services. Factory-style production is being outmaneuvered by "disruptive innovators" on their little surfboards who can offer these meaningful items. As Godin puts it, "Many consumers have decided to spend their money buying things that aren't factory-produced commodities. And they've decided not to spend their time embracing off-the-shelf ideas. Consumers have decided, instead, to spend time and money on fashion, on stories, on things that matter, and on things they believe in."

Because techno-tribe economics are so fluid, each of us can belong to many tribes, and potentially lead a tribe. As a wayfinder, you're in a prime position to be a leader. The most enthusiastic tribes are made up of folks who need the same kinds of help, because they're mired in the same sort of hell. Whatever created your own hellish mender-training experience—loss, disillusionment, poverty, abuse, addiction, failure, constrictive undergarments, angry birds—also affected other people. Those people are out there seeking comfort and guidance. Nowadays even your grandmother no longer turns to the phone book or the library to get information about her worst problems. Virtually everyone either Googles their particular issue or talks to someone who Googles it for them.

You can be a successful mender in today's world without going online. That said, the Internet is such an easy place to form a tribe that it's a little silly not to use it. For example, a coach I helped train, Abigail Steidley, specializes in helping women with pelvic inflammatory disease. If Abigail had set up a hometown practice in, say, 1980, she might have rented an office and created a big old sign, PELVIC PAIN CENTER, to bring in customers. She probably would have listed her services in the Yellow Pages, maybe splurged to put some ads in newspapers, even set up a billboard on the highway into town. It would have been expensive, and still the odds of several thousand needy pelvic pain patients finding Abigail would have been vanishingly small. But today those folks are Googling up a storm, and before long Abigail's name pops up in front of them. They can send her a note with just a few clicks. Ta-da! Abigail has a client, and a suffering tribe member gets Abigail's helpful coping tips, information, and coaching.

This is called "inbound marketing." Instead of going out and flogging your product or service, you're best served by creating a very specific niche, offering something that is unique and helpful for a tribe whose members are seeking help. Instead of *generalizing* your product and trying to reach umpteen million people, of whom a few might become customers, you *specialize* your offering, allowing the people who need you to surf their way over to you. For example, if you write a cookbook, calling it *Good Food Everyone Will Like* is going to attract far fewer inbound customers than a book called *Vegetarian Recipes for Kosher Diabetics.* Nobody Googles "good food for everyone," but any kosher diabetic vegetarian will be snooping the Internet, inputting search terms that will connect them with your unusual recipes.

MENDER ART AND
TECHNOLOGICAL DELIVERY SYSTEMS

Today's wayfinder business model is based on one simple truth: human technology changes many orders of magnitude faster than human biology. That means that in an age dominated by machines and cities, we still have the brains, bodies, and basic needs of our ancestors, people who lived in small groups, close to one another and to nature. A rule for success in today's wild new economic world is this: *use the most innovative technologies to deliver the most primal products and services.*

This turns old-fashioned pricing schemes on their head. In the old days (from caveman times through the twentieth century) most objects and services were created with primitive tools or processes by individuals who had to show up physically to get the job done. Simple, hand-made items were low-class and low-price. High-tech items and processes, things made or done by machines, were considered fancy and fine. The higher the technological sophistication of the content-creation system, the more money people paid for whatever was being created. Now the opposite is true. Where the rule used to be "high tech = high price; low tech = low price," the current trend is "high tech = low price; low tech = high price."

OLD WAY	NEW WAY
HIGH TECH = HIGH PRICE	HIGH TECH = LOW PRICE
NEW WAY	OLD WAY
LOW TECH = HIGH PRICE	LOW TECH = LOW PRICE

For example, a book zapped to you on your wireless ebook is probably pretty cheap, while a *hand*-calligraphed book written by monks on *hand*-made paper, bound by *hand* with *hand*-tanned leather, is worth a bundle. Downloading a video of Jay Leno telling a joke costs you nothing. (If you borrow someone else's computer, you get the product without even needing your own machine.) But getting Jay Leno to show up in person—a flesh-and-blood human in real time, the most basic of physical connections—will cost you a pretty penny. Going to see lions in an expensive city zoo (high tech) is considerably cheaper than going to Londolozi and seeing lions out where God put them (low tech).

To survive as a wayfinder, you can either deliver a lot of low-priced things through high-tech distribution (like popular bloggers who get money through subscriptions or advertising), or you can deliver a few higher-priced things through primal distribution methods (like a personal trainer who shows up at your door and demands that you squat repeatedly). If you love new technologies, go for the high-volume, low-price model; if you're a nature baby, create a niche and use just enough magical technology to give interested customers access to your art. Here are two examples:

My friend Sebastian was an awkward, geeky boy who spent most of his time in a newfangled place called a "computer lab," punching paper cards to run what was basically a massive calculator. By the time he reached college, he was able to program well enough to create simple games. He majored in computer science and got better at programming, reaching his ten-thousand-hour limit by the time he was old enough to drink legally.

Unfortunately—you saw this coming—Sebastian was not exactly Mr. Popularity. Almost pathologically shy, he had endless romantic daydreams in which he was a knight-errant, showing up to help damsels by programming a computerized robot to kill a dragon. During his senior year, Sebastian teamed up with an artist friend to make a dragon-killing game, and they sold the idea to a gaming company for a tidy sum. In the meantime, everyone had begun using computers. Even the ladies. All over the world, beautiful women were gnashing their teeth in frustration as their Internet connections crashed, their documents disappeared, or their screensavers froze.

Ultimately, it was the idea of saving women from a dragon that led Sebastian to a clever marketing campaign that "rescued" people from problems in their computers. Still living in his college town, Sebastian started one of the first "geek services," where people could phone him to ask for technical assistance with techno-breakdowns. Not only has Sebastian made an abundant living helping people manage the "dragons" in their machines, he came out of his social shell when he was helping people. He found that his love of coming to the rescue made him gentle and patient as a tech consultant, while many techies treated their less computer-literate customers with disdain. Sebastian eventually hired a female assistant—also a geek—who is now his wife. By applying his ten-thousand-hour art (programming and fantasizing about being a rescuing hero) to his hell-and-back exercise (being lonely and shy), he found his way to the career, the relationships, and the life that made him happy.

On the other side of the spectrum is a mender named Fernando. He grew up in the canyons of northern Mexico, learning ancient skills like tracking and blending with nature to avoid being killed by drug runners, the only "civilized" people in the area. Fernando learned to love running through the mountains, and in the 1980s, when running became a craze in the United States, he was already a locally famous ultramarathoner (though that term meant nothing to him).

Fernando began coaching North American runners, who came to learn his "techniques" and soon learned that for Fernando, running wasn't about covering distance at speed, but about dropping into Wordlessness through the path of sacred play. He joined with one of his American students to begin offering "clinics" to lay athletes, teaching them to run all the way into Oneness, open their Imagination, and allow their passions to guide the Forms of their life. Thirty years later Fernando's professional schedule is booked solid, despite being so reclusive he asks his clients never to tell anyone anything about him. Through a silent inbound network of people connected by First World technologies, his influence is spreading to every corner of the world.

If you're selling a low-tech art, it will need to carry a healthy price, because it's scarce, high touch, and not replicable. You need only a small tribe for that, but they must be committed. If you're selling a high-tech thing that's a breeze to reproduce, like a daily blog, you can charge very little because you can reach billions of customers with virtually no effort. Either way, the more specific your mender art, and the more passionate your tribe, the more successful you'll be. (Remember, "passionate" means they're either fascinated, suffering, or both.) Your tribe will spread the word about your product or service. The tsunami of change will lift you and throw you forward. All you'll need to do is stay balanced on your board.

EXAMPLES: MENDERS USING THE MAGICAL TECHNOLOGIES TO DISTRIBUTE THEIR ARTS

Because every wayfinder is different, you can't copy anyone else's business byte for byte (in the case of a high-tech product like a video blog) or bite for bite (in the case of a low-tech product like excellent cookies). However, as you contemplate other successful menders, you'll find ways of cracking your own career puzzles. Examples can spark your Imagination, helping you dream up a business model you can then create in the world of Form. So here are a few true stories of modern menders.

Right now, on the far right side of the screen where I'm typing, is a live streaming broadcast of an eagle's nest in Decorah, Iowa. It's broadcast by unknown Earth menders under the name Raptor Resource Project. They can fund research by running brief ads on the live-feed site. Right now—this very moment!—I can watch three fuzzy eaglets flop around the nest while their devoted dad tidies their dry-grass bedding. A month ago I watched them hatch, and—oh, wait! Mom just got home! She's caught a fish! Now she's feeding the babies, patiently holding strips of meat in her huge beak as the little ones bumble around, trying to coordinate their heads. I love watching this eagle family. And so do more than fifty thousand other people who are logged on to the broadcast right now. Our tribe of eagle watchers is spread all over the globe, but in a very real sense we're also sitting together high in a single tree—without disturbing the eagles at all.

Now that the eagles have lured me online, I might as well navigate over and buy one of my favorite shirts from a company called Chewy Lou, founded by a woman named Alyssa Dinowitz after her mother was diagnosed with breast cancer. Alyssa was standing in the shower, looking for something to feel good about, when her Imagination handed her an image: beautifully designed, high-quality T-shirts decorated with encouraging words and delicate Swarovski crystals. Alyssa decided to hire people with cognitive disabilities to help make her T-shirts. Her shirts are not quite like anything else available. When I wear them, people invariably ask about them. I tell them about Chewy Lou, and they find the shirts online to buy their own. Alyssa's art heals in many ways: raising money for cancer research, employing a disadvantaged group, and delighting customers like me.

Having purchased a new sparkly T-shirt, I celebrate by visiting the site of one Allie Brosh, a young woman with a hilarious sense of humor and a knack for drawing cartoons. (You can tell she's been drawing for at least ten thousand hours.) When one of Allie's friends suggested she write a blog, Allie didn't know what a blog was. Long story short: now Allie's website, Hyperbole and a Half, has hundreds of thousands of followers and generates a healthy income, and she's working on a book. Offering hilarity and mental refreshment to a happy tribe just by being herself, telling her stories, and drawing her pictures, is Allie's wayfinding art.

After reading Allie's latest post, I trot over to the virtual home of Michael Trotta, a tribe leader I've mentioned several times in this book. His website offers wilderness survival and nature awareness experiences. Though I can connect with it through my computer, the complete physical Form of Michael's business—that is, the physical space where people gather to learn skills and ideas—is literally any wild place on Earth: the woods of the American Northeast, the deserts of the Southwest, the Canadian Great Plains. If you'll pardon the pun, Michael works virtually everywhere.

Now it's time for me to start writing for the day, so I decide to get encouragement by visiting another author (online). Amanda Hocking spent her childhood writing fantasy novels, first longhand, then on a computer. Unfortunately—no wait, make that fortunately—no publisher ever bought any of Amanda's books. She eked out her living by working at a group home for people with disabilities, writing more magical novels in her free time. (Can you say "mender archetype"?) Finally Amanda decided to publish her books online, all by her ownself. That was in April 2010. As I write this, in April 2011, Amanda has sold over 185,000 books and is lauded as a "Kindle millionaire." She has a passionate and growing tribe hungry for her art.

Are you starting to believe me? *Anyone who provides a valuable, innovative, or unique mender art can be a tribe's wayfinder and make a living in the process.* I'm lucky enough to work every single day with just such people, and though I'm writing this in the middle of a major financial crisis, they're thriving. If you have the true nature of a wayfinder, distributing the technologies of magic (Wordlessness, Oneness, Imagination, and Forming) with magical technologies (all the machines that are physically interconnecting humans in the physical world) is the easiest way to surf the economic tsunami of the wild new world. In fact it feels bizarrely easy if you get it right. And how, in this swirl of change, do you "get it right"? You actually use the technologies of magic I've described throughout this book to create the Form of your wayfinding career. Then you look for technologies—new ones so amazing they're almost magical—to distribute what you've created.

USING THE TECHNOLOGIES OF MAGIC TO ATTRACT AND SUSTAIN YOUR TRIBE

Of course, you must take physical action to make a physical living. But with new technologies, less and less physical action is necessary. Furthermore, today no amount of physical action alone carries sufficient power to create a successful career. As the world changes, more and more old-fashioned work—that is, the kind of work most people did up until the turn of the twenty-first century, the corporate or manual jobs we think of as "typical" occupations—is necessary to sustain old levels of economic prosperity. Trying to build businesses or careers that look the way most businesses and careers did in, say, the 1990s, is like shoring up a building as a tsunami is sweeping inward, tearing everything apart before you can finish creating it. *On the other hand, using Wordlessness, Oneness, and Imagination simultaneously creates so much targeted energy that when it's time to Form a physical career, the action required is minimal, gentle, joyful, and fun.* Surfing well is about mender magic, not sheer dogged effort.

I discovered this during the time I worked so frantically I forgot to sleep. Now I do business very differently. The meetings I attend with the staff of my little virtual company go something like this: Five to ten people dial into one conference number from wherever they happen to be in the world. (I keep the company small purposely. I don't want it to be a cement warehouse in a change tsunami.) My CEO calls the meeting to order by making sure everyone is wearing pajamas. Generally someone recommends a YouTube video of a golden retriever who dances the mambo (or similar). Then we discuss our business, which consists mainly of training coaches and creating audio and visual classes helping people heal various aspects of their lives and maximize their well-being.

As the meeting proceeds, my staff and I search for puzzles we might crack to make this business more of a win-win for us and our customers. We process feedback and consider ways to serve clients and coaches better. If solutions aren't initially obvious, the whole group sinks into a bit of Wordlessness and feels through the Oneness, getting our nonverbal brains primed to offer solutions, feeling for what "wants to happen." Then we all describe what we're Imagining. Almost invariably—to the point where it almost feels ridiculous—there's consensus on any significant idea about product creation, improved service, hiring, or whatever else needs doing. When there are differences of opinion, everyone examines his or her belief system to see which apparent "problems" (almost always unnecessary beliefs) are keeping us from seeing one another's viewpoint.

Once we're all on the same page, it's time to implement our ideas in the world of Form. This is important stuff, so it's crucial not to get serious, to realize that this is all fun and games. The attitude "business *is* serious, it's *not* fun and games" leads to financial failure, and I won't tolerate it in my company. If my staff and I get stuck trying to solve a puzzle, we ask two questions: Where could we make this more playful? and Where could we make this more restful? If we sense fatigue or exhaustion around any given issue, we all get off the phone and rest—for ourselves, for one another, for our customers. We'll meet again later and continue to crack puzzles. Playfully.

The energy of ease and enjoyment is the primary "deliverable" I monitor in my business. To put the energy of exhaustion and anxiety into anything I do at work would be like offering my customers rotten apples—and they know it, because even if they aren't aware of it, they can feel the truth of my life and the things I make. They're connected to me in the Oneness. So are you. To succeed financially in the wild new world, you eventually must learn to live according to the following instruction: *Rest until you feel like playing, then play until you feel like resting. Never do anything else.*

THE INFINITY LOOP OF REST AND PLAY

I realized I had to live this way on my leopard tortoise trip to Londolozi. I awoke from that sumptuous sleep knowing that when I care for myself, it helps me use the technologies of magic continuously, and my whole tribe feels the positive effects. The whole world of Form can then support me in a million ways: emotional, physical, and financial. When I awoke from my tortoise nap, I could see in my Imagination a visual symbol of a way-finder's life as an infinity sign, a never-ending, self-sustaining loop of rest and play. I quickly jotted down this image:

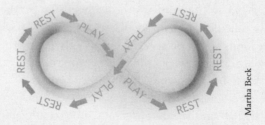

The infinity loop of rest and play (my version).

Even if you Do Everything Right, including all the exercises in this book, your mender career can't work if you allow yourself to slip into fear or exhaustion. Those pestilential feelings knock you right off your surf-board, casting you adrift in today's crashing financial waters. They don't mean you should get a corporate job; for a wayfinder in today's world, that would be energetic and financial suicide. They mean you need to rest and play. Grasping, grim, effortful energy kills the energetic foundation of any enterprise, drives away customers, ruins creativity, and makes success a thousand times more difficult.

You'd think it would be easy to stay in the infinity loop of restful, playful energy because it feels so wonderful. But for most of us, it's much easier to tune in to fear than to stay balanced in happiness. That's because a deep part of the brain, called the reptilian brain because it first evolved in reptiles, continuously creates what I call "lack and attack" fears: terror of not having enough and terror of something bad happening. I call your reptile brain your "inner lizard." A frightened inner lizard expects privation and opposition, so it grips anything it thinks will keep it safe from lack or attack, and desperately shoves away anything that makes it even slightly nervous. In career terms, this grasping energy creates exactly what the lizard imagines: fear-based financial and social catastrophe.

When I awake from my long night of sleep to find the leopard tortoise still resting happily next to the veranda of my room, I know with unprecedented clarity that my "lizard fear" has kept me away from the cycle of rest and play my whole life. I've been researching the technologies of magic for several years, but I haven't put my faith in them. I still think I need constant, exhausting work to keep afloat financially. Work is my solid structure. My inner lizard is afraid to let go and surf, to rest when I feel like resting and play when I feel like playing. As I sit contemplating this, a small lizard scuttles its way onto my veranda.

"Hello," I say. "Are you the symbol of my fear?"

At that moment, I swear to God, a small, beautiful snake ripples onto the veranda. Before I know what to think, the snake has squished the lizard in its coils, killing it almost instantly. Then the snake swallows the lizard, slithers up a tree, and arranges itself into this configuration, which I photograph with my camera phone.

Yes, on this particular trip, the world of Form is definitely speaking to me in Reptile. It will speak to you too, in myriad ways, the moment you begin to release your fears and trust in a new but ancient, natural, joyful, delicious way of thriving.

Here are some puzzles to crack, games you can play as you surf through your life as a mender. *If you feel any stress or anxiety as you do these exercises, you must calm your inner lizard.* You do that by finding ways to be more playful (if your energy is high) or more restful (if your energy is low). And remember, though these puzzles require you to operate in the world of

Martha Beck

The infinity loop of rest and play (reptile version).

Form, you will find effective solutions only to the extent that you can sustain the nonverbal awareness of Wordlessness, the loving comfort of Oneness, and the delirious swooping fun of a free Imagination.

GAMES YOU CAN PLAY TO DO YOUR JOB BETTER, BY GETTING YOUR ART TO YOUR TRIBE

Wayfinder Forming: Package Your Art

1. Recall the mender art or arts you defined in the previous chapter, your ten-thousand-hour activity and how you used it to survive your worst experience.

2. Think of other people who are suffering from the same sort of terrible challenge you once survived (your "hell and back" experience). They are your tribe. Feel them.

3. Imagine helping these people heal from their hellish experience using the strategies that helped you, especially those connected

to your ten-thousand-hour activity. In your mind's eye, watch yourself do this.

4. Imagine three objects you could make—check the **"Forms Your Art May Take"** chart to prime your Imagination—that would convey your art to your tribe. Be silly and playful about this if you want the ideas to work optimally. Get together with a friend and brainstorm. List your first three ideas here:

a. _____

b. _____

c. _____

5. Using the same playful energy, Imagine three activities you could lead—again, check the **"Forms Your Art May Take"** chart for ideas—that would teach your tribe to heal by using your art.

a. _____

b. _____

c. _____

6. Start asking around—playfully. Find people who may be in your tribe and describe your ideas to them. Request feedback about what you could do to make your products or services more helpful and valuable to them. Imagine this until you find something you can create in the world of Form.

Wayfinder Forming: Research Ways to Get Your Art to Your Tribe Using Magical Technologies

You've probably already Googled something related to your worst experience. Do it again, this time to see how other wayfinders are already offering products and services to your tribe. Notice what appeals to you. Use this to fuel your Imagination about ways to communicate your art to your tribe. This isn't about copying content; your content creation will always be unique. It's simply about noticing how arts like yours are being distributed these days.

Wayfinder Forming: Rest and Play, in Kind Defiance of Your Inner Lizard

Several times a day, say once an hour, bring your attention to the energy you feel as you go about your work. If you feel tired or fearful, you're obeying your inner lizard. It's not a useful strategy in today's world. If you find your energy is low, that you're tired or frustrated, ask yourself, "What can I do right now that would feel more restful?" You might want to lie down for a while or do some "intentional resting," Dan Howard's method of directing the mind toward rest so that the body rejuvenates more effectively. Any form of rest, no matter how minimal, will improve your inner life and productivity.

If your energy is high, ask yourself, "What can I do right now that would feel more playful?" Tell jokes. Watch a silly video on YouTube. Compete with your children to see who can make the most realistic animal sounds. *Have fun!* Should your inner lizard become nervous or panicky about all this rest and play, just breathe deeply and continue the exercise. Your lizard needs to be swallowed up in the infinity loop of rest and play. Only then can you discover how successful your career as a wayfinder is meant to be.

Wayfinder Forming: Rest for Your Tribe

Lie down and think of all the people who are suffering your "hell and back" experience. Imagine the Earth from space, and each person in your tribe as a pinpoint of light somewhere on the globe. Rest intentionally for yourself, and then silently repeat the sentence, "I am resting for my tribe now." Feel the depth of your connection with these people. This strange exercise is the best way I've found to contact your tribe, and thus (to put it in rather icky twentieth-century terms) grow your business.

THE FUN OF SUCCESS

Once the world of Form has communicated with me through three reptiles—the leopard tortoises, the lizard, and the snake—I decide to trust these animal messengers and take a leap of faith. I begin using the technologies of magic more often, especially when I'm doing my "work." What happens to me then has also happened to literally hundreds of other people I've coached: I become healthier and more relaxed, and begin enjoying my everyday life more than I ever thought possible. Every morning I get up to play, feeling healthier and more delighted than I have since early childhood. I feel as if I'm doing far, far less work, but instead of collapsing, my business improves, pushed forward by the fluid forces of the wild new world.

My message from Oneness on my "reptile trip" is that though leopard tortoises can't swim that well, they really love to surf. If your purpose is to mend things, Oneness is sending you similar messages right now, teaching you just such marvels. Open your eyes to the messages. Look around you for the most delicious fun you can have. Believe that this joyous play, and not the withering "work" you thought was your fate, is your ticket to safety and prosperity. We live in a liquid world, where the waves grow bigger every day, and that is a profoundly good thing. Your destiny is not to drown. It is to ride those waves.

The rest-meister.

Bigstock Photo

CHAPTER FIFTEEN

LEAPING INTO THE WILD NEW WORLD

Once again I'm being dandled by a tree in pitch darkness, surrounded by members of the Team. This time, however, the trees are here in Form, not just in a rain forest shaman's song or in my fevered Imagination. Along with Boyd, Koelle, and ten clients, I'm sitting on a wooden platform high in the boughs of an acacia, several miles from the Londolozi camp. It's four o'clock in the morning. No one moves. No one makes a sound.

I wonder if the clients around me are enjoying this, or fervently wishing they were home clutching a bag of nachos in one hand and a TV remote in the other. I hope they're all on a fast track to the technologies of magic, dropping into Wordlessness through the path of stillness, and perhaps also—given our fatigue, mild chill, and the pins-and-needles limb discomfort—through the path of torment.

Of course, the path of delight is here as well. Watching the blazing wheel of the Milky Way spin across the sky, hearing birds and animals call through the darkness, breathing the scent of night-blooming flowers: all of these are experiences our ancestors carried in their cells, something our culture drowns in the crash of garbage trucks and the hum of air conditioners. Mind you, I'm deeply grateful for garbage trucks and air conditioners, and I wouldn't want to do a sitting meditation in an African tree every night. But I'd regret spending a whole lifetime on this planet without ever doing it at all.

These thoughts arise in my consciousness and then disappear like smoke. A moment of Wordlessness follows them, and I feel the familiar rush of energy reminding me that I'm One with the inky expanse around me. The river far below us becomes my bloodstream, the gentle wind my breath, the rhythmic chanting of ten thousand lovesick frogs my heartbeat.

Then I feel something watching me.

The hair prickles on my neck. All my senses converge on a spot in the branches several yards away. It's far too dark to see, and I hear nothing. But I can sense the attention of an animal, the texture of feet on bark and bark on feet, as if I were both the beast and the tree. Then very, very faintly—I might be wrong—a scent like the lobby of a rather seedy movie theater grazes the back of my nose. My heart begins thumping like a drum, because the last time I smelled that scent, something killed me.

It was only a dream, but one of those dreams that feels so real you wonder for weeks if it's truer than your waking life. The dream was simple, straightforward, and utterly terrifying. In it, I opened the flap of a tent where I'd been sleeping to find a leopard crouching in the grass just outside. My joy at seeing this breathtaking animal disappeared as it was born, because as soon as our eyes met, the leopard charged me. The weight of its body against the heavy canvas of the tent flap was crushing, overpowering, horrifying. I woke up disoriented and covered with sweat. It was more than an hour before I could fall asleep again. When I did, the leopard was waiting.

In the second dream I'd barely begun to open the tent flap when the leopard smashed through it. I felt teeth on my throat as the hind claws hit my belly and raked into me. I could smell the brassy scent of my own blood under the thick, buttered-popcorn odor that clung to the leopard. I wrenched myself out of that dream with the strangled gasp of someone pulling a child from quicksand. This time I didn't try to go back to sleep. There was no doubt in my mind that the leopard would return the moment I did. I crossed my legs and tried to meditate, remembering the horrible catch-22 sensation I'd experienced as a nightmare-plagued child, terrified of the sleep I desperately needed.

After about half an hour, the right hemisphere of my brain burped up a thought so simple and obvious I burst out laughing. What we resist persists, so all I had to do to end the nightmare was stop fighting. I flopped back onto my pillow, fell asleep, and immediately reentered the same dream. This time I methodically unzipped the tent flap, folded it back, and stood in the opening. I looked out to see the leopard's beautiful, beautiful eyes gazing into mine. The leopard charged. I went limp. I felt its jaws close around my neck as its hind legs clawed me open, and at that moment I was absorbed into the leopard as the leopard was absorbed into me. I woke up into an overwhelming sense of clarity, calm, and peace—and, riding on the breeze from the slightly open window at the Londolozi cottage, the buttery smell of a movie theater.

When I confided in an African friend about my strange leopard dreams, he told me three things I later corroborated in books and by firsthand experience: (1) in many traditional cultures, the shift from an ordinary life to the life of a mender is marked by dreams or visions of being killed and/ or eaten; (2) the beast that shows up to eat the acolyte is often a solitary large cat; and (3) in real life, leopards actually do smell like popcorn.

I recall all of this in the darkness of the acacia tree, on the wooden platform where my friends and clients are meditating silently around me. As I strain my senses, scanning for that movie theater scent in every inhale, I begin to wonder why I ever agreed to this treetop vigil. Suddenly a nightlong treetop "serenity meditation" seems about as smart as a kindergarten field trip to a maximum-security prison. I want it all to go away *right now:* the darkness, the chill, the uncertainty, the fatigue, the prickling unease. I want my TV remote.

LEOPARD NIGHTS OF THE SOUL

There are nights like this in every wayfinder's life. You could be experiencing one right now. You may be in an unfamiliar, uncomfortable moment of your personal saga, a situation where you can't possibly know what's coming but absolutely know it could be bad. Your job or your whole profession may be fading into the mists of history. Your family may be shattered. Your body may be failing. Conflicting emotions may be breaking you in half. It's quite possible you've forgotten why you ever set out on the adventures that brought you to this point. Inspirations and motivations that seemed electrifying at some earlier time are now obviously idiotic and doomed.

I wish I could tell you that it's possible to head back to some safe, sane, civilized world where everything will work out for you tidily and predictably. But I can't. We happen to be on this planet now, and there's no going back to a slower, more pedestrian, less magical way of being. The only way for a born mender to live peacefully and abundantly in our wild new world is to let go of old models of thinking, working, decision making, and relating to others. If that doesn't work, the only option is to let go even more. Surrender to the way things want to happen next, even though this often involves a vast and terrifying loss of control. Trust the magic that was born into your soul. Let the leopard kill you, kill your present self, so that the nature of your true self can emerge.

LEAPS OF FAITH

The word for a collective of leopards (as in a *herd* of cows, a *flock* of birds, or a *school* of fish) is "leap." Leopards have incredible jumping ability; I've seen one gracefully bound ten feet into a tree carrying an antelope carcass almost as big as he was. The group term "leap" is also highly appropriate for wayfinders, whose familiar is the leopard. Anyone who embraces the mender's way of life must proceed through continual, infinite, breathtaking leaps of faith. Each time you face an unknown future with creativity rather than grasping at known quantities, you leap. Each time you dare to believe your art can sustain you financially, you leap. Each time you trust your tribe of menders, you leap. Each time you embrace a love that lays you bare in body, heart, or soul, you leap. And whenever you begin to disbelieve in yourself, your destiny, your ability to heal some part of the world, you must leap instead into the branches of magic.

The life you will lead as a wayfinder will be filled with far more joy, love, and abundance than the existence you'd create by clinging to outdated ways of being and doing. But to find your true self's way through our wild new world, you can't just *contemplate* the worldview of the mender. You have to risk embracing it. You must actually believe that what looks like magic exists, and that you can work it. You'll have to make decisions that fly in the face of everything you may consider safe and logical, all on the basis of evidence that sounds weird and woo-woo, not because science doesn't support the concept of an energetically interconnected, responsive universe (it does), but because the concept of an energetically interconnected, responsive universe isn't considered normal in the culture that socialized you.

In fact, if you choose to live the archetype of the wayfinder, you'll not so much defy your culture as leap into a new one, based on saner, sounder realities than what we now call "common knowledge" and "common sense." This new culture has already begun to awaken—not only in you, in your longing and your hope, but in the physical world of Form. It blends the wisdom of ancient menders with astonishing new machines. It doesn't ravage the true nature of humans, animals, and the Earth, but heals, restores, nurtures, and celebrates all nature, within us and around us. It spreads not through policies, laws, and enforcement, but through stories and laughter and adventures born from the companionship of dearest friends, through the technologies of magic dispensed through magical technologies. Wherever you go, it will find you. It is out there in the dark-est part of your life, hunting you, right now.

SAMPLES FROM MY PAST FEW WEEKS

Perhaps, while researching this book, I've immersed myself so deeply in thoughts about the technologies of magic and the magic of technology that I see them all around me, the way a medical student sees symptoms or a shopaholic sees clearance sales. Or maybe, with all that practice using the methods I've learned and with all that attention to the blend of ancient and modern, I'm actually Forming situations that validate my theories about the Team and its mission. Then again, it may be that the wayfinders really are feeling their destiny, learning their craft, and practicing their gentle art in countless surprising Forms all over our blue planet. Whatever the explanation, something is going on. Let me give you some examples I've noticed just during the time I was writing this chapter.

Example Number One: On a fine hot day in Phoenix, I spent an after-noon coaching a young woman who'd won a contest sponsored by a national retail chain. I'm not even sure what the contest entailed, only that an hour with me was part of the prize. (I can only suppose that sec-ond place entailed getting beaten with a bed slat. There's no accounting for what people think is worth winning.) I took along a notebook and pen, preparing for a brief return to "normal" coaching, which I abandoned years ago in favor of spending all my time with the Team.

The contest winner was a highly organized young lady named Kyria. We sat down in her hotel suite, and she told me she'd like advice about getting publicity for her business training service dogs for people with dis-abilities. Kyria's dogs helped not only the blind, but also people with epi-lepsy, paralysis, and posttraumatic stress. In fact, many of the dogs she had trained were serving veterans returning from the Middle East. They were in such hot demand that Kyria was being pushed through an emergency master's degree so she could legitimately teach her methodology to bud-ding mental health professionals in college and graduate school.

"You see," said Kyria, sounding oddly cautious, "these dogs do some-thing for these people, and it's not just guarding or helping them physi-cally. It's . . . ," her voice trailed off.

"It's not something you can describe in words?" I prompted.

"Exactly," said Kyria. "I know this may sound crazy, but the dogs are doing something you can *feel*—they're *fixing* something." Another moment of silence. "And I don't know why, but I have to do this work," she said, looking at me helplessly. "I've known it since I was a little kid. I have to."

"Have you ever had a mysterious chronic illness?" I said.

Kyria blinked. "How did you know that?"

"Do you feel like you're part of something huge that's meant to happen soon?"

The tears in her eyes made any comment unnecessary.

"Child," I said, "buckle your seat belt."

I abandoned my notebook and pen to spend an hour spewing as much information about the Team as I could. I taught Kyria all four technologies of magic in one fell swoop, finished with "And that's how we save the world," and then stopped to wipe my fevered brow and hope that the poor woman wasn't too alarmed at being locked in a hotel room with a lunatic.

Kyria took in a long breath and let it out slowly. "Everything you're saying makes perfect sense to me," she said, in the most ordinary voice. "I've just never talked to anyone about it. What are our next steps?"

Go Team!

———————

A few days later I received a surprise, last-minute invitation to attend the very last taping of *The Oprah Winfrey Show.* Blithely shoving my writing deadlines aside, I went to Chicago full of gratitude and anticipation. As the audience waited for the taping to begin, the preshow warm-up from the producers revved a studio full of fans into a true screaming mob of passionate devotion. As the countdown to the show began, my eardrums went numb from the cheering. It occurred to me that the Kleenex packs, thoughtfully placed under each seat to wipe tears of farewell off a hundred faces, could also be used to sponge adrenaline out of people's clothing. Then the producer gave the special hand signal that means SHE'S COMING!

The screaming immediately contracted into an excited hush. All eyes turned toward the door at the back of the studio, where Oprah customarily made her entrance. Thirty seconds passed as the crowd inhaled, ready to launch another deafening pandemonium of adoration. A minute went by. Some of us began breathing again. Another minute. The expression on people's faces went from wide-eyed to calm. Another minute, and the whole place began to relax. I don't know if that's what Oprah was waiting for, but that's when the curtains behind the stage parted and she calmly walked out.

I'm sure there was cheering, but I don't remember it. All I remember was that the lone woman on that stage was holding the deepest Wordlessness I'd encountered outside of a full-on wilderness. Her energy locked the entire crowd into One being, held by that Wordless power. The queen of television spent the last hour of her show not spotlighting celebrity appearances or massive material giveaways, but quietly speaking about the energy of the divine as it flows through each human being, about the way Imagination shapes everything we experience. She was bringing a simple and powerful message into Form, not so much by talking about it as by embodying it. I don't know how the very last *Oprah* show translated through the magic of technology that is television, but on site it left people wandering around looking reverent, thoughtful, stunned with peace, hit by a tsunami of healing.

Go Team!

From Chicago I went straight to another city where a prominent client, Andrew, was facing a gigantic leap of faith. To follow his heart, Andrew would have to leave a position of enormous power and influence, walk away from more money than most of us can imagine, break ties with several intimates who had betrayed his trust, and inevitably create the level of public scrutiny that can make fame a living hell. The social pressure against Andrew's leap of faith was indescribable. The only thing goading him forward was a thin, bright thread of hope—and, oh yes, a guide from South America who was heir to a long line of rain forest shamans and who triggered such a strong "You! You! You!" reaction in me I almost swooned.

Rodrigo prefers not to use the word "shaman" because it's been tainted by overuse and misunderstanding. He calls himself a guide. I, of course, call him a wayfinder. He spent part of his life deep in the Amazon forests, living with a tribe that had never experienced contact with the modern world. After malaria forced him to leave the jungle, he earned three Ph.D.s. Then he set out to bring ancient methods of healing to soul-sick people in the developed world. Though he never advertises—in fact he asks his clients for discretion—Rodrgigo has worked with many of the most influential people on Earth, people you'd never suspect of going to a jungle-trained soul-guide for comfort and advice.

I reached Andrew's Park City penthouse just in time to watch Rodrigo begin a healing session that would last well into the small hours of the night. It was like a very intense form of therapy, that progressed with bewildering speed because Rodrigo appears to be able to read people's thoughts, very specifically, by looking into their eyes. As he began helping Andrew process his impending leap of faith, Rodrigo articulated events and feelings from his client's past that Andrew had never told anyone. The guide switched fluidly between methods from clinical psychology: gestalt therapy, Rogerian theory, and several other theoretical traditions I recognized from well over ten thousand hours I've spent learning from books, specialists, and classes.

From a very different experience base, I also recognized the movement of Rodrigo's body as he crouched on the floor, staring directly into Andrew's eyes, gently asking and answering questions, barely blinking for hours at a time. He moved like a huge cat. He *looked* like a huge cat. He was stalking, his eyes tracking his client's thoughts, but with the sole intent of bringing comfort and peace. Rodrigo in action was love on the hunt.

Go Team!

THE POSSIBLE DREAM

Sometime during that long night Rodrigo and I left the others to go in the other room and have a sandwich. It felt to me like the hundredth meal we'd shared rather than the first. (You! You! You!) Though he's much more skilled than I'll ever be, Rodrigo and I have the same passion: calling to something deep, beautiful, primeval, and completely new that waits to arise within a human consciousness. We have the same objective: to expand this healing form of consciousness from each individual human to other people, other creatures, other systems. And we have the same eclectic approach: learning and using any human knowledge available, whether it comes from the traditions of ancient cultures or from peer-reviewed academic journals hot off the press.

"I'm still watching Andrew, by the way," Rodrigo said, nodding toward the unseen room where Andrew sat with his friends. "Sorry if I seem a little distracted."

"No, no, I totally get it," I said. "You're on the Team." I didn't even worry that he might not know what I meant. "I love watching Team people do their stuff. I call it your art. I know some in Africa who are healing ecosystems." I knew I was babbling, but it didn't matter. It felt as if I were filling in a family member on the activities of other siblings.

"Wonderful!" Rodrigo beamed. "Have you met the ones from China?"

"I didn't know there were any in China!" I said. "That's fantastic news!"

"Yes, they're in every country," he said. "There's a group of us meeting soon in Canada."

I did a double-take. "You've actually been to Team meetings?"

"Oh, yes," said Rodrigo, taking another bite of his sandwich. "Meetings in many places, with many different groups. Call it whatever you want. You'd be surprised who's on the Team." He mentioned a few names of people who had told him that he could speak freely about them, names that left me staring in astonishment. Then, as he dabbed a french fry in ketchup, he looked into my eyes and answered the question whirling around in my bleary midnight brain, even though I hadn't asked it out loud. "Yes, of course this is really happening," said Rodrigo with his gentle smile. "Of course it is."

Go Team!

YOUR VERY OWN WILD NEW WORLD

Like all of these wayfinders and hundreds more I've met, you may feel something calling you to become the change you wish to see in the world, *now*. You'll do this by healing your own true nature, and then any other aspect of true nature that calls to you. Start immediately. I mean this very moment. There's no need to wait for any external institution or teacher to show you the ropes. There aren't any fixed structures on the wayfinder's path, and there is no institutionalized way of training. You can find other menders—in fact you'll draw them to you—but the only ropes they can show you are the ones they're weaving as they go along. Wayfinders, by definition, create paths where there are none and find destinations no one knew were there. You can do things that turn your own technologies of magic into a way of living, as well as a way of being, and you will be the first to do it in your particular way.

If you are currently on your highest life purpose, comfortably back from your personal hell and sure of your navigational skills, then for God's sake, begin guiding the rest of us. If, on the other hand, you're peering into the darkness ahead of you without a clue where you're going, take the leap. Choose the mender's way through the wild world, a method of designing your life taught by people throughout all of human history who didn't so much reach goals as bring goals into existence. The wayfinder's travel is rooted in stillness, yet it will take you through the most wildly active corners of the wild new world. Here's a brief summary to remind you how you might walk through this very day as a wayfinder, tracking purpose and healing in whatever part of the wild world now holds you, from the breathing plains of Africa to the concrete canyons of Manhattan.

Wayfinding Your Way through the Day, Step One

As soon as you wake up—whether from sleep, a bad mood, or the chaos of others' needs—drop into Wordlessness. This may happen at any time of day. It may happen because you've had plenty of rest or because you're so tired you can't stay focused on your mind-bendingly boring job for one more second. You may be awakened by a strong cup of coffee, the sting of an argument, a failed project, or a beautiful face. However it happens, as soon as it happens, as often as it happens, use any method you know to reach that silent space where no story interferes with your awareness of the moment that is your whole life, right now.

If there is suffering in you that an animal wouldn't understand, let Wordlessness show you that this pain is made of lies. As Jill Bolte Taylor said, "step to the right" of your brain, where observation and energy rule so powerfully that painful stories can't be sustained. Deep-practice the skill of leaping out of the language of words and into the language of love. Do this in the faith that by releasing your mind's supposed control, you will drop into the truth, paradoxically finding the healing you've sought along all your trains of verbal thought.

Wayfinding Your Way through the Day, Step Two

As Wordlessness brings you into the present moment, the priorities by which you choose your course through today—and through life—will change. You'll feel the calm of the One that can supply all your particular needs. This will leave you with gratitude for everything and grasping for nothing, a complete reversal of the way fear teaches most humans to think. Where you once would have lashed back at your grumbling spouse, frantically worked to meet a deadline, and ignored the hummingbirds building a nest outside your kitchen window, today you may go outside to watch the birds and let everything else slide. Instead of sending your children to school, you may lie down with them in a layer of autumn leaves.

Stay Wordless and calm as you do this, because Oneness doesn't take you down paths that feel safe. More often than not it leads you to the edge of a cliff and pushes you off. Leap. Don't think about the landing, and don't worry about the fall, because you are falling in Love. As you fall through the One, you'll make the wild choices for which lovers, saints, and menders have always been famous: You'll see the best in everyone. You'll know that you are safe, powerful, beautiful. These truths will heal your wounds and make you what Rumi called "a mighty kindness."

Wayfinding Your Way through the Day, Step Three
As Wordlessness and Oneness clear your inner life of brooding, defensiveness, and fear, you'll free up vast quantities of emotional and physical energy. Your next wayfinding task is to see how far you can open your mind at this moment, how huge and beautiful a net you can cast with your Imagination. Use your life's puzzles to practice freeing your creative powers. Imagine the best possible outcome in the discussion with your still grumpy spouse, the work deadline that still looms, the schoolwork your children missed as they lay with you in the leaves making bright memories that will last long after their schoolwork is forgotten. Picture what would happen in each instance if you and everyone you encounter lived entirely in a state of Wordless Oneness. Then see that in their true natures, everyone already lives this way. Imagine that.

Take care, as you send your Imagination into the cosmic Web, not to label today's events "problems." Solve them as puzzles that are there to teach and enlighten you. Kindly dismiss your expectations about the terrible things that might result if these things never happen. Recognize that what you see as a negative outcome may in fact be an incentive to Imagine even more beautiful things. Put your favorite pastime next to your puzzling situation and ask yourself, *How is this like that?* Toss a thousand random facts into your brain and head outside for a rambling walk, letting your right hemisphere create a Eureka moment.

Not everything you Imagine today will appear in the world of Form, but by Imagining what could go right, you begin bringing fortuitous circumstances, new friends, and good fortune across the bridge from the

Everywhen to the physical world. And these days there are fewer limits than ever on the power of each individual to create an Imagined outcome. As Arthur C. Clarke said, "The only way of discovering the limits of the possible is to venture a little way past them into the impossible." With the technological magic and unprecedented cross-fertilization of ideas on Earth right now, it takes a limitless Imagination to even picture the impossible. Picture it anyway. Leap.

Wayfinding Your Way through the Day, Step Four

Once your Imagination is working as the servant of Wordless Oneness, you can devote your physical energy to Forming the material version of whatever you've Imagined. Never forget, this must be accomplished by playing until you feel like resting, then resting until you feel like playing. If you find yourself doing anything else, such as working, killing time, or looking for ways to escape, you are in the grip of language. Stop. Breathe. Leap back into Wordlessness as if your life depended on it. Anything else will stop your wayfinding magic, getting you hopelessly lost. If this happens, go back to the last "hot track," the last moment you found the mender's relaxed and joyful way of being. Proceed from there.

As you play in the world of Form, you'll realize that the best games involve persistent effort—often very challenging effort, at the limit of your ability—without attachment to the outcome so much as enjoyment of the process. The divine lilt of play and rest themselves are the reason we act. The results, the things we once called "accomplishments," are only amusing byproducts of the real purpose, which is the process of doing magic.

If you Form out of a Wordless energy connected to Oneness, with your Imagination cranking on all cylinders, your art will bring new things into the world this very day. Your tribe will find you. They will help you create new ways of making a living as a mender, transmitting your magical creations through magical inventions. The process goes slowly at first, when your Imagination is still shaped by what you expect, but if you deep-practice the technologies of magic, you'll see miracles begin to happen. Your body, your sense of security, your relationships will grow more robust in ways that will often seem too perfect to be coincidental. You'll find yourself healing things, within you and around you, that you thought were gone forever, broken beyond repair. You can't believe this until you've tried it, but if you try it, you'll begin to believe it. Take the leap.

LEADING THE WAY

This is the way we save the world: one peaceful word, one act of compassion, one long sweet nap, one burst of laughter at a time. And if you embrace this way of living, even in the most ordinary and prosaic-looking ways, word will spread. Your purpose may be only to find your own path, but others will feel calmed and healed by your art, your way of creating it, your simple presence. The messages you broadcast through the energetic Internet, as well as in the world of Form, will spread far and fast.

This is what has happened to countless Team members I know. Kyria is shocked by the number of people who want to support her vision of dogs healing veterans, and the speed with which they're moving to help realize her Imagined purpose in the world of Form. Many television talk-show hosts have tried to duplicate "the Oprah effect," but without the mender energy she broadcasts into the world, the things they've Formed don't have her healing effect and don't catch popular attention the way she did as an unknown talk-show host in Chicago. Rodrigo asked me over sandwiches, "Why do so many people pay me to do what I do? Am I really that different from other counselors?" This makes me laugh. I've met many therapists, but few who use the technologies of magic like Rodrigo does, or who can look into my eyes and follow my thoughts as easily as if I'd spoken them aloud. It's this ancient healing power, combined with rationalist techniques, that has Rodrigo booked solid two years in advance by some of the most powerful people on Earth.

If you truly leap into the archetype of the wayfinder, if you learn and practice the technologies of magic, transmitting them through whatever magical technologies our amazing civilization creates, the same kinds of inexplicable successes will happen to you. This will not only help you find your own way through the wild new world; it will help you lead the way for many others. Without intending it, you will soon look behind you and see that your Teammates are following.

When you feel a call to lead your tribe into a healing way of thinking and acting, you must leap. You must serve the whole world through leadership based on humility, like the sea to which, as Lao Tzu says, all streams flow because it is lower than they are. You must gently teach others not to follow your footprints, but to track their own purpose with the wayfinding capacities hidden in their bodies and souls. There is no one stable path to humanity's best future: we live in the time of infinite paths. The only thing we need to share is our commitment to traveling the wild new world through presence, compassion, imagination, and creation—and to the joy of playing with a few million of our closest friends.

If enough people accept this leadership, if a critical mass of human beings begin to live as wayfinders, a new dominant worldview could soon arise on our planet. Is this a quixotic, ridiculously optimistic vision? Of course it is. I'm not asking you to believe it—wouldn't even suggest such a thing. I'm only asking you to Imagine it.

That's easy for me, because since I decided to play with the Team, I've been surrounded by hundreds of menders, people whose presence fills me with gratitude so overwhelming I can barely remember to think. A future created by a whole culture of such people would be mind-bogglingly different from our brutal, internecine past. Here are a few comparisons between the worldview that is coming perilously close to destroying the world and the worldview that could save it:

AREA OF LIFE	THE SPENT OLD WORLD	THE WILD NEW WORLD
Inner experience of individuals	Dominated by fearful stories	Saturated with the present moment
Relationships	Faithful to arbitrary social standards of various cultures	Faithful to the truth of love within and between people
Careers	Dependent on the repression of a human's true nature	Dependent on the expression of a human's true nature
Industries	Huge organizations win by controlling distribution of goods	Individuals and small groups create win-win ideas for innovative content creation
Technological innovation	Machines designed to hoard and exploit nature, devouring resources	Machines designed to heal and preserve nature, renewing resources

You could go on Imagining the differences between the old and new consciousness forever. In fact I highly recommend that you do. The more we Imagine a world peopled by menders, the more we make choices that may just possibly create such a world in Form. As you heal your own true nature, not only will the things you Imagine appear more frequently and powerfully, but you will also draw more quiet attention and help more people find their own way home. Your art, whatever it is, will bring your tribe, whoever they are, more deeply into healing magic.

FINDING YOUR WAY BEFORE THE WAY APPEARS

Because I try, in my clumsy, bumbling way, to live through my own day with a mender's intentions and methods, I frequently end up in situations so strange and unexpected that I wonder whether I'm dreaming. Sometimes it's wonderful. But sometimes I slip back into my pre-mender consciousness. Then, until I find my way back, I remember what nightmares are like.

———————

This dark vigil in the African acacia tree with my wayfinder friends is shaping up to be one of the bad times. Hour after hour I grow more cold, exhausted, disillusioned, and scared. The weird feeling that a leopard is watching me never abates, and try as I do to reconcile myself to letting it kill me, this isn't working nearly so well on a wooden platform as it did when I was lying in a warm bed, asleep and dreaming.

I struggle to use what I've learned about living as a wayfinder. I try to drop into Wordlessness, looking for the peace that will magically calm my fears and bring me into a state of enlightened bliss. I can't make it happen.

The thing that finally ends my miserable night isn't magic; it's simply morning. A thin gray line on the horizon flares slowly into yellow, washing the tree with light and showing me that there's no exotic shaman animal crouching near us.

The funny thing is, I still smell popcorn.

For the rest of the day, that faint suspicion of a scent won't leave my memory. After wishing all night that I could get away from that platform, I can't stop wanting to go back. Finding your way through the wild world often feels like this. While it's happening, the leap of faith—the move to another city, the massive creative project, the birth of a child—does *not* feel like something you'll want to repeat. Then it's over, and suddenly you can't stop thinking about how wonderful it was. Throughout the day, as my fellow coaches and I play with our guests, I hanker to return to the Platform of Hell. Fortunately the people of my particular tribe are very understanding of such things, so during a break in our coaching day, when I ask Boyd to take me back to the acacia tree, he agrees without question.

As we approach the tree, Boyd cuts the power to the Land Rover and lets it coast down a gentle incline. We come to a stop. There's a long moment of deep quiet, the indescribable whispering peace of the African bush. Finally I'm able to drop into Wordlessness. The distinction between myself and everything around me disappears. As the present moment floods my senses, I let go of everything I imagined during the long night.

Then I see a flicker of motion in my peripheral vision.

Out of the grass, just a few feet from us, steps a walking jewel, a flame on four feet, a golden shaman straight out of the Everywhen. The leopard moves past us, so close we can hear the whisper of her breathing, of her huge soft paws touching the earth. In three great leaps up the massive tree she reaches the platform where my human friends and I spent the night sitting in darkness. So she was there all along—but not to harm. To help. She'd heard the Wordless call of human wayfinders echoing through the One, and she'd come, as leopards have done from time immemorial, to be the menders' familiar in Form.

She strides the length of the platform, a feline runway model on a literal catwalk, lifting her head to display the necklace of black around her white, white throat. Just above the Land Rover she stops and settles onto her belly, her head held regally high, and deliberately looks each of us in the eyes.

Meeting that gaze sends a spear of love straight through me. The eyes of a wild leopard are so clear, deep, fierce, and pure that nothing false can survive an encounter with them. Once you've looked into a leopard's eyes and the leopard has looked into yours, you have a choice: you can struggle to pretend that nothing remarkable has happened, or you can surrender to believing in magic. The leopard will never blame you for choosing "normality," for giving up the archetypal way of the mender. But if you want to travel in her magical company, you will have to leap.

Your leopard is already near you. She waits in the darkness of your most miserable nights, patiently guarding you until day dawns and you let her lead you through the wild new world. She stalks you in the Form of a new yearning, a strangely fascinating book, a YouTube video that catches your attention. You may never go near the continent of Africa. You may never leave the city where you were born. You may be violently allergic to every kind of cat. But if you choose to live as a wayfinder, at some point today you will look into your leopard's eyes. Love is hunting your true nature, and it is very near, and it will never stop.

FINDING YOUR WAY FROM RIGHT HERE

Look around you, right this instant. What's happening? Where is the rustle in the grass, the buttery scent of something magical waiting to greet you? You may sense it as a longing, a magnetic pull, a heart-stopping possibility, a warm glow. Whatever it is, Imagine it. Form it. Commit to it with a wayfinder's passion and persistence. Practice the technologies of magic, and use them to bring your wildest visions into the realm where you can touch them, live them, share them.

I'm writing this on the veranda of the Varty cottage at Londolozi, the healed land named for the "protector of all living things" and healed by the technologies of magic, combined with magical technologies. I didn't consciously intend to finish this book here, but in hindsight I expected it. I Imagined it.

Just a few days ago Koelle, Boyd, Solly, and I went rhinoceros-tracking again, but this time we brought several more Team members to share the experience. The only thing sweeter than letting the wild world awaken your sense of purpose is sharing that experience with your tribe. In the recurrent dream that is my life, five years after the mother rhinoceros almost charged me, I found myself looking up again to see great gray shapes moving silently through the bush. We did manage to avoid getting quite so close, and the rhinos stayed much calmer. It was a dream come true, only better.

Did I make this happen? In a way. Along with my Teammates, I felt into the Everywhen and Imagined having a chance to do this for a living. We all participated to create that vision in the world of Form. Together we designed an outrageously inaccessible African seminar. Koelle and I got ourselves back to Londolozi. Boyd and Solly located trackable rhinos with almost supernatural skill. And the other menders with us each took a huge leap of faith by finding the resources to join us here. My gratitude that this actually worked—and for everything that's happened to me since I saw that first rhino—is inexpressible. But it doesn't surprise me. Not any more. I've tested the mender's methods empirically and found them effective so often, in so many ways, I would be lying to question them.

This morning, when I woke up, I dropped into Wordlessness, felt through the Oneness for my leopard familiar, and found her. Then I Imagined another leopard walking past me today, as I wrote. The odds of this happening were infinitesimal. Five minutes ago, I swear on my life, it happened. Monkeys and birds began to alarm, and I saw a flicker of gold rippling through the tall grass. A friend came to ask if I'd seen the leopard. He confirmed that she'd strolled past the cottage and on through the camp, drawing the attention of rangers all the way. Not only did "my" leopard walk past me in broad daylight, but at the moment she did, my computer registered a wireless Internet connection in a place where that wasn't supposed to happen. I could immediately send word of my familiar's visit to the whole wild new world.

It made me laugh out loud, but not swoon with shock. For me, such events have become normal—dazzlingly wondrous, yes, but also normal.

Tell me: What would you like to be normal for you? You can create it, starting in this moment. Leap.

In the silence that comes when your feet leave the earth, you can hear the wild new world calling to your true nature. The One is whispering to you that what you thought was lost is still yours, that whatever is broken in you can be healed. The longing hidden in your heart, for however many years, is nature waiting to restore itself. Give it space, give it love, and it will grow strong again. And in the meantime, especially in the long cold nights of the soul, know that you are protected by the very power you fear most.

As within, so without: what's true for your inner life is also true for every part of the interconnected One Being that is nature. As a wayfinder friend told me long ago, we move at dawn, and dawn has arrived. All around you on this delicate sphere of a planet, the Team is waking up, shaking stiff cold limbs, smiling into one another's eyes. On the horizon the gray light grows, brightening to a symphony of reds and purples and golds. In the brush the hornbill calls, the lion roars, the leopard breathes. The day for you to mend your life, to find your true nature's way through the wildest world human history has ever seen, has begun.

And oh, oh, oh, my Teammate, what a glorious morning it is.

Bigstock Photo

The vision.

Shutterstock Photo

The Vision.

About the Author

Martha Beck is a writer and life coach who specializes in helping people design satisfying and meaningful life experiences. She holds a bachelor's degree in East Asian Languages and Civilization, and a master's degree and Ph.D. in sociology, all from Harvard University. She worked as a research associate at Harvard Business School, studying career paths and life-course changes in today's economic and social environment. Before leaving academia to be a full-time writer and life coach, Dr. Beck taught sociology, social psychology, organizational behavior, and business management at Harvard and the American Graduate School of International Management. She has published academic books and articles on a variety of social science and business topics.

Her nonacademic books include the *New York Times* bestselling memoirs *Expecting Adam* and *Leaving the Saints,* as well as self-help bestsellers *Finding Your Own North Star: Claiming the Life You Were Meant to Live* and *Steering by Starlight.* Dr. Beck has been a contributing editor for many popular magazines, including *Real Simple* and *Redbook.* For the past ten years, she has been a monthly columnist for *O, the Oprah Magazine.* She lives in Phoenix with her family.